C000047153

Fernanda

Cambridge English

Pag 53 - homework

EMPOWER

INTERMEDIATE
STUDENT'S BOOK

Despatched

B1+

Adrian Doff, Craig Thaine
Herbert Puchta, Jeff Stranks, Peter Lewis-Jones
with Rachel Godfrey and Gareth Davies

Lesson and objective	Grammar	Vocabulary	Pronunciation	Everyday English
Unit 1 Talk				
Getting started Talk about communication				
1A Talk about different forms of communication	Subject and object questions	Communication	Sound and spelling: /ɪ/ and /iː/	
1B Describe experiences in the present	Present simple and present continuous	Gradable and extreme adjectives	Sentence stress: gradable and extreme adjectives	
1C Give and respond to opinions		Word groups		Giving and responding to opinions
1D Write a guide				
Review and extension More practice		WORDPOWER *yourself*		
Unit 2 Modern life				
Getting started Talk about the workplace				
2A Talk about experiences of work and training	Present perfect simple and past simple	Work	Present perfect and past simple: *I've worked / I worked*	
2B Talk about technology	Present perfect simple and present perfect continuous	Technology	Sentence stress: main verb / auxiliary verb	
2C Make and respond to suggestions			Sentence stress	Making and responding to suggestions
2D Write an email giving news				
Review and extension More practice		WORDPOWER *look*		
Unit 3 Relationships				
Getting started Talk about relationships				
3A Talk about a friendship	Narrative tenses	Relationships	Linking sounds	
3B Talk about families	*used to, usually*	Family; Multi-word verbs	Sentence stress: multi-word verbs	
3C Tell a story			Stress in word groups	Telling a story
3D Write about someone's life				
Review and extension More practice		WORDPOWER *have*		
Unit 4 Personality				
Getting started Talk about people				
4A Describe people and their abilities	Modals and phrases of ability	Ability	Stress in modal verbs	
4B Describe feelings	Articles	*-ed / -ing* adjectives; Personality adjectives	Sound and spelling: final *-ed* in adjectives	
4C Offer and ask for help			Intonation in question tags	Offering and asking for help
4D Write an informal online advert				
Review and extension More practice		WORDPOWER *so* and *such*		
Unit 5 The natural world				
Getting started Talk about endangered animals				
5A Talk about the future	Future forms	Environmental issues	Sound and spelling: *a*	
5B Talk about *if* and *when*	Zero conditional and first conditional	The natural world	Consonant clusters	
5C Give reasons, results and examples			Voiced and unvoiced consonants	Giving reasons, results and examples
5D Write a discussion essay				
Review and extension More practice		WORDPOWER *problem*		

4

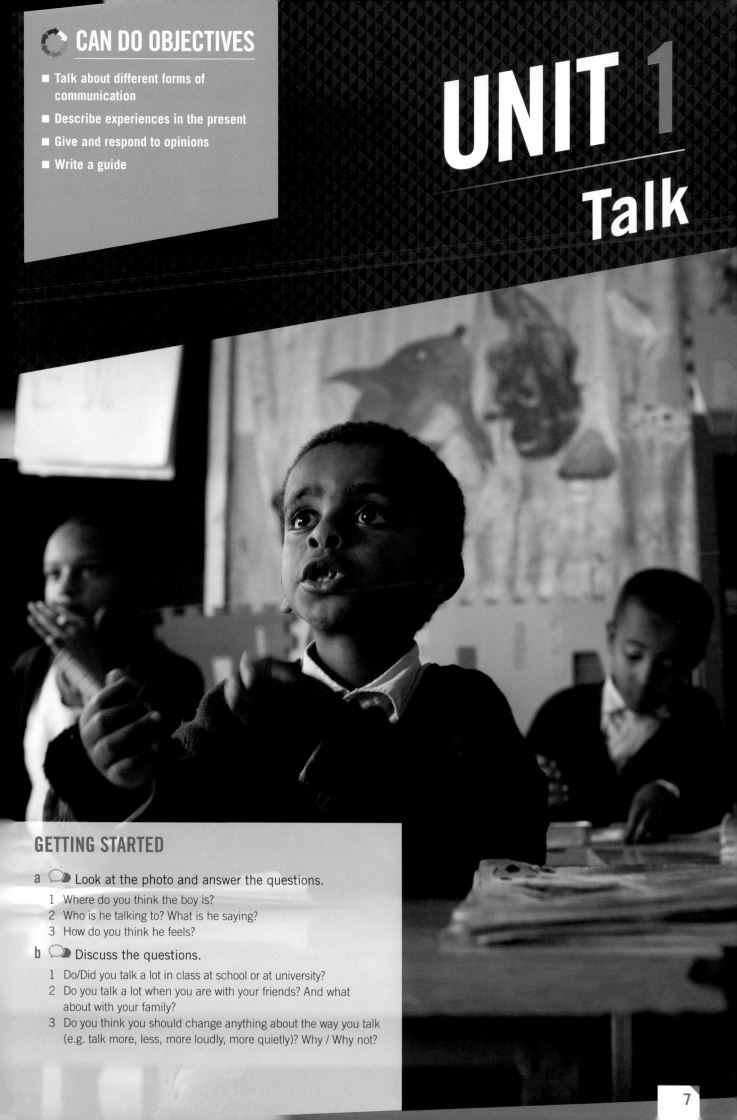

CAN DO OBJECTIVES

- Talk about different forms of communication
- Describe experiences in the present
- Give and respond to opinions
- Write a guide

GETTING STARTED

a 💬 Look at the photo and answer the questions.

1 Where do you think the boy is?
2 Who is he talking to? What is he saying?
3 How do you think he feels?

b 💬 Discuss the questions.

1 Do/Did you talk a lot in class at school or at university?
2 Do you talk a lot when you are with your friends? And what about with your family?
3 Do you think you should change anything about the way you talk (e.g. talk more, less, more loudly, more quietly)? Why / Why not?

1A Keeping in touch

1 VOCABULARY Communication

a 💬 Look at photos a–e below and answer the questions using words from the box.

1 How are the people communicating?

> face to face   expressing feelings
> giving a presentation   interviewing
> telling a joke   keeping in touch
> speaking in public   giving opinions

2 When was the last time you were in a similar situation to each of the photos?
3 Which situations in the photos do you enjoy? Which don't you enjoy? Why?

b ▶1.2 **Pronunciation** Do the underlined vowels have a long or a short sound? Listen and check.

1 expressing f<u>ee</u>lings   4 k<u>ee</u>ping in touch
2 int<u>e</u>rviewing   5 g<u>i</u>ving opinions
3 sp<u>ea</u>king in pub<u>li</u>c

c ▶1.2 Listen again and repeat the phrases.

d ▶ Now go to Vocabulary Focus 1A on p.152

2 READING

a 💬 Read *How do you communicate?* on p.9 and answer the questions.

1 Which generation are you?
2 How many of these generations are there in your family?
3 Which generation are most of the people where you work or study?

b 💬 Read the article again and match quotes 1–4 with generations a–d.

1 ☐ 'Let's talk about this over lunch tomorrow.'
2 ☐ 'I had a lovely letter from Emma. I'll write a long letter back at the weekend.'
3 ☐ 'My Facebook status got 62 likes!'
4 ☐ 'Sorry, I haven't got time for this. Just tell me what you want.'

a Veterans
b Baby Boomers
c Generation X
d Millennials

c 💬 Think about yourself and people of different generations that you know. Do you agree with the descriptions?

HOW DO YOU COMMUNICATE?

What do we all want from life? As well as love and money, most of us want someone to understand us. But we don't communicate in the same way. People born at different times have very different styles of communication. Which generation are you?

VETERANS

Born before 1945, 'Veterans' are the oldest and most experienced members of society. They think that family life is important and prefer traditional forms of communication. 'Veterans' are the richest generation, possibly because they worked hard and were loyal employees.

BABY BOOMERS

A large number of babies were born after 1945. (In the USA, the peak of the baby boom was in 1957, when eight babies were born every minute!) This increase in births was called a 'boom', which gave the name to a generation. These people have money and good jobs. Many are in positions of power. They are optimists and like face-to-face communication.

GENERATION X

'Generation X' was born after 1965. They are independent thinkers and want to be different from their parents. They have seen the introduction of the home computer, video games, satellite TV and, of course, the internet, so they are good at adapting to changes. This generation is busy – they don't want to wait to hear what you say.

MILLENNIALS

'Millennials' were born after 1980. They are confident, they like computers, and work well in teams. Family and friends are more important than work, but they spend a lot of time online. In fact, 65% of Millennials say that losing their phone or computer would change their daily routine more than losing their car.

---

3 GRAMMAR
Subject and object questions

a Look at the questions and answers and <u>underline</u> the correct words in rules a–c.

1 Which of the generations **grew up** in the digital age?
   Millennials.
2 What do we **want** from life?
   Someone to understand us.

   a The answer to question 1 is the *subject / object* of the verb in **bold**.
   b The answer to question 2 is the *subject / object* of the verb in **bold**.
   c We use the auxiliary verbs *do*, *does*, *did* in *subject / object* questions.

b Are the questions below subject or object questions?

1 Who do I give this to?
2 What happened to your leg?
3 Which of these books do you want to borrow?
4 Who gave you the flowers?
5 Which car uses less petrol?
6 What did he say to you?

c ▶ Now go to Grammar Focus 1A on p.132

d Make questions with the words below.

1 Who / phone / you / yesterday?
   _____
2 Who / you / email / yesterday?
   _____
3 What / you and your friends / talk about?
   _____
4 What / make / you and your friends / laugh?
   _____
5 Which of your friends / you / see / every day?
   _____
6 Which of your friends / know / you / best?
   _____

e 💬 Discuss the questions from 3d. Ask follow-up questions.

Who phoned you yesterday?

My mum phoned me.

What did you talk about?

4 LISTENING

a 💬 Talk about family, friends or colleagues. What problems do you think different generations might have when they communicate?

> Older people sometimes think younger people are rude because they use more informal language.

b ▶️1.7 Listen to someone talking about communication across the generations. Tick (✓) the things he mentions.

1 ☐ Millennials like connecting with people online.
2 ☐ Millennials and Veterans usually hate each other.
3 ☐ Generation Xers and Baby Boomers are similar because they both express how they feel.
4 ☐ Men and women have different ways of communicating.
5 ☐ We shouldn't get upset because other generations don't do what we expect.
6 ☐ It's important to use correct spelling when writing an email or text.
7 ☐ Different generations can learn a lot from each other.

c ▶️1.7 Listen again and answer the questions.

1 Which generation is the speaker from?
2 What does Generation X believe communication is important for?
3 Which two generations don't want to talk about their personal goals?
4 What do Millennials expect other people to tell them?
5 What can younger generations offer to older generations?

d 💬 Which of the things are you best at? Which do you find very difficult? Talk about your ideas.

- talking to older people
- talking to younger people
- talking to people from different countries
- expressing my opinions
- expressing my feelings
- listening when people criticise me
- avoiding arguments

> I like talking to older people, but I'm not very good at talking to children.

5 SPEAKING

a Tick (✓) the things you have done recently. Make notes about the experience.

☐ met someone new
☐ had a communication problem with someone from another generation
☐ spoken to a large audience
☐ spoken a foreign language outside class
☐ met a famous person
☐ communicated with someone you don't know online
☐ sent or received a letter

b Look at the experiences your partner ticked and write three questions to ask them.

> *met someone new*
> *Who was it?*
> *Where were you?*
> *What did you talk about?*

c 💬 Ask your partner about their experiences.

> Who was the person you met?

> It was a new neighbour.

> What did you talk about?

> We talked about the neighbourhood. She asked me to recommend some shops in the area.

1B I'm using an app for learning English

Learn to describe experiences in the present
- **G** Present simple and continuous
- **V** Gradable and extreme adjectives

1 SPEAKING

Dy bannee diu • Guten Tag • **Gouden Dai** • **Salut**

Сәлем! • **Bonjour** • **Halito** • Salute

Hallo • Håfa ådai • **Ç'kemi** • Guuten takh

Héébee • Bon die! • Servas • Tungjatjeta

Ola • Ahoj • **Вітаю** • Góðan dag • Hoi

Salud • Hola / Bonos díes • **Bon dia**

a 💬 Discuss the questions.
1 How many languages can you say 'Hello' in?
2 How many languages can you order a meal or have a simple conversation in?
3 What language are you best at (apart from your own)?

b Choose one idea below and continue using *because*. Write your idea.

Learning a new language is like …
- falling in love
- going on an endless journey
- being a child
- growing plants in a garden
- learning a musical instrument

Learning a language is like falling in love, because it's exciting at the beginning, and then it becomes hard work.

c 💬 Read your sentences to each other. Do you agree with each other's ideas?

d 💬 Look at photos a–d and discuss the questions.
1 What are the advantages and disadvantages of each way of learning a language?
2 Which have you tried? Have you tried any other ways?

11

2 READING

a Read *Can you really learn a language in 22 hours?* quickly and answer the questions.

1 What is Memrise?
2 Why is Jon Foster using it?
3 How much has he learnt?

b Read the article again and choose the correct answers for questions 1–4.

1 The writer wants to learn Lingala because he …
   a loves new languages.
   b wants to talk with the people who speak it.
   c wants to try Memrise.
2 Ed Cooke wants learners to …
   a enjoy learning more.
   b improve quickly.
   c do more vocabulary practice.
3 'Mem' is …
   a the Lingalese word for 'engine'.
   b a translation of a new word.
   c a picture that helps people remember new words.

4 Where do the mems come from?
   a Ed Cooke creates them.
   b Users can create mems for themselves and other users.
   c Every user creates mems only for themselves.

c Match the words in **bold** in the article with meanings 1–8 below.

1 getting better
2 changes a word from one language into another
3 what someone wants to do
4 learnt something so that you remembered it exactly
5 something difficult which tests your ability
6 able to communicate freely and easily
7 to make someone remember something
8 do something again

d 💬 Would you like to use Memrise? Why / Why not?

CAN YOU REALLY LEARN A LANGUAGE IN 22 hours?

WE ALL KNOW THAT PEOPLE LEARN BETTER IF THEY ENJOY LEARNING.
Jon Foster reports on an app that makes learning a new language like playing a game.

I've never been much good at languages. But next month, I'm travelling to a remote area of Central Africa and my **aim** is to know enough Lingala – one of the local languages – to have a conversation. I wasn't sure how I was going to manage this – until I discovered a way to spend just a few minutes, a few times a day, learning all the vocabulary I'm going to need.

To be honest, normally when I get a spare moment at home, I go on Facebook or play games on my phone. But, at the moment, I'm using those short breaks for something more useful. I'm learning a foreign language. And thanks to Memrise, the app I'm using, it feels just like a game.

'People often stop learning things because they feel they're not **making progress** or because it all feels like too much hard work,' says Ed Cooke, one of the people who created Memrise. 'We're trying to create a form of learning experience that is fun and is something you'd want to do instead of watching TV.'

And Memrise is fun. It's a **challenge**. It gives you a few new words to learn and these are 'seeds' which you plant in your 'greenhouse'. (This represents your short-term memory.) When you practise the words, you 'water your plants' and they grow. When the app believes that you have really remembered a word, it moves the word to your 'garden'. You get points as your garden grows, so you can compare yourself to other Memrise users. I want to get a high score and go to the next level. And if I forget to log on, the app sends me emails that **remind** me to 'water my plants'.

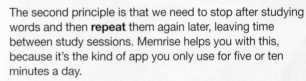

The app uses two principles about learning. The first is that people remember things better when they link them to a picture in their mind. Memrise **translates** words into your own language, but it also encourages you to use 'mems' – images that help you remember new words. You can use mems which other users have created or you can create your own. I **memorised** *motele*, the Lingalan word for 'engine', using a mem I created – I imagined an old engine in a motel room.

The second principle is that we need to stop after studying words and then **repeat** them again later, leaving time between study sessions. Memrise helps you with this, because it's the kind of app you only use for five or ten minutes a day.

I've learnt hundreds of Lingalan words with Memrise. I know this won't make me a **fluent** speaker, but I hope I'll be able to do more than just smile and look stupid when I meet people in the Congo.

Now, why am I still sitting here writing this? I need to go and water my vocabulary!

3 GRAMMAR
Present simple and continuous

a Match present simple sentences a–c with uses 1–3.

  a When I get a spare moment at home, I normally **go** on Facebook or **play** games on my phone.

  b I **know** this won't make me a fluent speaker.

  c People **learn** better if they enjoy learning.

We can use the present simple:

1 to talk about things which are generally true (sentence ___)

2 to talk about habits and routines (sentence ___)

3 with state verbs – verbs about thoughts (e.g. *understand*), feelings (e.g. *want*) and possession (e.g. *own*). (sentence ___)

b Match present continuous sentences a–c with uses 1–3.

  a I**'m learning** a foreign language.

  b Now, why **am** I still **sitting** here writing this?

  c Young people **are spending** more and more time playing on the computer.

We can use the present continuous to talk about:

1 actions in progress at the same time as speaking/writing (sentence ___)

2 actions in progress around (before and after) the time of speaking/writing (sentence ___)

3 changing situations (sentence ___)

c ▶ Now go to Grammar Focus 1B on p.132

d 💬 Make questions with the words below. Then discuss the questions.

1 you / think / you / communicate / well in your own language?

2 How often / you / hear / foreign languages where you live?

3 you / think / you / have / a good memory?

4 What / help / you / learn / English grammar?

5 What / you / think / about / right now?

6 you / prepare / for an exam at the moment?

7 more people / learn / languages in your country than before?

> Do you think you communicate well in your own language?

> I think so, but I prefer writing to speaking.

e ▶ Communication 1B 💬 Student A: Look at the picture on p.127. Student B: Look at the picture on p.131. Describe your picture to your partner. Find eight differences between your pictures.

4 VOCABULARY
Gradable and extreme adjectives

a ▶1.10 Listen and <u>underline</u> the correct words.

1 James is *a bit / very* tired.

2 Linda *likes / doesn't like* the book.

3 Tony thinks the girl can do something *quite / very* impressive.

4 The teacher thinks Olivier *will / won't* be able to pronounce 'squirrel'.

b ▶1.10 Complete the sentences with the words in the box. Listen again and check.

exhausted	fantastic	impossible	useless

1 I'm absolutely _____ .

2 This book's _____ .

3 That's _____ ! I can only speak one language.

4 It's _____ ! I'll never get it right.

c Read about gradable and extreme adjectives. Complete sentences 1–6 with *absolutely* or *very*.

> - With some adjectives (*good, bad, difficult*), we can use words like *quite, very, really* and *extremely* to make their meaning stronger or weaker (e.g. *His pronunciation is quite good. The exam was extremely difficult.*).
> - Other adjectives already have a strong or extreme meaning (e.g. *perfect, useless*). We can use words like *completely* or *absolutely* before these adjectives to add emphasis (*Her English is absolutely perfect.*).

1 Online dictionaries are often _____ **useful**.

2 That cake's _____ **enormous**.

3 I think Anna's _____ **confident**.

4 I went for a swim in the river and the water was _____ **freezing**.

5 There are only seven houses in my village – it's _____ **tiny**.

6 It's _____ **important** to learn pronunciation as well as vocabulary.

d ▶1.11 **Pronunciation** Listen and check. Then answer the questions below.

1 Which word is stressed in each sentence?

2 Do we usually stress gradable adjectives or extreme adjectives?

e ▶1.11 Listen again and repeat the sentences.

f ▶ Now go to Vocabulary Focus 1B on p.153

5 SPEAKING

a 💬 Talk about learning a foreign language. Use the questions below.

- What do you want to be able to do with English?
- What level of English do you hope to reach?
- How often do you review what you have learned?
- How often do you watch or read things in English?
- How often do you communicate with native speakers?
- What are you doing at the moment to learn English?
- Are you having any problems with English at the moment?

b Report back to the class about what you found out.

1C Everyday English
Well, if you ask me …

1 LISTENING

a 💬 Discuss the questions.

1 Do you enjoy meeting new people?
2 Do you usually decide what you think of someone from a first impression? Or do you get to know them first?

b 💬 Look at the photo above. What do you think the customer is buying?

c ▶1.14 Watch or listen to Part 1 to check.

d ▶1.14 Watch or listen again and underline the correct answers.

1 Becky is buying flowers because she's *going to someone's house* / *getting married*.
2 She doesn't want roses because *she doesn't like them* / *they're too romantic*.
3 She *likes* / *doesn't like* the tulips.
4 She will *buy flowers in another shop* / *come back later*.

e 💬 Look at the photo below right and answer the questions.

1 Where are the people?
2 What are they doing?

f ▶1.15 Watch or listen to Part 2 to check.

g ▶1.15 Watch or listen again and answer the questions.

1 What will happen to the bookshop?
2 What problem will this cause for Rachel?
3 What is Mark's advice?
4 What does Rachel say happened at work?

2 USEFUL LANGUAGE
Giving and responding to opinions

a ▶1.16 Listen and complete the sentences with one word.

1 Well, in my _____, roses are always a good option.
2 I _____ something like tulips might be better.
3 I _____ it's going to be impossible with another florist's in the same street.
4 Well, if you _____ me, it's not worth worrying about until we know for sure.

b Put the words in the correct order to make more formal phrases for giving an opinion.

1 it / me / seems / that / to   2 as / as / concerned / far / I'm

c Look at five ways of responding to an opinion. Does the speaker agree (A) or disagree (D)?

1 I know what you mean, but … ___
2 I know exactly what you mean. ___
3 I'm not so sure about that. ___
4 That's right. ___
5 I see where you're coming from, but … ___

d Tick (✓) the sentences you agree with. Change the other sentences so you agree with them.

1 ☐ English is an easy language to learn.
2 ☐ It's difficult to communicate with older people.
3 ☐ First impressions are important when you meet someone.

e 💬 Give your opinions from 2d and respond.

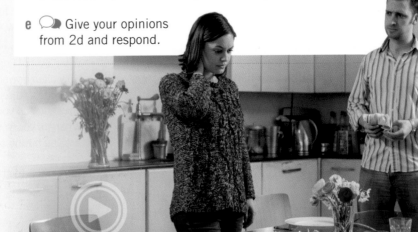

3 PRONUNCIATION Word groups

a ▶**1.17** Listen to these sentences. Notice where the speaker pauses to make the message clearer.

I'm really worried. Jo phoned today with some bad news.

b ▶**1.18** Listen to this similar sentence. Does the speaker pause?

I'm really worried I won't make enough money.

c Look at the conversation. Write // where you think the speakers pause.

Rachel	Oh, I'm sorry, love. I'm just a bit worried. Jo phoned today and said that the old bookshop is going to be turned into another florist's.
Mark	The bookshop on the corner? I didn't know they'd sold it.
Rachel	Me neither. But what am I going to do? It's hard enough already to make money, but I think it's going to be impossible with another florist's in the same street.

d ▶**1.19** Listen and check.

4 CONVERSATION SKILLS
Using *me too* / *me neither*

a ▶**1.20** Listen and <u>underline</u> the correct words.

1
Mark	The bookshop on the corner? I didn't know they'd sold it.
Rachel	Me *too* / *neither*.

2
Mark	Hey, don't worry about it. Let's just forget about work. Personally, I need a relaxing evening!
Rachel	Me *too* / *neither*.

1 We use *Me too* and *Me neither* to say we agree or are in the same situation.
2 We use *Me too* after a positive sentence.
3 We use *Me neither* after a negative sentence.

b Complete the exchanges with appropriate responses.

1 **A** I need a nice cup of tea.
   B _____ .
2 **A** I don't really like watching football.
   B _____ .
3 **A** I wasn't invited to the wedding.
   B _____ .
4 **A** I'm looking forward to the party.
   B _____ .
5 **A** I don't really eat chocolate.
   B _____ .
6 **A** I hate going out in the rain.
   B _____ .

5 LISTENING

a 💬 Look at the photo. What is happening? What do you think will happen next?

b ▶**1.21** Watch or listen to Part 3 and check your ideas.

c 💬 Discuss the questions.

1 How would you feel in Becky's situation?
2 How would you feel in Rachel's situation?
3 Have you ever made a bad first impression?

6 SPEAKING

a Think of an example of:
- a good way to meet new people
- a good way to make a good first impression
- a good topic of conversation with someone you don't know well
- a good reason to dislike someone you've just met.

b 💬 Discuss your ideas in 6a.

If you ask me, the best way to make a good impression is to use people's names a lot.

I'm not so sure about that.

◯ Unit Progress Test

CHECK YOUR PROGRESS

You can now do the Unit Progress Test.

1D Skills for Writing
Different ways of learning

1 SPEAKING AND LISTENING

a 💬 What do you think are some good ways to learn new vocabulary in English? Talk about the ideas in photos a–e, or your own ideas.

b ▶1.22 Listen to Maria and Gilberto talking about learning vocabulary. Are you more like Maria or Gilberto?

c ▶1.22 Listen again and answer the questions.
1 What system does Maria use for learning vocabulary?
2 What system does Maria's sister use?
3 Does Gilberto think either system will work for him?

d Read the descriptions of each style. What kinds of learners are Maria and Gilberto?

Visual learners

They prefer to learn by seeing or reading things and need to see new information written down.

Auditory learners

They prefer to learn by listening to new information. They also like to talk about the new things they've learnt.

Kinaesthetic learners

They prefer to learn by doing something. They don't like sitting still for very long.

e 💬 Talk about what kind of learner you are and why.

2 READING

a Read *What kind of learner are you?* on p.17. Answer the questions.
1 Which of Maria's ideas is mentioned?
2 Does the article talk more about understanding new information or remembering it?

b Read the article again. Make notes about the key study techniques for each learning style.
- visual
- auditory
- kinaesthetic

WHAT KIND OF LEARNER ARE YOU?

Different people learn in different ways. In order to find the most useful way to learn new information, it's a good idea to think about the kind of learner you are: visual, auditory or kinaesthetic. Knowing your learning style helps you study more effectively, so you remember what you have learnt more easily. Remember, you don't just learn when you study – this advice can also be useful for learning at work or in your free time.

VISUAL LEARNERS

It helps to study in a quiet place so that you can concentrate. To learn new information, try to think of an image in your head, or make a diagram to highlight different points. [1]**This technique helps your memory and it means you can find the information easily when you look at your notes again.**

AUDITORY LEARNERS

Going to a lecture is a good way for you to learn. Read your notes aloud, then cover them and try to say them again from memory. Also, try to use new words when you're talking to people. If you are studying words on a particular topic, you can listen to podcasts that include this vocabulary. [2]**These ideas should help you remember what you need to know.**

KINAESTHETIC LEARNERS

In order to learn new information, you need to be doing something. It helps to study in a place where you can walk around the room, touch things and move as freely as possible. Make sure you take regular breaks and go for a walk. [3]**This will help you to concentrate and remain interested in what you are studying.**

These descriptions are only a guide. Most people have a mixture of learning styles. To study successfully, you need to experiment and find the most suitable method.

3 WRITING SKILLS
Introducing a purpose; referring pronouns

a Look at these sentences from the article. Circle the words or phrases in the <u>underlined</u> parts which introduce the purpose in each sentence.

1 <u>In order to find the most useful way to learn new information</u>, it's a good idea to think about the kind of learner you are …
2 Knowing your learning style helps you study more effectively, <u>so you remember what you have learnt more easily</u>.
3 <u>To learn new information</u>, try to think of an image in your head.

b <u>Underline</u> other examples of purpose words/ phrases in the article.

c Join the sentences using purpose words/ phrases. More than one answer is possible.

1 I write the new words in a vocabulary notebook. I remember them.
2 I practise pronunciation. I record myself saying words on my phone.
3 I write grammar rules on a piece of paper. I understand them better.

d Look at sentences 1–3 in **bold** in the article and <u>underline</u> the correct words in the rules.

a *This* and *these* refer to *ideas already mentioned / new ideas.*
b In sentences 1 and 3, *this* refers back to *one word / a complete idea.*
c We sometimes put *a noun / an adjective* after *this* and *these.*

4 WRITING A guide

a Think of a skill you know how to do well. It can be something to do with study, work, sport or a free-time activity. Make notes using these questions.

1 How easy is it to learn this skill?
2 What are the problems people have when learning it?
3 What are good ways to learn this skill?
4 Why are they good ways?

b Write a guide on how to learn this skill. Use words/phrases to introduce purpose and *this* or *these*, if possible, to refer back to ideas.

c 🗩 Work in pairs. Read your partner's guide. How easy do you think it would be to learn their skill?

UNIT 1
Review and extension

1 GRAMMAR

a 💬 Complete the questions. Then ask and answer the questions.

1 You live with someone.
  Who ___*do you live*___ with?
2 Something woke you up this morning.
  What _____ this morning?
3 You talk to someone every day.
  Who _____ every day?
4 You read something yesterday.
  What _____ yesterday?
5 Something has made you laugh recently.
  What _____ recently?
6 Someone speaks to you in English.
  Who _____ in English?
7 You know different ways of learning English.
  Which different ways of learning English _____?
8 Some ways of learning English work best for you.
  Which ways of learning English _____?

b Four of the sentences below have a mistake.
  Tick (✓) the four correct sentences.

1 ☐ John's having a shower.
2 ☐ I think we need a new laptop. Are you agreeing?
3 ☐ I'm hardly ever writing letters.
4 ☐ You look sad, Maria. What do you think about?
5 ☐ Monkeys communicate with sounds.
6 ☐ I don't know at the moment.
7 ☐ Carrie doesn't work this week because she's ill.
8 ☐ I'm getting cold.

2 VOCABULARY

a Complete the sentences with the verbs in the box.

argue   complain   give   express
keep   persuade   speak   tell

1 Are you going to _____ about the terrible food?
2 Let's _____ in touch.
3 Can you _____ a joke?
4 I don't want to _____ a presentation.
5 He prefers to _____ his opinions in writing.
6 She's trying to _____ me to go on holiday with her.
7 When did you last _____ in public?
8 I try not to _____ with my boss – even when he's wrong!

b Match the extreme adjectives in the box with gradable adjectives 1–8.

awful   brilliant   enormous   exhausted
filthy   freezing   furious   tiny

1 big   _____   5 tired   _____
2 dirty _____   6 angry   _____
3 small _____   7 bad   _____
4 cold   _____   8 good   _____

3 WORDPOWER *yourself*

a Match sentence beginnings 1–6 with endings a–f.

1 ☐ Why do you keep **talking**
2 ☐ This room needs a lot of work, but you can **do**
3 ☐ Come in! **Make yourself**
4 ☐ Good luck at the interview! Just **be**
5 ☐ Bye! Have a wonderful time! **Look**
6 ☐ Are you OK? Have you

a **after yourself** and have fun – **enjoy yourself**!
b **yourself** and **tell yourself** 'I can do this!'.
c **to yourself**? Is it because you're **teaching yourself** German?
d **hurt yourself**?
e at home, and **help yourself** to food and drink.
f **it yourself** – you don't need to pay someone.

b Underline the correct words in the rule.

We use *yourself* in the phrases in **bold** in 3a because the object of the verb is *the same as* / *different from* the subject of the verb.

c Underline the correct words.

1 Is it possible to *help* / *teach* yourself how to swim?
2 You could pay someone to clean the car or you could *do* / *do it* yourself.
3 There's a lot of food in the fridge. Please *help* / *make* yourself.
4 Don't copy other people. *Be by* / *Be* yourself.
5 Sit down. Make yourself *to* / *at* home!
6 You should *tell* / *tell to* yourself 'I'm wonderful!' every day.

d Complete the questions with the correct form of the verbs in the box and *yourself*.

enjoy   hurt   look after   talk to   teach

1 Have you ever _____ how to do something? What was it? Was it easy or difficult to learn?
2 Do you _____? Do you eat well and get enough sleep?
3 Have you ever _____ at home? Did you have to go to hospital?
4 Do you ever _____? What do you say?
5 Are you _____ right now? If not, what would make you happy?

e 💬 Discuss the questions in 3d.

⟳ REVIEW YOUR PROGRESS

How well did you do in this unit? Write 3, 2 or 1 for each objective.
3 = very well   2 = well   1 = not so well

I CAN ...

talk about different forms of communication.	☐
describe experiences in the present.	☐
give and respond to opinions.	☐
write a guide.	☐

CAN DO OBJECTIVES

- Talk about experiences of work and training
- Talk about technology
- Make and respond to suggestions
- Write an email giving news

UNIT 2
Modern life

GETTING STARTED

a ▶ 1.23 Look at the photo. Where do you think the woman is? Listen and check your ideas.

b 💬 Discuss the questions.

1 What else do you think there might be in this office building? (Think of the furniture, rooms and entertainment.)
2 Would you like to work in an office building like this? Why / Why not?
3 What would your ideal workplace be like?

2A They've just offered me the job

Learn to talk about experiences of work and training

G Present perfect simple and past simple
V Work

1 READING

a 💬 Discuss the questions.

1 Have you ever had a job interview?
2 Was it a good experience? Why / Why not?

b Read *Not the best interview I've ever had!* Who got the job? Who didn't get the job?

c Read the stories again. Match a–d with headings 1–4.

1 ☐ Wrong word!
2 ☐ Better to tell the truth
3 ☐ The interviewer probably felt worse than me!
4 ☐ An unlucky call

d 💬 Tell your partner which story you liked best. Have you had any embarrassing experiences like the ones in the stories?

> I've received a phone call at a bad moment.

> Really? What happened?

Not the best interview I've ever had!

Most people feel nervous when they go for a job interview, but some interviews are worse than others. Fortunately, they don't all end in disaster!

a 'They wanted to test how fast I could type. My fingers were over the keyboard, ready to type. The interviewer said 'Right click to open the file', but all I heard was 'Write click' so I typed 'click' on a window that was already open. I felt so embarrassed when I realised my mistake, but we both laughed and I got the job. I've worked there for eight months now.'
Laura

b 'I've never forgotten to switch my phone off in the cinema, but for some reason I forgot when I went for my first job interview. My friend phoned me to wish me good luck – right in the middle of the interview. Oops! I didn't get the job.'
Andy

c 'I've had lots of good interviews, but this one was a disaster. I had put on my CV that I could speak 'some French'. I learnt some French at school, but I've never really used it and my listening skills are really bad. The three interviewers began the interview by speaking to me in French, and I didn't understand a word. No, I didn't get the job, and yes, I've changed my CV!'
Dan

d 'I had a job interview with two people last week. One of them was leaning back on his chair when suddenly it fell right back and it was soon clear that he couldn't get up again. I didn't know if I should try to help or not and I was worried I was going to start laughing. Fortunately, the other interviewer asked me to wait outside the room for a minute, and then the interview carried on as if nothing had happened. Guess what? They've just offered me the job!'
Ellie

20

2 VOCABULARY Work

a Look at photos a–f below and match them with sentences 1–6.

1 ☐ Hundreds of people **applied for** the job but only six **candidates** were invited for an interview.
2 ☐ It's hard to balance family life and a **career**.
3 ☐ I'm proud of my practical skills and medical **knowledge**.
4 ☐ There are 200 **employees** in this organisation, but I'm only **in charge of** a small team.
5 ☐ I've got good **grades** but I haven't got much experience to put on my **CV**.
6 ☐ I've got a lot of **business contacts** who work for **employers** in different countries.

b Match the words in **bold** in 2a with these meanings.

1 the jobs you do during your working life
2 people you know who might be able to help your career
3 contacted a company asking for a job
4 people who work for a company
5 the results of your exams at school or university
6 the things you know from experience or study
7 people who are trying to get a job
8 responsible for something or someone
9 the people that you work for
10 a document which describes your education and the jobs you have done

c 💬 What do managers look for when they employ someone new? Choose the four qualities that you think are most important.

- creative thinking
- good grades
- work experience
- self-confidence
- good problem-solving skills
- a friendly personality
- the ability to work in a team
- a positive attitude to work
- practical skills

3 GRAMMAR
Present perfect simple and past simple

a Look at these sentences from the stories on p.20. Which verbs are in the present perfect and which is in the past simple?

1 I**'ve** never **forgotten** to switch my phone off in the cinema.
2 I**'ve had** lots of good interviews, but this one was a disaster.
3 I **had** a job interview with two people last week.
4 They**'ve** just **offered** me the job!

b Underline the correct words to complete the rules.

1 We use the *past simple / present perfect* to talk about recent past events that have an effect on the present.
2 We use the *past simple / present perfect* to talk about our experiences.
3 We use the *past simple / present perfect* when we give details (e.g. when, where, etc.) or talk about specific past events.

c ▶1.24 **Pronunciation** Listen and choose the sentence you hear, a or b.

1 a I worked there for eight months.
  b I've worked there for eight months.
2 a I had lots of good interviews.
  b I've had lots of good interviews.

d ▶1.25 Listen and practise saying the sentences.

e ▶ Now go to Grammar Focus 2A on p.134

f Complete the sentences with the present perfect or past simple form of the verbs in brackets.

1 I _____ (never/have) a really terrible job interview.
2 Once, I _____ (forget) to switch off my phone when I was at the cinema.
3 I don't have very much work experience, but
  I _____ (be) in charge of a small team.
  I _____ (be) the leader on a project at school.
4 I _____ (get) some useful work experience last year.
5 I _____ (study) hard this year, so I hope I can pass my exams.
6 I _____ (always/be) able to express myself clearly since I was a child.
7 I _____ (already/work) for more than three organisations.
8 I _____ (know) what career I wanted when I was a child.

g 💬 Tell your partner which sentences are true for you and give more information.

> Number 1 is true for me. I've only had two or three job interviews, but they've all been OK.

4 LISTENING

a 💬 Think of five reasons why an employer might <u>not</u> offer a candidate a job. Compare your ideas with a partner.

b ▶1.29 Listen to the beginning of a radio interview. Answer the questions.

1 Are any of your ideas in 4a mentioned in the report?
2 What one quality does Nancy believe all employers are looking for at a job interview?

c ▶1.29 Listen again and complete each sentence with one or two words.

1 People with likeability can _____ with other people.
2 Nancy believes likeability is more important than other abilities in the first _____ of a new job.
3 She advises job hunters to spend time with _____.
4 Nancy encourages people to apply for jobs even if they don't have the right _____.
5 During an interview, it's important to _____ the interviewers by showing that you're friendly, positive and can communicate well.

d ▶1.30 Listen to five speakers. Do they agree that being likeable is more important than other skills? Write A (agree) or D (disagree).

Speaker 1 _____   Speaker 3 _____   Speaker 5 _____
Speaker 2 _____   Speaker 4 _____

e ▶1.30 Listen again and answer the questions.

1 According to Speaker 1, why don't people know that likeability is important?
2 According to Speaker 2, what's the advantage of developing your 'soft skills'?
3 How does Speaker 3 behave towards his patients?
4 What problem does Speaker 4 have with 'soft skills'?
5 According to Speaker 5, what are the most important things you can offer an organisation?

f 💬 Discuss the questions.

1 Which do you think is more important when getting a new job – likeability or good qualifications? Why? Think of different kinds of jobs.
2 Do you think schools and colleges should help students develop 'soft skills'? How could they do this?

5 SPEAKING

a You are going to talk about your experiences. Tick (✓) three things you have done. Then make notes about your experiences.

- ☐ learned practical skills (what?)
- ☐ got qualifications (which?)
- ☐ studied/worked in a foreign country (where?)
- ☐ chosen a career
- ☐ worked for no money
- ☐ visited an interesting office or factory
- ☐ written a CV
- ☐ given a talk or presentation
- ☐ done some online learning
- ☐ studied or worked as part of a team
- ☐ been in charge of a project

b 💬 Take turns to talk about your work and training experiences. Ask questions to find out more information.

> I've been in charge of a project. It was a small team and we all worked well together.

> Was this at work or at school?

2B I've been playing on my phone all morning

1 VOCABULARY Technology

a 💬 Think of things you can do on a smartphone. Compare ideas with other students. Who has the most ideas?

b Match words 1–5 with definitions a–e.

1 ☐ app   3 ☐ icon   5 ☐ username
2 ☐ browser   4 ☐ text message

a a name you need to type (with a password) to start using something
b a written message that you send from one phone to another
c a computer program that you use to read information on the internet
d a small picture on a computer/phone screen that you click on to open a program or an app
e a small computer program that you can download onto a mobile phone or other device

c Cross out the wrong verb in each group.

1 *turn off* / *send* / *delete* an email
2 *download* / *press* / *share* a video
3 *install* / *share* / *upload* some photos
4 *install* / *download* / *press* a new app
5 *turn off* / *turn on* / *delete* a phone
6 *upload* / *press* / *click on* a button or icon
7 *connect to* / *send* / *browse* the internet
8 *type* / *change* / *turn on* a password

d 💬 Think of five things that you've done recently using phrases from 1c. Tell a partner.

> I've just changed my email password.
>
> Why? Did you forget it?

e 💬 Discuss the questions.

1 What apps have you got on your phone or tablet?
2 Which apps do you like or use most?
3 Look at the apps on this page. What do you think they do?

2 READING

a Read *What's your favourite app?* below and answer the questions.

Which app … ?
1 is good for music lovers
2 helps you learn about the stars
3 keeps you interested because you can keep improving
4 helps busy people organise themselves
5 helps you create and keep photos online
6 helps you make funny photos
7 is useful if you've got too many apps on your phone
8 records your fitness information

b Read the article again and answer the questions.

1 What do you get from ThingsToDo at the end of each week?
2 How do you find a planet with SkyWatch?
3 What changes can you make to photos with Imagegram?
4 Why does Enzo play Balloon Pop every day?
5 What information does ActivityTracker give you when you run?
6 What information can Tunespotter tell you about a song?
7 How can StopApp make your phone work better?
8 What kinds of photos does Luke think are funniest on Crazy Faces?

c 💬 Discuss the questions.

1 Do you use any apps like the ones in the article? Which ones? How useful are they?
2 Would you like to use any of the apps in the article? Which ones? Why?

3 GRAMMAR Present perfect simple and continuous

a Read sentences a–d. Then answer questions 1–5.

a **I've seen** photos where people have baby faces on adult bodies.
b **I've been playing** it on the bus every day.
c **I've been recommending** it to all my friends.
d **I've just installed** the ThingsToDo app.

1 Which sentences use the present perfect continuous?
2 Which sentence talks about one completed past activity (without mentioning a time)?
3 Which sentence talks about something the speaker has experienced?
4 Which sentences talk about activities which started in the past and are not finished yet?
5 Which sentences talk about something which happened regularly or more than once?

What's your favourite

I've just installed the ThingsToDo app. It's so easy to use – which is really important when you've got lots of things to do and not much time! You just create a list and then add items to it. Once a week it sends you a list of everything you've done. **Juan**

My favourite game at the moment is Balloon Pop. You select groups of coloured balloons and pop them. I've been playing it on the bus every day, because I always want to get to the next level – it's very addictive! **Enzo**

Have you heard about SkyWatch? It's great. You just point your phone at the night sky and it tells you what the stars are. You can also type in the name of a planet and the program tells you where to look for it. **Katya**

ActivityTracker is a great app for running. You just press the start button when you begin your workout and the app records your speed, distance and heart rate. After the workout, you can then upload your information to social networking websites and compare with your friends. I've never found an app as good as this before. **Fay**

I love Imagegram and I've been using it more and more recently. You can use different effects to make photos look different, like old-fashioned photos, or with brighter colours. Then you can store them online and share them with your friends. **Paul**

I've just downloaded Tunespotter. If you hear a song you like but you don't know what it is, you can use this app. It identifies the name of the song and the singer. And if you like it, you can buy the song really easily. I've had it for a week and I've been using it a lot. **Martin**

b Complete the sentences with the present perfect simple or present perfect continuous form of the verbs in brackets.

1 I _____ a new phone. (just/buy)
2 I _____ for my own name online. (never/search)
3 I _____ a lot of films in the last two weeks. (watch)
4 I _____ for a new tablet, but I haven't got enough money yet. (save up)
5 I _____ about not using my smartphone for a few weeks, just to see if I can survive! (think)

c ▶ **1.31** **Pronunciation** Listen to sentences 1–4 and <u>underline</u> the correct words in the rule.

1 I've used an app.
2 I haven't used an app.
3 I've been using an app.
4 I've just been using an app.

In present perfect sentences, we usually stress the *main verb / auxiliary verb*. If it is a negative sentence, or we add a word like *just*, then we *also / don't* stress the main verb.

d ▶ **1.31** Listen again and repeat the sentences.

e ▶ Now go to Grammar Focus 2B on p.134

f 💬 Are the sentences in 3b true for you? Change the false sentences so that they are true for you. Tell your partner about your sentences.

4 SPEAKING

a You are going to find out which of your classmates is most addicted to technology. Think of six questions to ask about what people have used recently. Use the topics below or your own ideas.

apps/mobile phones   computer games
the internet   social-networking sites

How often have you been on Facebook in the last two days?
What apps have you been using recently?

b 💬 Use your questionnaire to interview different people in the class. Who has used the most and least technology recently? Who in the class do you think is a technology addict?

StopApp is a really useful app and I've been recommending it to all my friends. If too many apps are open on your phone, your phone can be really slow. This app turns them off, which can make your phone faster. **Anna**

I've been using Crazy Faces a lot recently. It's very silly, but it's fun. You just take photos of your friends and then you can change their faces. You can make them look older or younger, fatter or thinner, and you can add beards, moustaches and glasses. I've seen lots of photos where people have put baby faces on adult bodies and they make me laugh every time! **Luke**

2C Everyday English
Could you take it back to the shop?

Learn to make and respond to suggestions

P Sentence stress
S Sounding sympathetic or pleased

1 LISTENING

a 💬 Talk about a problem you have had recently. What was the problem? Did you solve it? How?

b 💬 Look at the photos. What has just happened?

c ▶1.33 Watch or listen to Part 1 to check.

d 💬 What do you think Rachel and Becky will do next?

e ▶1.34 Watch or listen to Part 2. Do they mention any of your ideas?

f ▶1.34 Watch or listen again. Are the sentences true (T) or false (F)?

1 Becky's screen is still working. F
2 Rachel thinks removing the SIM card might help. T
3 Becky is worried about losing all her phone numbers. T
4 Becky bought the phone very recently. F
5 Becky has got insurance. F
6 Rachel heard on the radio about using rice to dry phones. F

2 USEFUL LANGUAGE Making suggestions

a Choose the correct words.

1 Have you tried *turning* / *turn* it off and on again?
2 What about *taking* / *take* the SIM card out and drying it?
3 Could you *taking* / *take* it back to the shop?
4 Can you *claiming* / *claim* on your insurance?
5 You could *trying* / *try* that.

b ▶1.34 Watch or listen to Part 2 again and check your answers to 2a.

c Complete the responses with the words from the box.

| why idea worth give |

1 **A** How about just leaving it until it dries out?
  B I'll give it a try. What have I got to lose?
2 **A** Why don't you try drying it with a hair dryer?
  B That's worth a try, but wouldn't the heat damage the phone?
3 **A** Shall we phone Mark and see if he has any ideas?
  B Yes, why not? He might know what to do.
4 **A** Let's go to the phone shop and ask for advice.
  B That's a great idea. They should be able to help.

d What solutions can you think of for these problems? Make notes.

1 You missed your bus home and the next one is in an hour. It's raining.
2 You don't have any ideas about what to buy your friend for his/her birthday.
3 You've spilt coffee on your shirt and you have an important meeting in 20 minutes.
4 The battery in your phone is low and you need to make an important call in an hour.

e 💬 Take turns to ask for advice and make suggestions.

3 LISTENING

a 💬 Look at the photo. Who do you think Becky is talking to?

b ▶️ **1.35** Watch or listen to Part 3. Does the phone work now? Why / Why not?

4 CONVERSATION SKILLS
Sounding sympathetic or pleased

a ▶️ **1.36** Listen and complete the conversations.

1 **Rachel** How's the phone?
  Becky Not good. The screen's frozen.
  Rachel _____! Have you tried turning it off and on again?

2 **Becky** I hope I haven't lost all my contacts. I haven't saved them anywhere else.
  Rachel Oh no, _____.

3 **Becky** My phone's working. That rice trick worked.
  Rachel That's _____! I'm really _____ to hear that.

b Look at the completed conversations in 4a. Which phrases sound sympathetic? Which phrases sound pleased?

c 💬 Take turns to say sentences 1–6 below. Respond, sounding sympathetic or pleased. Then ask for more details.

1 I've lost my phone.

2 I've found a new place to live.

3 My car has broken down.

4 I was woken up very early this morning.

5 My sister is coming to visit.

6 I've been offered a great new job.

5 PRONUNCIATION Sentence stress

a ▶️ **1.37** Listen to these sentences. <u>Underline</u> the stressed syllables.

1 Have you tried turning it off and on again?
2 What about taking the SIM card out and drying it?
3 Could you take it back to the shop?
4 Can you claim on your insurance?

b We usually put stress on the words which are important for our message. Which syllables do you think are stressed in these sentences?

1 I can't find my phone!
2 My computer's broken. I've lost all my work!
3 I have a very annoying colleague at work – he complains about everything.
4 I'm really worried. I have a big exam tomorrow.
5 My car has been making a strange noise recently. I hope there isn't a problem.

c ▶️ **1.38** Listen and check. Then practise saying the sentences.

6 SPEAKING

a Think of a problem you have or might have (e.g. with a colleague, your studies, a car, your computer). Make notes about the problem.

b 💬 Take turns to explain your problem and make suggestions.

○ Unit Progress Test

CHECK YOUR PROGRESS

You can now do the Unit Progress Test.

1 SPEAKING AND LISTENING

a What changes would you like to make to your life? Make notes about one of the topics below.

> your job   the apartment/house you live in
> the town/city you live in   your free-time activities
> your studies   your friends

b 💬 Talk about the changes you would like to make to your life. Give reasons.

c ▶1.39 Listen to two friends, Tania and Lin, talking in a café. What two changes is Tania thinking about?

d ▶1.39 Tania writes an email to an IT company in Hong Kong called PayHK. Listen to the conversation again and complete gaps 1–6 in the application email above right.

e 💬 Ask and answer the questions.

1 How common is it for people in your country to work abroad?
2 What are the main reasons they go?
   - better work opportunities
   - more money
   - a cultural experience
   - language learning
   - other reasons

2 READING

a Read Tania's email to Lin about Hong Kong and answer the questions.

1 Has Tania got good or bad news?
2 When does she hope to see Lin?

b Read the email again and answer the questions.

1 What did Tania do the day after the interview?
2 What kind of apps will she create in her new job?
3 Will she only work on the company's current products?
4 Is the new job well paid?
5 What else would she like to do in Hong Kong?

---

application

Dear Sir/Madam,

I'm writing to enquire about the possibility of work in your company. I'm an application software developer. I've been ¹working for my current company for just over ²a year now, but I'd like a change. I'm good at ³creative thinking and I have excellent ⁴problem-solving skills. In addition, I also have a positive ⁵attitude towards my work and colleagues.

I don't speak Cantonese, but I'm very interested in ⁶Chinese culture and would love the opportunity to live and work there. I'd be interested in any information you can send me.

Please find my CV attached.

Yours faithfully,

Tania Sampson

Hong Kong!!!

Hi Lin,

I'm sorry I haven't been in touch for the past few days, but it's been a very busy time.

On Monday I had a job interview with PayHK, the IT company in Hong Kong that I emailed. Then the next day, I had to do a practical test. ¹**You won't believe this, but** they've just rung to offer me the job!

The work sounds really interesting – they want me to work on developing apps that can be used for making mobile payments. ²**And what's really exciting is that** they also want me to think of ideas for new products. The job offer is very generous. Apart from giving me a good salary, they're also going to pay me a bonus if I do well. And they'll pay for my flights and help me with accommodation when I arrive.

³**But the best thing is that** I'm going to live in Hong Kong! Besides the food, I'm also looking forward to learning Cantonese. Everyone at PayHK speaks English, but I'd like to be able to talk to local staff in their first language. I've always wanted to learn a second language well, and I'm sure I'll be able to do it when I'm living there.

We must get together before I leave, so you can tell me all about Hong Kong. Would you like to meet up for dinner some time in the next week? Let me know a day that suits you.

Tania

3 WRITING SKILLS Adding new information

a Look at **bold** phrases 1–3 in the second email. Why does Tania use them? Choose the correct reason.

1 to summarise her news
2 to introduce new information
3 to show she is very busy

b Rewrite phrases 1–3 in the second email using the words in brackets.

1 _You will never believe this,_
    (will never)
2 _And what's really fascinating is that_
    (fascinating)
3 _But the most fantastic thing is that_
    (most fantastic)

c Put the words in the correct order to make sentences.

1 but I've / believe this / bought a house / you'll never

2 is / more amazing / what's even / the location

3 it wasn't / thing is that / too expensive / but the best

d Read sentences a–c and <u>underline</u> the correct words in the rules below.

a I have good problem-solving skills. **In addition**, I also have a positive attitude towards my work.
b **Apart from** giving me a really good salary, they're also going to pay me a bonus.
c **Besides** the food, I'm also looking forward to learning Cantonese.

- We can use phrases like *in addition (to)*, *apart from* and *besides* when we want to add information.
- We use them at the ¹*beginning* / *end* of a sentence.
- We use *in addition (to)* in more ²*formal* / *informal* writing.
- After *apart from* and *besides*, we use an ³*infinitive form* / *-ing form* or a noun.
- In the other part of the sentence, we can use ⁴*and* / *also* to emphasise that we are adding information.

e Read the sentences. Do the words/phrases in **bold** mean *as well as* or *except for*?

1 They're going to pay all my expenses **apart from** meals.
2 **Apart from** my travel expenses, they're also going to pay for my meals.
3 **Besides** the food, I'm also looking forward to learning Cantonese.
4 I've done everything I can to prepare, **besides** learning Cantonese.

f Rewrite these sentences using the words in brackets. Write two sentences if necessary. There may be more than one possible answer.

1 I have a degree in software development and I have a diploma in interactive media design. (in addition)
2 They'll pay for a hotel when I arrive and they'll pay the first month's rent on an apartment. (apart from)
3 They're going to give me a return airfare now and they're going to pay for another return airfare in the middle of my contract. (besides)

4 WRITING An informal email

a Imagine you have some exciting news. Choose one of the topics below or your own idea. Make notes about extra things you can say about this news.

1 You've won a trip to a tropical island.
   (How did you win it? When are you going?)
2 You've got a new job.
   (What's the job? Why did you apply?)

b 💬 Compare your ideas with a partner.

c Write an email to a friend explaining your good news. Use phrases to introduce new information, if possible.

d Work in pairs. Read your partner's email. Is their news similar to yours? Do they use phrases to add information correctly?

UNIT 2
Review and extension

1 GRAMMAR

a 💬 Underline the best answers. Then ask and answer the questions.

1 What job *did you want* / *have you wanted* to do when you were a child?
2 How long *have you used* / *have you been* using this book?
3 How many emails *have you written* / *have you been writing* today?
4 Have you ever *lost* / *been losing* your phone?
5 How long *have you known* / *have you been knowing* your colleagues or classmates?
6 *Have you taken* / *Have you been taking* a driving test yet?

b Complete the text using the present perfect simple, present perfect continuous or past simple.

¹ Have you ever imagined _____ (you/ever/imagine) what it's like to be a successful games designer? That's my goal.
I ² 've always _____ (always/love) playing games. In fact, I ³ 've been playing _____ (play) computer games since I was just three! I ⁴ left _____ (leave) school at 18 and studied computer animation at college. Then I ⁵ worked _____ (work) for a software company. I ⁶ developed _____ (develop) some useful skills there, but it wasn't the right job for me.
Then, six months ago, I got an apprenticeship with a games company. It doesn't pay very much, but I ⁷ 've already gained _____ (already/gain) a lot of experience.
I ⁸ 've been working _____ (work) on an idea for a game in my free time for the last six months. When it's ready, I'll present it to my company. I know I'll be a success.

2 VOCABULARY

a Complete the words.

1 We have 72 e m p l o y e e s at this company. Some of them have worked here for a long time.
2 We have two c a n d i d a t e s for the job. We need to choose one.
3 Schools should teach p r a c t i c a l skills, like cooking and driving.
4 He's got great p r o b l e m-s o l v i n g skills.
5 My uncle had a long c a r e e r in the army.

b Match the words in the box with definitions 1–6.

app   browser   device   display   keyboard   password

1 a software program that allows users to find and read information on the web browser
2 a secret phrase that you use to log in to a website password
3 you type by using this keyboard
4 a computer program designed for one purpose app
5 a tablet, laptop or mobile phone device
6 the screen on a phone, tablet or computer display

3 WORDPOWER *look*

a Match questions 1–8 with answers a–h.

1 [d] What do employers usually **look for**?
2 [f] Did you see John's office?
3 [b] What does 'disconnect' mean?
4 [g] What are you **looking at**?
5 [c] Are you coming to the meeting tomorrow?
6 [h] How do you feel about your trip to Moscow?
7 [a] What do you think of my new SmartWatch?
8 [e] **Look out**! Didn't you see that bicycle?

a It **looks** good. Can I try it?
b I don't know. **Look** it **up** online.
c No, I have to **look after** some customers.
d Someone who is reliable and hard-working.
e No! It came out of nowhere!
f No, we didn't **look around** the building.
g It's an advert for a sales job.
h I'm really **looking forward to** it.

b Match the phrases in the box with definitions 1–8.

look + adjective   ~~look after~~ someone/something
~~look at~~ someone/something   look around (somewhere)
look for something/someone   ~~look forward~~ to something
look out   look (something) up

1 try to find look for
2 feel excited about a future event look forward
3 check a meaning or other fact in a book or online look up
4 explore look around
5 be responsible for look after
6 seem look adjective
7 be careful look out
8 watch look at

c Complete the sentences with the correct form of *look* and a particle (*after*, *up*, etc.) if necessary. Sometimes, more than one answer is possible.

1 Do you like looking at trees, flowers and other plants?
2 Do you enjoy looking after small children?
3 Have you ever looked around a factory?
4 Do you know anyone who's looking for a job at the moment?
5 Where do you usually look up new English words?
6 What are you looking forward to doing this year?
7 Does the weather look good today?
8 In what situation would you shout 'look out!' to someone?

d 💬 Discuss the questions in 3c.

🔄 REVIEW YOUR PROGRESS

CAN DO OBJECTIVES

- Talk about a friendship
- Talk about families
- Tell a story
- Write about someone's life

UNIT 3
Relationships

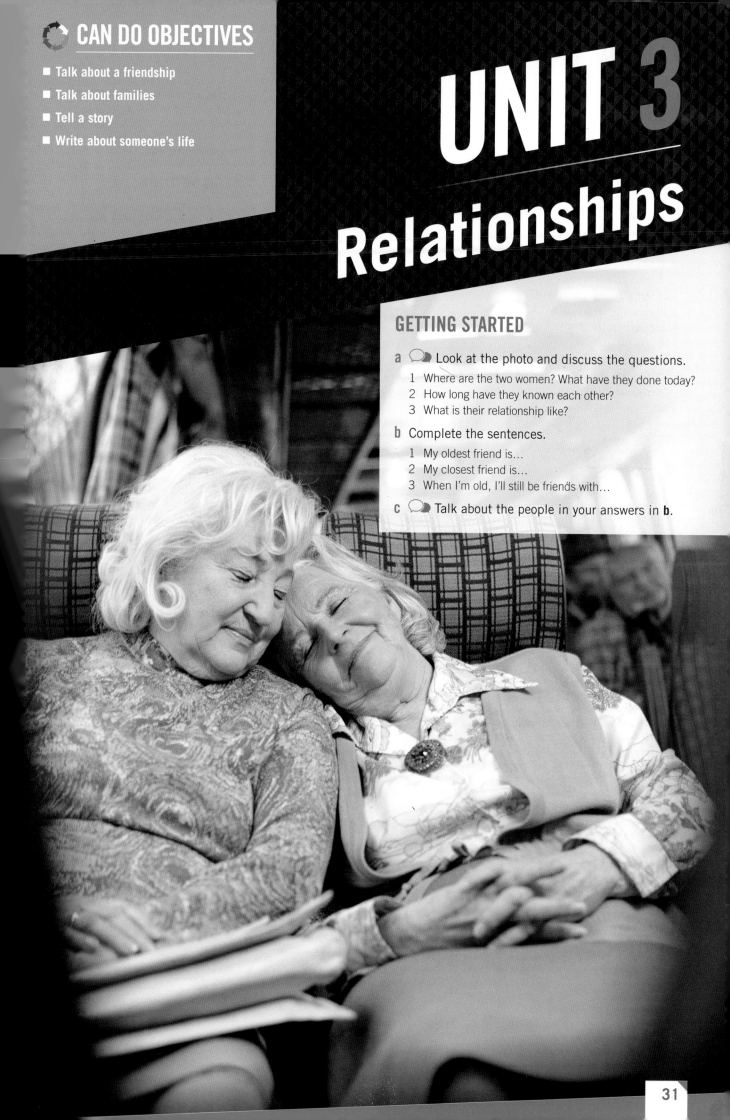

GETTING STARTED

a 💬 Look at the photo and discuss the questions.

1 Where are the two women? What have they done today?
2 How long have they known each other?
3 What is their relationship like?

b Complete the sentences.

1 My oldest friend is…
2 My closest friend is…
3 When I'm old, I'll still be friends with…

c 💬 Talk about the people in your answers in **b**.

1 VOCABULARY Relationships

a 💬 Write down the names of three people you know well and show them to your partner. Ask and answer the questions about each person.

1 How long have you known him/her?
2 When did you meet?
3 How often do you see each other?
4 What do you do together?

b Underline the correct answers.

1 My friends and I like the same music but that's the only thing we *have in common* / *get on*.
2 I don't like it when *strangers* / *relationships* start talking to me.
3 I generally *get on with* / *get to know* people of all different ages.
4 I have a good *friendship* / *relationship* with my cousins.
5 I think you can only *keep in touch* / *get to know* people well when you live with them.
6 I don't need emotional *friendship* / *support* from my friends. I just want to have fun with them.
7 Most of my friends come from the same *background* / *personality* as me.
8 A lot of my *relatives* / *strangers* live in the same town as I do.
9 I can be friends with anyone who has the same *sense of humour* / *relationship* as me.
10 I'm not very good at *getting on* / *keeping in touch* with friends who live far away.
11 My longest *friendship* / *relative* started when I was at primary school.
12 I have shared *interests* / *support* with most of my close friends.

c 💬 Which sentences in 1b are true for you?

2 PRONUNCIATION Linking sounds

> In a sentence, when one word ends in a consonant sound and the next word starts with a vowel sound, we often link these words. We say them without any pause between the words.

a ▶1.40 Listen to the sentences. Can you hear the linking between the words in **bold**?

1 That's the only thing we **have in** common.
2 I don't **need emotional** support.
3 I generally **get on** with people **of all ages**.

b Underline the words which you think will be linked in this way (consonant sound + vowel sound).

1 I fell in love with my husband the moment I saw him.
2 Kate lives in the USA, but we keep in touch online.
3 My friends and I have a very silly sense of humour.
4 I don't think a shared background is important.
5 My relatives are all very close.

c ▶1.41 Listen and check. Then practise saying the sentences.

32

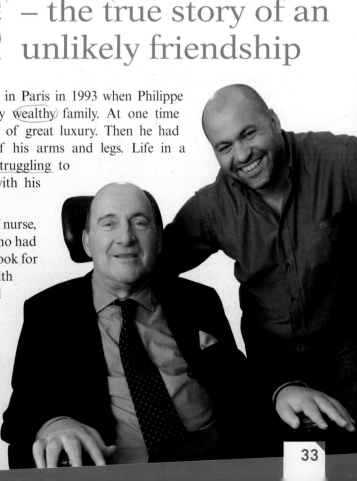

a QUAD Production

3 READING

a Look at the film poster on the right and the 'Film Facts' below and answer the questions.

1 What do you think the connection between the two men is?
2 Why is one man in a wheelchair?

b Read the first part of *Untouchable: the true story of an unlikely friendship* below and check your ideas.

c Before you read the rest of the article, guess the answers to these questions.

1 In what ways did Abdel help Philippe?
2 How long did Abdel work for Philippe?
3 In what ways did Philippe help Abdel?
4 What is their relationship like now?

François Cluzet Omar Sy

Untouchable

Written and directed by Eric TOLEDANO and Olivier NAKACHE

ANNE LE NY AUDREY FLEUROT CLOTILDE MOLLET DIRECTOR OF PHOTOGRAPHY MATHIEU VADEPIED ORIGINAL MUSIC LUDOVICO EINAUDI
EDITOR DORIAN RIGAL-ANSOUS 1st ASSISTANT DIRECTOR HERVÉ RUET CASTING GIGI AKOKA SET FRANCOIS EMMANUELLI
SOUND PASCAL ARMANT LINE PRODUCER LAURENT SIVOT PRODUCED BY NICOLAS DUVAL ADASSOVSKY YANN ZENOU and LAURENT ZEITOUN
a QUAD GAUMONT TF1 FILMS PRODUCTION TEN FILMS CHAOCORP COPRODUCTION WITH THE PARTICIPATION OF CANAL + and CINECINEMA
IN ASSOCIATION WITH APIDEV 2 and CINEMAGE 4 DEVELOPPEMENT INTERNATIONAL SALES AND DISTRIBUTION GAUMONT
QUAD Gaumont TF1 TenFilms CHAOCORP

Film Facts

 Untouchable (2011)

 Directed by Olivier Nakache and Éric Toledano

 France's number one film for ten weeks

 France's second biggest box office hit

 Nominated for nine Césars

Made over $160 million in France and $400 million worldwide

Untouchable
– the true story of an unlikely friendship

1 *Untouchable*, a charming French comedy about two friends who have almost nothing in common, has been a huge international success. But, before their story became a cinematic sensation, how exactly did a rich French aristocrat and an Algerian immigrant with a criminal past become good friends?

2 Philippe Pozzo di Borgo and Abdel Sellou first met in Paris in 1993 when Philippe was looking for a nurse. Philippe was from a very wealthy family. At one time he had been a successful businessman, living a life of great luxury. Then he had a terrible paragliding accident and lost the use of his arms and legs. Life in a wheelchair was lonely and boring. Philippe was struggling to imagine the future, and he needed practical help with his day-to-day life.

3 Philippe interviewed more than 80 people for the job of nurse, but none of them seemed right. Then he met Abdel, who had quit a life of crime in Algeria and moved to France to look for work. He was lively, intelligent and quick-thinking, with a crazy sense of humour. Philippe got on with Abdel immediately, and he offered him the job.

4 The two men didn't have much in common. Abdel loved pop music, but Philippe preferred classical music. Philippe loved modern art, but Abdel hated it. Philippe's family were sure that he had made a bad choice. They believed that Philippe needed someone much more sensible. Meanwhile, Abdel wasn't planning on staying in the job for long.

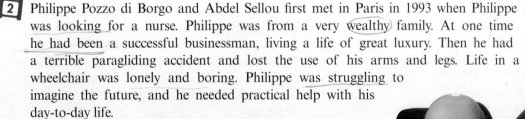

d Read the second part of the article and check.

5 However, their working relationship quickly developed into a close friendship. Abdel gave Philippe the support he needed. More importantly, his energy and sense of humour brought fun and excitement back into Philippe's life. Abdel helped Philippe make trips to other countries. Back home in Paris their adventures included travelling around the streets of Paris with Abdel on the back of Philippe's wheelchair or driving Philippe's Rolls-Royce – often much too fast!

6 In the end, Abdel worked for Philippe for ten years. Philippe believes it was Abdel's energy and sense of fun that kept him alive. 'I suddenly found I was enjoying life again,' he says. 'I felt like I didn't know what was coming next.' As for Abdel, getting to know Philippe had kept him out of prison and introduced him to a new way of life.

7 Philippe and Abdel now live in different countries, each with a wife and family. They keep in touch regularly. Over the years they have learnt, among other things, to enjoy each other's favourite music. All that really matters to their friendship, though, is their shared love of laughter and adventure.

e Find words or phrases with these meanings in the article.
1 someone from a high level in society (paragraph 1)
2 rich (paragraph 2)
3 sad because you are not with other people (paragraph 2)
4 full of energy (paragraph 3)
5 help or encouragement (paragraph 5)
6 ability to enjoy life and not be too serious (paragraph 6)

f Discuss the questions.
1 Why do you think people liked the film so much?
2 Do you have a lot in common with your friends? Or do they introduce you to new things and ideas? Which is more important?
3 How long can a friendship last when you keep in touch but don't spend time together?

4 GRAMMAR Narrative tenses

a Underline the correct words.

The two men ¹*first met / were first meeting* in Paris in 1993, when Philippe ²*looked for / was looking for* a nurse. At one time, he ³*was / had been* a successful businessman, living a life of great luxury. Then, after a terrible paragliding accident, he ⁴*had lost / lost* the use of his arms and legs. Philippe ⁵*struggled / had struggled* to imagine the future. Philippe ⁶*liked / had liked* Abdel immediately and he ⁷*offered / had offered* him the job of being his nurse.

b Answer the questions.
1 Did Philippe look for a nurse once or for a long time?
2 When was Philippe a businessman: when he met Abdel or before he met Abdel?

c Find and underline two more examples of the past continuous and two more examples of the past perfect in the first part of the article on p.33.

d Complete the story with the correct form of the verbs in brackets. Use narrative tenses (past simple, past continuous, past perfect).

I ¹_____ (meet) my friend Amy in 2009. She ²_____ (work) in a café at the time and I ³_____ (go) there quite often. She ⁴_____ (not be) very happy because she ⁵_____ (just/finish) a degree in Art History and she couldn't find an interesting job. One day she ⁶_____ (notice) that I ⁷_____ (read) a book about Leonardo da Vinci and we ⁸_____ (start) talking about art. We realised we had a lot in common, including a love of Italian art. A few months later, Amy ⁹_____ (hear) about an Art History course in Italy and we ¹⁰_____ (decide) to do it together. We both still live in Rome and we love it here.

e ▶ Now go to Grammar Focus 3A on p.136

5 SPEAKING

a Think about yourself and a close friend, or two people you know who are close friends. Prepare to tell the story of how the friendship started. Make notes about these topics:
- life before you/they first met
- what happened when you/they met
- what happened next
- things in common.

b Take turns to tell your stories.

> I met my best friend at high school. We had been at the same primary school, but we were in different classes.

3B We used to get together every year

Learn to talk about families

G used to, usually
V Family; Multi-word verbs

1 VOCABULARY Family

a 💬 Look at the photos and guess the family relationships between the people. Make at least two guesses for each picture.

> They could be sisters.
>
> Perhaps they're cousins.

b Match sentences 1–8 with photos a–h.

1. [g] I haven't got any brothers or sisters, so I'm an **only child**.
2. [c] My brother has got a son and a daughter, so I've got a **nephew** and a **niece**. They're twins.
3. [f] Judy was born a year before me, so I've got an **older sister**.
4. [a] My brother is two years older and my sister is three years younger. I'm the **middle child** in our family.
5. [h] I've got five brothers and sisters who are all younger than I am. I'm the **oldest child** in the family.
6. [e] My family lived in Malta until I was 12 years old, so I spent all my **childhood** there.
7. [b] Helena has given up work to stay at home and **raise** her young children.
8. [d] I've just become a grandmother, so there are now three **generations** in our family!

c 💬 Use the **bold** words and phrases in 1b to talk about your family.

> I'm not an only child – I've got an older sister.
>
> I spent my childhood in the country.

35

2 LISTENING

a 🗨 Discuss the questions.

1 Do you know any twins? If so, how well do you know them? How similar/different are they?

2 What do you think are the advantages and disadvantages of having a twin?

b ▶1.45 Listen to two twins talking about their lives. Answer the questions.

Charlotte

1 What were the twins like when they were children?

2 What changed in their relationship when they were teenagers?

3 What's their relationship like now?

Megan

1 What kind of sister was Charlotte?

2 What changed in their relationship when they were teenagers?

3 In what ways are they similar now?

c 🗨 Do you think Megan and Charlotte like being twins? Why / Why not?

d ▶1.45 Listen again and answer the questions. Write C (Charlotte), M (Megan) or B (both).

Who says … ?

1 she can tell what the other twin is thinking _C/B_

2 they used to swap clothes _M_

3 they looked very similar when they were children _B/M_

4 they didn't use to argue very much _B/M_

5 they wanted to be different from each other when they were teenagers _B_

6 they get in touch frequently now _C_

e 🗨 Discuss the questions.

1 Do you have brothers and sisters? Is your relationship similar to the relationship between Megan and Charlotte?

2 Would you like to have a twin? Why / Why not?

3 VOCABULARY Multi-word verbs

a Match the multi-word verbs in **bold** in sentences 1–9 with meanings a–i.

1 [h] As we **grew up**, we created our own identities.

2 [b] We usually speak on the phone two or three times a day, and we **get together** as often as we can.

3 [e] We looked so similar – our parents used to **mix us up**.

4 [d] We didn't use to argue much, but in our teenage years we started to **grow apart**.

5 [f] We saw that we'd both **cut** all our hair **off**!

6 [g] We wanted to **hang out with** each other more.

7 [c] My parents **ring** me **up** every Sunday night for a chat.

8 [i] My grandmother **brought** me **up**, so I'm very close to her.

9 [a] I think I mainly **take after** my dad – we look similar and we're both good at science.

a to be similar to an older member of the family

b to meet (when you have organised it before)

c to make a phone call to someone

d to gradually have a less close relationship

e to think one person/thing is another person/thing

f to remove or make shorter, using scissors or a knife

g to spend time with someone

h to gradually become an adult

i to look after a child until he/she is an adult

b Complete rules 1–3 with the verbs in **bold**.

- I mainly **take after** my dad.
- We started to **grow apart**.
- We'd both **cut** all our hair **off**.
- We'd both **cut off** all our hair.
- We'd both **cut** it **off**.

1 Some multi-word verbs have no object (e.g. _____).

2 Some multi-word verbs are separable (e.g. _____). This means that the object can go either between the verb and the particle or after the particle. (When the object is a pronoun (e.g. *you*, *him*, *it*), it must go between the verb and the particle.)

3 Some verbs are not separable (e.g. _____). When we use a pronoun with these, it goes after the particle.

c ▶1.46 **Pronunciation** Listen to these sentences. Which word in **bold** is stressed?

1 As we **grew up**, we wanted to create our own unique identities.

2 We wanted to **hang out with** each other.

3 We saw that we'd **cut** all our hair **off**!

We usually stress the particle in multi-word verbs, not the main verb. If the multi-word verb has two particles, we stress the first one. If the multi-word verb is separated by an object (e.g. *all our hair*), then we often stress the object.

d ⏵**1.46** Listen again and repeat the sentences.

e 💬 Discuss the questions.

1 Where did you grow up?
2 Who brought you up?
3 When did your whole family last get together?
4 How much do you take after your parents?

4 GRAMMAR *used to, usually*

a ⏵**1.47** <u>Underline</u> the words used in the recording. Then listen and check.

1 Megan *dressed / used to dress* as differently from me as she could.
2 Megan *started / used to start* wearing flowery dresses!
3 We *were / used to be* very close.
4 We *usually speak / used to speak* on the phone two or three times a day.

b Complete the rules with the words in the box.

always   the past simple   *usually*   *used to*

1 We can use _____ to talk about events that happened only once in the past.
2 We can use _____ + infinitive to talk about past habits.
3 We can use _____ and _____ with the present and past simple to talk about present and past habits.

c ▶ Now go to Grammar Focus 3B on p.136

d Complete the sentences so they are true for you.

• The whole family usually … once a year.
• My mum/dad/parents used to … when I was a child.
• My mum/dad/parents didn't use to … when I was a child.
• My grandmother/grandfather/uncle/aunt used to …
• My brother/sister usually …
• Families in my country usually …
• Families in my country used to …

e 💬 Talk about your sentences from 4d.

> The whole family usually gets together once a year.

> Really? How big is your family?

> There are about 20 of us.

5 SPEAKING

a You are going to talk about a tradition in your family. Make notes using these questions and use the ideas in the photos to help you.

• What's the tradition?
• How often does it happen?
• When/Where does it happen?
• Which family members are involved?
• How did the tradition start?
• Was there anything you used to do which you don't do now?
• Do you like the tradition?
• Do you think the tradition will carry on in the future?

b 💬 Tell each other about your family traditions. Are your traditions similar?

> We always go out for dinner on my birthday. We used to go for a pizza, but now I usually choose a Japanese restaurant – I love sushi!

3C Everyday English
You won't believe what I did!

Learn to tell a story
- **P** Stress in word groups
- **S** Reacting to what people say

1 LISTENING

a 💬 Discuss the questions.

1 When was the last time you bought a present for a friend or relative? What was it? Did they like it?

2 Do you do a lot of shopping online? Do you buy different things online and in 'real' shops? Which do you prefer?

b 💬 Look at the photo below and the words in the box. What story do you think Mark is telling Tom?

a desk   Mark's dad   online shopping
very small   for children

c ▶**1.49** Watch or listen to Part 1 and check your ideas. What mistake did Mark make?

2 CONVERSATION SKILLS
Reacting to what people say

a ▶**1.49** Watch or listen to Part 1 again. Match Mark's comments 1–4 with Tom's replies a–d.

1 ☐ You won't believe what I did.	a	Great!
2 ☐ It was a fantastic price too.	b	What?
3 ☐ So I ordered it.	c	Sounds good.
4 ☐ It turned out I'd ordered a desk for a child.	d	No way!

b Match responses a–d in 2a with the descriptions below.

1 responding positively ___ , ___
2 showing surprise ___
3 asking for more information ___

c Underline two other ways to show surprise in the exchange below.

A I've just bought my sister's birthday present. She loves running, so I got her a sports watch.

B Wow! That's a coincidence. I ordered one for myself yesterday.

A Really? What make did you get?

d Complete the sentences so they are true for you.

1 I like / don't like …
2 Last week, I …
3 I really want to …
4 I haven't been to …

e 💬 Take turns to say your sentences and then react to what your partner says. Use the phrases in 2a and 2c.

> I don't like chocolate cake.

> Really? I thought everyone liked chocolate cake.

3 LISTENING

a What do you think Mark did when he discovered his mistake?

b ▶**1.50** Watch or listen to Part 2. What did Mark do next? Did he get a desk for his dad in the end?

c ▶**1.50** Watch or listen again. Are the sentences true (T) or false (F)? Correct the false sentences.

1 The company Mark bought the desk from didn't offer a refund. F
2 Looking on a freecycling website for a new desk was Rachel's idea. T
3 Freecycling is where people can give away unwanted things. T
4 Tom already knew about the website Freecycle. F
5 Mark is waiting for the desk to be delivered. F

d 💬 Have you ever had any problems with online shopping? What happened?

4 USEFUL LANGUAGE
Telling a story

a ▶ 1.51 Complete each sentence with one or two words. Then listen and check.

1 **You won't** *believe* **what** I did.
2 **The _____ thing** is, it was really, really small.
3 **It _____** I'd ordered a desk for a child.
4 But _____, I still had to find a desk.
5 **In the _____**, Rachel suggested I try one of those 'freecycling' websites.
6 I found the perfect desk straight away, and **the _____ thing is** it's free.

b Add the phrases in 4a to the list below.

* starting a story:
You'll never guess what (happened to me last week).

_____

* adding new information:

_____
_____
_____

* finishing a story (or part of a story):

_____
_____

c ⬤ Tell each other stories using the notes below and the phrases in 4b.

1 • went to the shops
 • saw an old friend I hadn't seen for years
 • had lunch
 • she knew my wife/husband from work
2 • went shopping
 • wanted new clothes for wedding
 • found perfect dress/suit
 • got 25% discount

5 PRONUNCIATION
Stress in word groups

a ▶ 1.52 Listen to these sentences from the conversation. Notice how the speaker pauses between word groups. Use // to mark where the speaker pauses.

1 The funny thing is, it was really, really small.
2 In the end, Rachel suggested I try one of those 'freecycling' websites.
3 Well, I phoned the company to explain and luckily they agreed to give me a refund.

> Notice how, in each word group, one syllable is stressed more than all the others in the group. This is the main stress.

b ▶ 1.52 Listen again. Underline the syllable in each group which is stressed more strongly than the others.

c ▶ 1.52 Listen again and repeat the sentences.

6 SPEAKING

a Think of an interesting thing that happened to you (or someone you know) recently. Choose from the topics below or your own ideas:

* making a stupid mistake
* meeting a new person
* going on an interesting trip

Make notes about what happened. Think about which phrases from 4a you can include when you tell your story.

b ⬤ Tell each other your stories. Make sure you react to what your partner is saying.

🔄 **Unit Progress Test**

CHECK YOUR PROGRESS

You can now do the Unit Progress Test.

1 SPEAKING AND LISTENING

a 💬 Discuss the questions.

1 How much do you know about past generations of your family?
2 Do you know more about your mother's or your father's side of the family? Why?

b ▶1.53 Bryan is talking to his cousin, Susie, about their family. What relatives are they talking about?

c Look at the photos. How do you think Bryan and Susie's relatives met?

d Make notes about someone in your family who interests you. Why do they interest you?

e 💬 Tell a partner about the person in your family.

2 READING

a Read Bryan's email to Susie. Why did their grandparents decide to live in Canada?

Mail

Hi Susie,

I've done a bit of investigating about Gran and Grandad, and how they ended up living in Canada. I told you that Grandad worked as a chef on cruise ships from 1937 until 1939, when World War II started. And you know that while he was working on one of the ships, he met Gran. She was the ship's nurse.

Well, apparently, that ship's destination was Vancouver. When the ship arrived, they spent a couple of days there. That's when Grandad proposed to Gran, and she said yes. During their stay in Vancouver, they decided that they really liked the city and that they would start a new life in Canada.

However, World War II started and Grandad had to go back to England and join the British army. Meanwhile, Gran stayed in Canada, because it was much safer. They were separated for five years and missed each other very much. Gran was quite lonely at first, but after a couple of months she got a job in a hospital and she made friends there – she was always very friendly and good at talking to people.

In 1946, Grandad returned to Canada and they got married. Five years later, my father was born. And then two years after that, your mother was born.

Gran and Grandad lived in the same house for 30 years. I used to go and visit them in Vancouver over the summer when I was at school. Would you like me to take you to see the house one day?

Bryan

40

b Read the email again and put pictures a–e in the correct order.

1 ☐   2 ☐   3 ☐   4 ☐   5 ☐

3 WRITING SKILLS Describing time

a Look at the words in **bold** in the examples. Do they all describe a *point* in time or a *period* of time?

1 **From** 1937 **until** 1939, he worked as a chef on cruise ships …
2 **While** he was working on one of the ships, he met Gran …
3 **During** their stay in Vancouver, they decided that they really liked the city …
4 They were separated **for** five years …
5 **Meanwhile,** Gran stayed in Canada and Grandad went back to England …
6 I used to visit them **over** the summer.

b Underline the correct words to complete the rules.

1 We can use *while* / *during* before a noun or noun phrase.
2 We can use *while* / *during* before a verb phrase.
3 We *can* / *can't* use 'during' before lengths of time (e.g. six months).
4 *Meanwhile* / *Over* means 'at the same time' and is always at the start of a sentence.
5 *Meanwhile* / *Over* can mean the same as 'during'.

c Underline the correct words.

1 I lived alone *from* / *until* 1993 *from* / *until* I got married.
2 I worked as a chef *while* / *during* the 1990s.
3 I usually go abroad *over* / *from* the winter months.
4 I lived in London *while* / *meanwhile* I was working for the government.
5 I had a job in Los Angeles *from* / *for* about two years. *Meanwhile* / *While*, I was planning to move to New York.

d Complete the sentences.

1 He was a soldier in the army _____ five years.
2 He went to India twice _____ he was working on the boat.
3 He was in Italy _____ 1943 until 1945.
4 She was in Rome for about six months. _____, her husband stayed in Milan.
5 From 1950 _____ two years later, he worked as a chef in an Italian restaurant.

e Make notes about some important events in your life (e.g. your job, your studies, the people you know, etc.).

Over the summer holidays, I worked at a swimming pool.
I started work four years ago. Meanwhile, I was studying for a diploma.

f 🗨 Take turns to read your events to your partner. Ask questions to find out more.

4 WRITING

a You are going to write a biography of someone you know or know about. Choose who to write about and make notes about these topics:

1 why this person is important to you
2 what you remember most about this person
3 what the key events in this person's life are.

b Write the biography. Use words and phrases to describe time (*from*, *while*, etc.).

c 🗨 Work in pairs. Read your partner's biography. Do they use time words correctly? Ask a question about the person they described.

UNIT 3
Review and extension

1 GRAMMAR

a Complete the sentences with the past simple, the past continuous or past perfect of the verbs.

1 When I _got_ (get) home, everyone _was waiting_ (wait) for me. My family and friends _had planned_ (plan) a surprise party for my birthday!

2 When I _woke up_ (wake up) this morning, I _had_ (have) a shock. The wind _had blown_ (blow) a tree down and it _had blocked_ (block) the front door.

3 As soon as the doctor _showed_ (show) me the X-ray, I _knew_ (know) I _had broken_ (break) my leg.

4 As I _sat_ (sit) on the grass, I _realised_ (realise) I _had_ (put on) odd socks. I _felt_ (feel) very silly.

b Underline the correct words.

1 We *occasionally* (used to)/ *had* a big family party.

2 My parents *used to give* /(*gave*)me a bike on my eighth birthday.

3 Did you *used* /(*use*) to be shy when you were a child?

4 Terry and his twin brother *always wear* /(*used to wear*) the same clothes. They wear the same clothes to work and at the weekend, too.

5 My sister and I *always*(*used to walk*)/ *walked always* home from school together when we were young.

6 My aunt doesn't *used to* / (*usually*)celebrate her birthday, but I always phone her.

7 I didn't (*use to*)/ *hardly ever* like George, but now we're best friends.

8 My grandfather says, 'Young people (*used to be*)/ *always were* more polite than they are now'.

2 VOCABULARY

a Complete the words.

1 Someone with no brothers or sisters is an o_nly_ ch_ild_.

2 Your brothers, sisters, parents, cousins, uncles, aunts and grandparents are your r_elative_s.

3 Someone who you don't know is a s_tranger_.

4 Your brother or sister's daughter is your n_iece_.

5 Your brother or sister's son is your n_ephew_.

b Complete the sentences with a multi-word verb which has a similar meaning to the words in brackets.

~~bring~~	grow	cut	hang	grew
apart	off	out	~~up~~	up

1 It's a book about how to _bring_ _up_ children. (raise)

2 When did he _cut_ all his hair _off_? (remove)

3 Where did you _grow up_? (live when you were a child)

4 We used to be good friends, but we _grew apart_ when she changed schools. (become less close)

5 I often _hang out_ with Martin and his cousin. (spend time relaxing)

3 WORDPOWER *have*

a Complete the conversations with sentences a–g.

a Yes, we did, but we **had an accident** in the car we rented.

b Yes, I did. Well, I **had a go**. I wasn't very good!

c Shall we **have lunch** out today?

d Neil **has three brothers**, doesn't he?

e I **have no idea**. What Spanish restaurant?

f Does he **have brown eyes and a beard**?

g You should **have some lessons**.

A 1 _d_

B Yes, but I only know the oldest one, Carl. I sometimes **have a drink** with him after work.

A 2 _f_

B Yes, he does.

A How was your holiday? Did you **have fun**?

B 3 _a_

A 4 _c_

B Yes, I'd like that. Where's that new Spanish restaurant?

A 5 _e_

B It's a new place. Let's go into town and **have a look**.

A How was the wedding? Did you dance?

B 6 _b_

A 7 _g_

B Yes, maybe I will.

b Add the phrases with *have* in **bold** in 3a to the table.

eating/drinking	possession	experience	other phrases
have a drink have lunch	brown eyes beard	have fun	have no idea have some lessons

c Complete the sentences with the correct form of *have* or *have a/an*.

1 How many cousins do you _have_?

2 When was the last time you _had_ special meal?

3 Are any of your friends or family _having_ language lessons at the moment?

4 Your sister's private diary is open on her bed. Do you _have a_ look?

5 Do you usually _have_ breakfast with your family or on your own?

6 Have you ever _had an_ accident in a car, or on a bike?

7 Did you _have a_ good time last weekend? Why / Why not?

8 For fun, some people are trying to lift a 50kg weight. Do you _have to_ go too?

d 💬 Ask and answer the questions.

REVIEW YOUR PROGRESS

How well did you do in this unit? Write 3, 2 or 1 for each objective.

3 = very well   2 = well   1 = not so well

I CAN . . .

talk about a friendship.	☐
talk about families.	☐
tell a story.	☐
write about someone's life.	☐

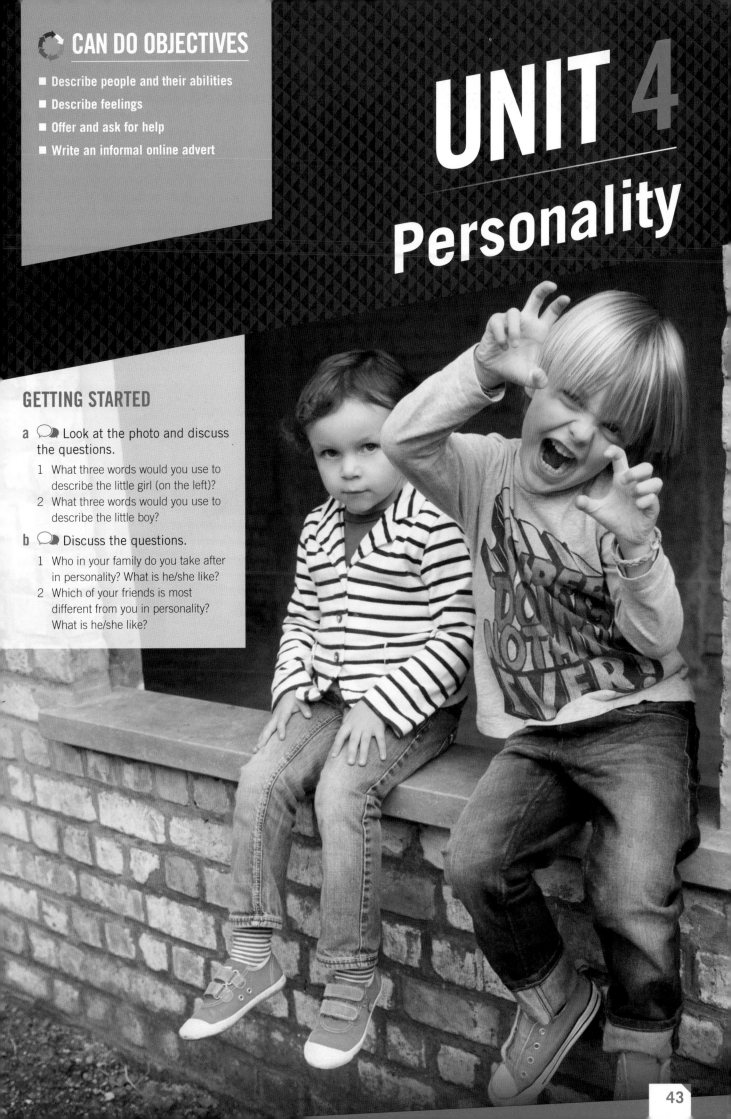

CAN DO OBJECTIVES

- Describe people and their abilities
- Describe feelings
- Offer and ask for help
- Write an informal online advert

GETTING STARTED

a Look at the photo and discuss the questions.

1 What three words would you use to describe the little girl (on the left)?
2 What three words would you use to describe the little boy?

b Discuss the questions.

1 Who in your family do you take after in personality? What is he/she like?
2 Which of your friends is most different from you in personality? What is he/she like?

Learn to describe people and their abilities

- **G** Modals and phrases of ability
- **V** Ability

1 VOCABULARY Ability

a Write down three things you are good at. How long have you been able to do these things?

b 💬 Talk about what you are good at.

> I'm good at drawing people's faces. I've always enjoyed drawing and painting.

c Read *What happens to talented children when they grow up?* Did the children become successful as adults?

d Read the article again and underline the correct words.

e Look at the words and phrases in the box. Which are about … ?
  1 how clever you are *brilliant, bright, intelligent*
  2 your feelings/emotions *confident, positive a.*
  3 what you have done *achievement, successful*
  4 stopping something *give up,*

  ~~talented~~ ~~confident~~ ~~brilliant~~
  ~~ability~~ ~~intelligent~~ ~~a positive attitude~~
  ~~successful~~ ~~achievement~~ ~~give up~~ ~~bright~~

  ---

f Complete the sentences with the correct prepositions.
  1 She is **good** _____ making friends.
  2 He's **brilliant** _____ playing the piano.
  3 I'm not very **talented** _____ art.
  4 It's important to have **a positive attitude** _____ your work.
  5 She has the **ability** _____ pass exams without even trying.

g Complete the sentences so they are true for you.
  1 It's important to have a positive attitude and not give up because …
  2 I'm talented at …
  3 I'm not very good at …
  4 If you want to be successful in life, you need to …
  5 One of my biggest achievements is …

h 💬 Talk about your sentences in 1g.

WHAT HAPPENS TO TALENTED CHILDREN WHEN THEY GROW UP?

Do successful children become successful adults? We look at two talented children and see what happened to them when they became adults.

ANDREW HALLIBURTON

Andrew Halliburton has an IQ of 145 and was very [1]*succeeded | talented* at maths at a young age. But, rather than making a fortune in banking or computers, he ended up clearing tables in a fast-food restaurant. As a child, his parents pushed him very hard, but he didn't spend enough time making friends. He thinks that the other children at school didn't like him because he was always so clever. He went to university to study computing, but he thought the course was too easy, so he [2]*gave up | succeeded* after six months. He got a job in a burger bar instead, and worked there for several years.

OPRAH WINFREY

Oprah Winfrey is a [3]*success | successful* TV presenter in the USA. She had a very difficult family life and she never had any money. But she was very [4]*intelligent | talent* and did well at school. She always had a [5]*positive attitude | positive thinking* towards life and she was [6]*determined | brilliant* to work on TV. At the age of 19, she got a job with a local radio station. In the mid 1970s, she became the first black female newsreader on American TV. This was the beginning of her [7]*successful | success* story. Her TV show, where she interviewed famous people like Tom Cruise, Michael Jackson and Barack Obama, became famous around the world. Now she is one of the richest women in America.

2 LISTENING

a 💬 Look at the photos below of four talented people and discuss the questions.

1 What is each person good at?
2 Do you think they always had this talent?
3 What age do you think they were when they became successful?

b ▶1.54 Listen to a radio programme about age, talent and success. Check your ideas from 2a.

c ▶1.54 Listen again. Are the sentences true (T) or false (F)?

1 Tsung Tsung first became famous when he appeared on a TV show. F
2 As a boy, Messi could play football better than the older boys. T
3 A recent study showed that most talented children do much better than other adults when they grow up. F
4 Vivienne Westwood used to be a teacher. T
5 Bocelli's solo classical album became an international success when he was in his 40s. T
6 Ed believes that talented people don't usually make mistakes. F

d 💬 Do you agree with these statements?

1 Talented children don't succeed as adults because they don't develop good social skills.
2 It's better to be successful when you are young – you can enjoy it more.
3 If you want success in a creative job, hard work is more important than talent.

Vivienne Westwood

Tsung Tsung

Lionel Messi

Andrea Bocelli

3 GRAMMAR
Modals and phrases of ability

a Underline the words and phrases used to talk about ability in these sentences.

1 Tsung Tsung <u>could</u> play the piano when he was three.
2 He wants to be able to play like Mozart.
3 He was so good that he was able to join the Barcelona junior team when he was 11.
4 Less than 5% managed to become very successful adults.
5 Andrea Bocelli has been able to sing well since he was a child.
6 Say to yourself: 'I can do it!'
7 She'll be able to play the piano when she's a bit older.

b Look at the sentences in 3a. Complete rules 1–5 with the words in the box.

be able to   can   will be able to
could   manage to   was/were able to

1 We use _____ and *be able to* to talk about ability in the present.
2 In the past, we usually use _____ to talk about general ability and _____ to talk about a single time.
3 There is no present perfect or infinitive form of *can*, so we use forms of _____ instead.
4 We can't say 'will can', so we say _____ instead.
5 The verb _____ means to succeed in doing something difficult.

c ▶1.55 **Pronunciation** Listen to this sentence from 3a. Which is stressed more: *could* or *play*?

Tsung Tsung could play the piano when he was three.

d ▶1.56 Now listen to this sentence. Which word is stressed the most?

Say to yourself: 'I can do it!'

e Underline the correct words in the rules below.

1 We *usually* / *don't usually* stress words and phrases to talk about ability, unless we are emphasising something.
2 We *usually* / *don't usually* stress the main verb we are focusing on (e.g. *play the piano*).

f Complete the sentences. More than one answer may be possible.

1 I took my exam today and I _____ finish all the questions before the end.
2 After trying for 20 minutes, we _____ open the door.
3 I've _____ ski since I was five years old.
4 Ellie _____ already read simple books when she was three years old.
5 I live near the sea, but I _____ swim.
6 My Spanish is getting better. I'll _____ speak to my Spanish friends on the phone soon.

g ▶ Now go to Grammar Focus 4A on p.138

h Make notes about these topics.

1 three things you could do when you were a child which you can't do now
2 two things you managed to do after a lot of hard work
3 one thing you want to be able to do better in the future
4 two things you didn't manage to do last week because you had no time

i 💬 Talk about the topics in 3h. Ask each other questions to find out more information.

4 SPEAKING

a Think about ways in which you have succeeded (e.g. learnt a new skill, passed an exam, solved a problem). Tick (✓) the things that helped you to be successful.

- ☐ a positive attitude
- ☐ patience
- ☐ working long hours
- ☐ knowing the right people
- ☐ good luck
- ☐ good health
- ☐ talent
- ☐ support from friends and family
- ☐ self-confidence
- ☐ intelligence

b 💬 Which of the things from 4a helped you to be successful? Which do you think are most important?

My parents helped me a lot when I was at university. You definitely can't succeed without the support of your family.

4B Are you an introvert?

1 VOCABULARY -ed/-ing adjectives

a 💬 Discuss the questions.

1 Do you prefer spending time alone or with other people?
2 Do you think you are an extrovert or an introvert? Why?

b Read the description and the reviews of *Quiet* by Susan Cain. What good things do you think the book says about introverts?

c Match the words in **bold** in the reviews with the meanings 1–7.

1 very unhappy
2 unhappy because something is not interesting
3 making you feel pleased because you have what you need or want
4 unhappy because something didn't happen
5 very afraid
6 not interesting or exciting
7 extremely interesting

d ▶1.58 **Pronunciation** Listen to these adjectives. How is the final -ed sound pronounced? Complete the table.

amused   bored   depressed   disappointed
fascinated   interested   relaxed   satisfied   terrified

/d/	/t/	/ɪd/

e ▶1.59 Listen and check. Repeat the adjectives.

f Match the sentence halves.

1 We use -ing adjectives
2 We use -ed adjectives

a to describe feelings.
b to describe the things or people that cause the feelings.

g Complete the sentences with the correct form (-ing or -ed) of the words in brackets.

1 Jo and I are going to a concert next week. Are you _____? (interest)
2 Some people find winter _____ but I like it. (depress)
3 Everyone says the new restaurant is very good but I thought it was very _____. (disappoint)
4 I thought Clare would like the picture, but she wasn't _____. (amuse)
5 When I saw the spider on my leg I was _____! (terrify)
6 Japan is a wonderful country. I'm _____ by the culture. (fascinate)

h Write short answers for these topics.

• a time you felt disappointed
• a book or film that you found really interesting
• music that you find relaxing
• something or someone that you find amusing
• something you think is boring
• what you do if you feel depressed

i 💬 Take turns to read out your answers.

Quiet

The Power of Introverts in a World That Can't Stop Talking

SUSAN CAIN

NEW YORK TIMES BESTSELLER

"Superbly researched, deeply insightful, and a fascinating read."
—GRETCHEN RUBIN, author of *The Happiness Project*

by Susan Cain (2013)

Are you an extrovert (confident and sociable) or an introvert (quiet and happy to be alone)?

Your personality type influences your friendships, your relationships and your career. It even affects your need for sleep and the way you learn.

In societies that value conversation and self-expression, introverts are often seen as 'second place' to extroverts. In this beautifully written book, Susan Cain explores the many good things that introverts bring to the world.

BOOK REVIEWS 📖

Home   Shop   Reviews   Login

by BookMan ★★★★
This is the most **fascinating** book I've read on the introvert/extrovert topic for a long time. Cain describes her personal experience of being an introvert as well as writing about famous introverts who have changed the world.

by JD ★★★★
As a child I was often **terrified** at school because of the emphasis on public speaking and discussion. Perhaps some of the ideas from Susan Cain's book will change the education system in the future.

by Alan Gibson ★★★
A well-written book. I found the ideas very interesting, but I was **disappointed** that Susan Cain only writes about society in the USA without exploring how other cultures view introverts and extroverts.

by BLil ★★★★★
A great book! Everyone who thinks that introverts are **depressed** or **boring** should read it!

by Thinker ★★★
I was a bit **bored** by all the stuff about business, but I'm an introvert myself so it was very **satisfying** to see such praise of my personality type!

2 READING

a Complete the quiz. Then go to p.128 to see your results. Do you agree with how the results describe you?

b Look at the four photos of famous people below and on p.49. Then answer the questions.

1 What do you know about them?
2 Do you think they were/are introverts or extroverts?

c Read *Why the world needs introverts* quickly to check your ideas.

d Read the article again and answer the questions.

1 What is the attitude that Susan Cain calls the 'Extrovert Ideal'?
2 How do people organise classrooms and offices to make them better for extroverts?
3 How are extroverts useful to introverts?

e 💬 Discuss the questions.

1 Do people in your culture think that being quiet is a good thing?
2 Are schools and offices in your country designed for extroverts? How?

Are you an introvert? 🕰 **Quiz**

Read each statement and tick *Yes* or *No*.

1 I can be alone for a long time without feeling lonely.
Yes ◯ No ◯

2 In class, I prefer listening to talking in groups.
Yes ◯ No ◯

3 I express myself better in writing than speaking.
Yes ◯ No ◯

4 I don't always answer the phone when it rings.
Yes ◯ No ◯

5 I prefer working on my own or in a small group of people.
Yes ◯ No ◯

6 I don't like other people seeing my work before I've finished it.
Yes ◯ No ◯

7 People often describe me as quiet.
Yes ◯ No ◯

Number of *Yes* answers = ☐

Why the world needs introverts

'It's good to be **sociable**! It's good to be confident! It's good to be loud!' In her book *Quiet*, Susan Cain points out how deeply this belief is held by society. Very often the qualities of extroverts – being **active** and **lively**, making quick decisions and working well in a team or group, for example – are valued more than the **shy**, serious and **sensitive** qualities of introverts. Susan Cain calls this attitude the 'Extrovert Ideal'. In her book she looks at the way society places such value on the Extrovert Ideal that many modern schools and workplaces are built around it. Desks in classrooms are pushed together so that students can work in groups more easily. In Europe and the USA, employees are frequently put in shared offices so that they can work in teams. Students and employees are also expected to be confident and **talkative**.

Mahatma Gandhi was an introvert, as were Van Gogh and Albert Einstein

Why are the needs of introverts ignored in this way when introverts have so much to offer? Introverts need less excitement around them than extroverts, it's true, but that doesn't make them less exciting people. Many of the world's greatest ideas, art and inventions have been produced by introverts. The Indian leader Mahatma Gandhi was an introvert, as were the artist Vincent Van Gogh and the physicist Albert Einstein.

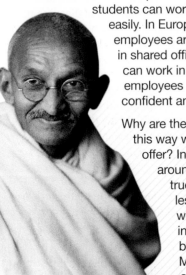

Then there was Rosa Parks, who started the US civil rights movement in 1955 by bravely and quietly saying 'no' when a white passenger wanted to sit in her seat on a bus.

Famous introverts in modern times include Angelina Jolie and Mark Zuckerberg. Jolie, a hugely successful actor, supports charities that help people in war zones. She describes herself as an introvert, saying she loves to spend time alone or with small groups of people because it helps her develop as a person.

And despite the huge success of his social networking site, co-founder of Facebook Zuckerberg remains a private person who doesn't like speaking in public.

But let's not forget that we need extroverts too. Because of course, introverts can come up with great ideas, but they also need help in communicating those ideas to the world. Songwriters need singers. Designers need sales people. In other words, extroverts and introverts need each other.

3 VOCABULARY Personality adjectives

a Complete the definitions with the personality adjectives in **bold** in the article on p.48.

1 _____ people talk a lot.
2 _____ people are easily upset and feel emotions deeply.
3 _____ people like spending time with other people.
4 _____ people do a lot of things or move around a lot.
5 _____ people are full of energy and enthusiasm.
6 _____ people are not confident, especially with new people.

b Read about these people. What adjectives describe them?

1 Bella loves romantic poetry. It often makes her cry.
2 Louis doesn't say much when he's with people he doesn't know.
3 Stefan always has something to say.
4 Jon loves parties and meeting new people.
5 Anna organises various clubs, and is always out doing new things.
6 Monica is always so energetic and busy.

4 GRAMMAR Articles

a Read the text and <u>underline</u> the correct answers. Ø means 'no article'.

I have always been ¹*an / the* introvert, but I pretend to be lively. At ²*the / Ø* school, I was always really shy, but I acted loud and confident. I have always preferred to spend hours alone with ³*the / a* good book or go for a long walk with my dog. I hate ⁴*Ø / the* clubs and groups. For example, I went to ⁵*a / the* birthday party last week, and I felt really shy and nervous. But I tried to look happy and active at ⁶*a / the* party because I didn't want people to think I was strange. My husband is ⁷*the / a* friendliest person in ⁸*a / the* world. He loves going out and being with people. And he appreciates the effort I make to fit in when we socialise. But every so often he says, 'You really don't like ⁹*Ø / the* people, do you?'.

b Complete the rules with *a/an*, *the* or *Ø* (no article).

1 We use _____ when it is clear what or who we are talking about.
2 We use _____ when we are not talking about one specific thing or person.
3 We use _____ when there is only one of something.
4 We use _____ when we talk about things in general, or the general idea of something.

c ▶ Now go to Grammar Focus 4B on p.138

d Write a short paragraph about one of the topics below. Try to use articles correctly.

• someone you know who is an extrovert/introvert
• an interesting book you would recommend
• a famous person you admire

e Read and check your partner's paragraph. Are there any mistakes with articles?

5 SPEAKING

a You are going to talk about a time when you experienced strong feelings. Choose one of the ideas in the box, or your own idea. Make notes about how you felt at different stages of the experience. Write down key words and phrases.

a time you helped someone	a terrible shock
an interesting journey	a nice surprise
an expensive mistake	a scary situation

b 💬 Tell your group about your experience. Has anyone else had a similar experience? If so, did they feel the same?

> I had to give a speech to 200 people. I'm quite shy, so I was terrified!

Learn to offer and ask for help
- **S** Question tags
- **P** Intonation in question tags

1 LISTENING

a 💬 Discuss the questions.

1 Do you think that you're a helpful person? Why / Why not?
2 Do you know anyone who's very helpful? Have they helped you?

b 💬 Look at the photo. What do you think Tom is offering to do to help?

c ▶ **1.61** Watch or listen to Part 1 and check your answers to 1b.

d ▶ **1.61** Watch or listen to Part 1 again. <u>Underline</u> the correct answers.

1 Becky is showing Rachel photos of her *holiday / house*.
2 Rachel asks Becky to take photos for *her website / fun*.
3 Mark is going to *buy / pick up* the desk on Saturday.
4 Becky suggests that *Mark goes alone / Tom helps Mark*.

e What favour do you think Tom might ask Rachel?

2 CONVERSATION SKILLS
Question tags

a ▶ **1.62** Listen to the questions below and look at the question tags in **bold**. Match the question tags with uses a or b.

1 ☐ That's the hotel you stayed in, **isn't it**?
2 ☐ You know I'm making a new website, **don't you**?

a a statement checking something you already think is true
b a real question

b Match 1–4 with a–d to complete the rules.

1 ☐ We usually use a positive question tag
2 ☐ We usually use a negative question tag
3 ☐ If there is an auxiliary verb (*do/have/be*), or the main verb isn't *be*,
4 ☐ If there is no auxiliary verb, or the main verb isn't *be*,

a after a positive sentence.
b after a negative sentence.
c use *do/don't* in the question tag.
d use the auxiliary verb in the question tag.

c Complete the question tags.

1 You don't drink coffee, _____?
2 It's cold in here, _____?
3 You've eaten, _____?
4 It was you I saw, _____?
5 Steve's gone to France, _____?
6 You didn't come to class yesterday, _____?

3 PRONUNCIATION
Intonation in question tags

a ▶ **1.63** Listen to this sentence. Here, the speaker thinks she knows the answer. Does the intonation go up or down on the question tag?

> That's the hotel you stayed in, isn't it?

b ▶ **1.64** Now listen to the same sentence with a different intonation on the question tag. This time, the speaker isn't sure about the answer. It is a real question. Does the intonation go up or down on the question tag?

> That's the hotel you stayed in, isn't it?

4 LISTENING

a ▶**1.65** Watch or listen to Part 2 and <u>underline</u> the correct words.

1 Tom wants Rachel to help him to *ask Becky to marry him / buy a ring*.

2 Rachel *agrees / refuses* to help Tom.

b 💬 Look at the photo. What do you think is happening?

c ▶**1.66** Watch or listen to Part 3 and check your ideas.

d 💬 Which of these things have you done to help a friend? Were you happy to do it? What happened?

- move furniture/help them move house
- use your creative skills (e.g. taking photos)
- talk through a problem they have
- buy a present
- give them a lift in your car

5 USEFUL LANGUAGE
Offering and asking for help

a ▶**1.67** Complete each sentence with one word. Listen and check.

1 **Do you think you** _____ take them?
2 **Do you** _____ **a hand?**
3 **Could I** _____ **you a favour** in return?
4 So **what do you** _____?
5 **I** _____ **if you could** come with me to buy the ring.

b Add the phrases in **bold** in 5a to the table.

Offers to help	Asking for help

c Add these questions to the table in 5b.

1 Can you do something for me?
2 Can you give me a hand (with something)?
3 Is there something I can do?
4 How can I help you?

d Complete the conversations with the phrases in 5b. There may be more than one answer.

1 **A** I'm having a fridge delivered this evening.
   B _____?
   A No, it's fine, thanks.

2 **A** _____ with this report?
   B Of course, what do you need?
   A _____ check it and see if it makes sense?

3 **A** _____?
   B Depends what it is.
   A _____ look after my plants while I'm away.

6 SPEAKING

a ▶ **Communication 4C** 💬 Student A: Go to 6b below. Student B: Go to p.128.

b You are going to have two conversations offering and asking for help. Read the information and think about what you are going to say.

> **Student A**
> 1 You need some help to buy a new computer. You think Student B knows about computers. You would like Student B to come shopping with you.
> 2 You have a bad back so you can't lift things. However, Student B is available at the weekend, but he's not available on Friday.

c 💬 Have conversations using the language in 5b.

🗘 Unit Progress Test

CHECK YOUR PROGRESS

You can now do the Unit Progress Test.

1 SPEAKING AND LISTENING

a 🗩 Discuss the questions.

1 Have you ever used the internet to … ?
- buy or sell something
- rent a room
- meet other people or join a group
- find work or offer other people work

2 What do you think are the advantages and disadvantages of using the internet for these things?

b ▶1.68 Listen to three people talking about websites they have used. What is the purpose of each website?

c ▶1.68 Listen again. What do the speakers in brackets say about each topic?

1 how she travelled in India (Sheena)
2 her personality (Sheena)
3 earning money (Alya)
4 teaching children (Alya)
5 his skills (Brad)
6 being serious (Brad)

d 🗩 Would you use websites like these? Why / Why not?

2 READING

a Read adverts a–c below and on p.53 quickly. Which of these topics does each advert mention?

dates or times   money   travelling   types of people   work

b Read the adverts again and answer the questions.

Advert a
1 Where is the trip? *North India / Hymalayas*
2 How many people are they looking for? *1 or 2*
3 What kind of person are they looking for? *m/F under 30*
reasonably fit / able…

Advert b
1 What are the main responsibilities of the job? *domestic duties teaching*
2 When does the work start? *Next month*
3 What kind of person are they looking for? *positive and outgoing*

Advert c
1 What does the job involve? *general work.*
2 What experience is needed? *No experience*
3 How long is it for? *2 weeks*

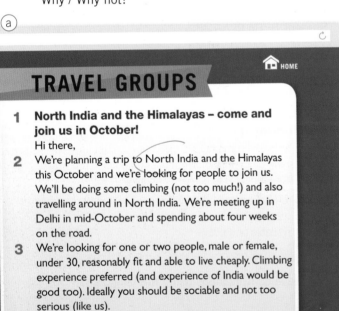

TRAVEL GROUPS 🏠 HOME

1 **North India and the Himalayas – come and join us in October!**
Hi there,

2 We're planning a trip to North India and the Himalayas this October and we're looking for people to join us. We'll be doing some climbing (not too much!) and also travelling around in North India. We're meeting up in Delhi in mid-October and spending about four weeks on the road.

3 We're looking for one or two people, male or female, under 30, reasonably fit and able to live cheaply. Climbing experience preferred (and experience of India would be good too). Ideally you should be sociable and not too serious (like us).

4 If this sounds like the trip for you, send a reply plus a photo and we'll get back to you!
Cristina, Matt and Rob
●●●● ▶

VC Volunteer Community Project

home   about us   community projects   accommodation   applications

Volunteer needed

Duties include teaching English, art, maths, etc., as well as leading educational play groups. Support will be given by local teachers or project staff. Occasionally, volunteers will be asked to help with domestic duties such as preparing meals and keeping the classrooms and gardens clean to help create a happy and healthy atmosphere for the children.

Volunteers should be available to start work next month. No qualifications required, but candidates should have a positive and outgoing personality and be good with young children.

Please send a CV and a short personal profile.

Homework :)

3 WRITING SKILLS The language of adverts

a Read about the language used in the adverts. Which adverts do sentences 1–6 describe? Write a, b or c.

1 Sentences start with *we* or *you*. __a, c__
2 Sentences start with impersonal nouns like *jobs* or *duties*. _____
3 Sentences use formal words like *candidates* or *volunteers*. _____
4 Passive verb forms are often used. _____
5 The advert uses conversational expressions (*Hi there*, *get back to*, *fixing things*). _____
6 Some sentences and phrases end in exclamation marks. _____

b Which features in 3a make the adverts seem …?

a more personal and friendly
b more impersonal and official

c Look at advert a. What is the purpose of each section? Match sections 1–4 with these descriptions.

a ☐ tells the reader what to do next
b ☐ gives details of the situation (work, travel, plans, etc.)
c ☐ shows briefly what the advert is about
d ☐ says what kind of person they're looking for

c

SHORT WORK
Home Profile Account

Wanted – help with garden and house

We're a big family (three small children) and we need help with work on our garden and house for two weeks.

Jobs that need doing include general work in the garden, painting in the house, fixing electrical problems.

No experience needed but you should be good at fixing things and happy to work hard. Payment to be arranged.

Reply to: Mel and Nick

---

d In adverts and messages, we often use fixed 'reduced' expressions. Find expressions in the adverts which mean the following:

1 You don't need any experience.
2 We'd prefer a person with climbing experience.
3 We need a volunteer.
4 We don't require you to have any qualifications.

e Look at some more examples of reduced expressions in writing. How can you express the same ideas in full sentences?

1 Assistance urgently needed.
2 Driving licence required.
3 Male or female under 40 preferred.
4 Accommodation included.

4 WRITING An informal online advert

a Write an advert. Choose one of these situations.

- You're travelling somewhere and you want more people to join you to make a group.
- You're organising charity work and you want to take on some volunteers to help you.
- You want to employ someone to work for you for a couple of weeks.

Follow this plan.

1 Give a heading to draw attention to the advert.
2 Describe the situation (the job, your plans, etc.).
3 Say what kind of person you're looking for.
4 Ask for a reply.

b Read and check your advert.

1 Do you think it's too formal, not formal enough, or about right?
2 Have you used any reduced expressions?

c Read another student's advert and write a reply.

1 Say you're interested.
2 Give details about yourself.
3 Ask any further questions.

UNIT 4
Review and extension

1 GRAMMAR

a Tick (✓) the correct sentences. Sometimes both are correct.

1 a ☑ I can kick a ball, but I can't play football!
   b ☐ I manage to kick a ball, but not manage to play football!
2 a ☑ Were you able to answer all the questions?
   b ☑ Did you manage to answer all the questions?
3 a ☑ Unfortunately, I couldn't relax.
   b ☑ Unfortunately, I wasn't able to relax.
4 a ☐ You need to can swim.
   b ☑ You need to be able to swim.

b Underline the correct words (Ø means 'zero article').

The colourful world of Aelita Andre

Aelita Andre is ¹a / Ø six-year-old artist from Melbourne, Australia. She loves ²the / Ø colours, and her paintings are bright and wild. She sometimes adds ³the / Ø small toys to her pictures, such as plastic dinosaurs and butterflies.
⁴A / The young painter has already earned more than £100,000, and ⁵Ø / the people have described her as 'the youngest professional artist in ⁶Ø / the world'. When Aelita was five, her work was on show in ⁷the / an art gallery in New York.
Aelita's mother says, 'You know how ⁸Ø / the young children paint for a few minutes and then lose interest? When Aelita was two, she often painted for an hour without stopping.'

c 💬 Complete the questions with *a*, *an*, *the* or *Ø*. Then ask and answer the questions.

1 Do you like spending time in the countryside?
2 How many times a year do you go to the cinema?
3 Can you remember the first time you went to school?
4 Have you ever called the police?
5 Did you go anywhere interesting Ø last week? If so, where?
6 Can you play the piano or any other musical instrument?
7 Would you like to be an artist? Why / Why not?

2 VOCABULARY

a 💬 Underline the correct words. Which sentences are true for you?

1 People think I'm *confidence* / *confident*, but I'm not.
2 I'd like to be a *successful* / *success* businessperson.
3 I've already *succeeded* / *achieved* a lot of my goals.
4 I'm very *patient* / *patience* with young children.
5 I'm very *talkative* / *sensitive*, so people often tell me to be quiet.

b Complete the sentences with the correct *-ing* or *-ed* forms of the words in brackets.

1 I hate this kind of music. It's really _ing_! (depress)
2 I thought the plane was going to crash. It was _ing_! (terrify)
3 Ivan was very _ed_ that he didn't get the job. (disappoint)
4 I like travelling by train. It's more _ing_ than driving. (relax)
5 I hope Jane was _ed_ with her exam results. (satisfy)

3 WORDPOWER *so and such*

a Match statements and questions 1–6 with responses a–f.

1 ☐ How many people were in the group?
2 ☐ Julie works **so** hard!
3 ☐ How many pages have you written?
4 ☐ Simon's a bit of an introvert.
5 ☐ You're getting married. That's **such** good news!
6 ☐ We're going to need a lot of stuff!

a Yes, paper, glue, paint, scissors **and so on**.
b About 20 **or so**, I think. I didn't speak to all of them.
c **So** he doesn't like working in big groups, then?
d Yes, I'm **so** happy!
e Ten **so far**, but I haven't finished yet.
f I know. And she's **such** a nice person, too.

b Find examples of rules 1–3 in 3a.

1 We use *so* + clause to describe a result. ____
2 We use *so* before an adjective or adverb to add emphasis. ____, ____
3 We use *such* before an adjective + noun to add emphasis. ____, ____

c Match the words in the box with the meanings.

> and so on   so far   or so

1 up to now ____
2 there are more things on the list ____
3 more or less ____

d Complete the sentences with one, two or three words. One of the words must be *so* or *such*.

1 Emma speaks ____ quickly!
2 We need to leave in 10 minutes ____.
3 It was too difficult ____ I asked for help.
4 She's ____ interesting person.
5 I've been trying to find a present for my brother, but I haven't had much success ____.
6 I don't like ____ hot weather.
7 We need simple food for the picnic, like bread, cheese, eggs, tomatoes ____.
8 It was ____ big achievement for me.

e 💬 Think of famous people who match the descriptions below.

1 ... is such an amazing singer.
2 ... is so funny.
3 ... is so rich.
4 ... does such good things for other people.

54

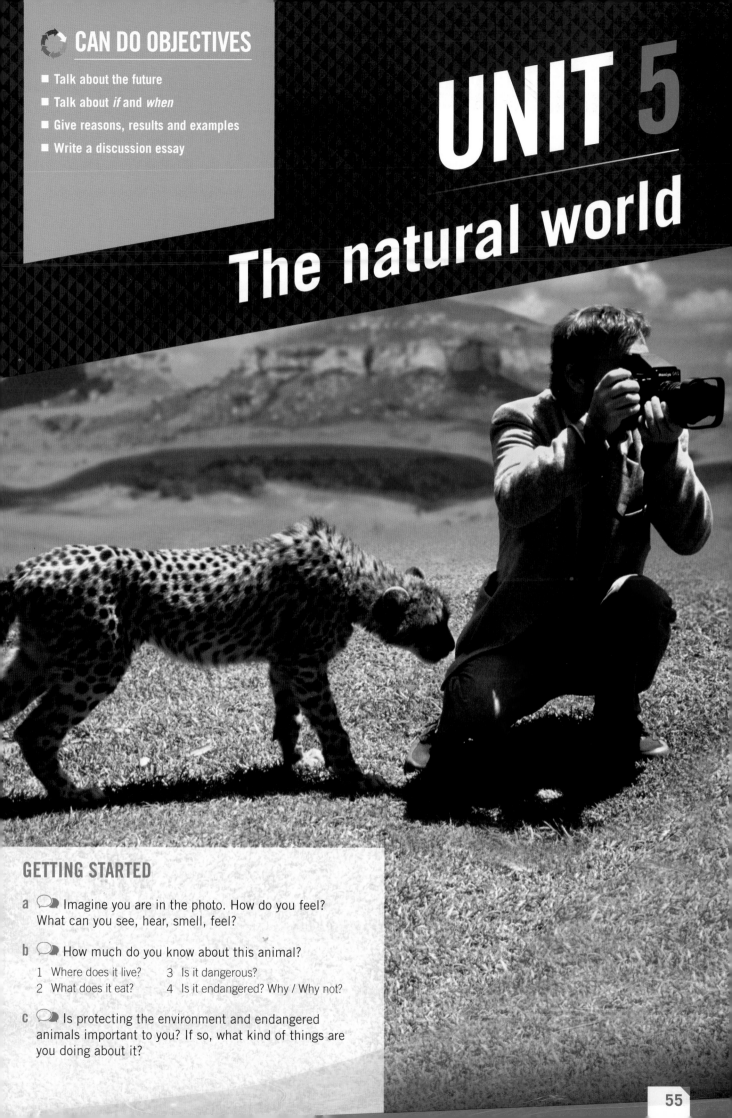

CAN DO OBJECTIVES

- Talk about the future
- Talk about *if* and *when*
- Give reasons, results and examples
- Write a discussion essay

UNIT 5
The natural world

GETTING STARTED

a 💬 Imagine you are in the photo. How do you feel? What can you see, hear, smell, feel?

b 💬 How much do you know about this animal?

1 Where does it live?
2 What does it eat?
3 Is it dangerous?
4 Is it endangered? Why / Why not?

c 💬 Is protecting the environment and endangered animals important to you? If so, what kind of things are you doing about it?

1 VOCABULARY Environmental issues

a Match the words in **bold** in sentences 1–8 with the descriptions in a–h.

1 Is air **pollution** a problem where you live? If yes, how can we **prevent** it?
2 What **wildlife** or natural environments are **endangered** in your country?
3 Are there any **conservation projects** to help **protect** these animals and plants or **save** these places?
4 Do most people support these projects?
5 Have new roads and buildings **damaged** the environment near you?
6 Do most people in your country care enough about **climate change**?
7 What can ordinary people do to help **the environment**?
8 Are you **environmentally friendly**? For example, do you **recycle** glass and paper?

a a noun that means the air, land and water where people, animals and plants live
b four verbs that are used to talk about solutions
c a verb which means 'destroyed' or 'hurt'
d two nouns that are environmental problems
e a noun that can be a solution to environmental problems
f a noun that means 'animals and plants'
g an adjective that describes animals and plants that may disappear
h a phrase that means 'not harmful to the environment'

b ▶2.2 **Pronunciation** How is the underlined letter *a* pronounced in each word below? Complete the table. Listen and check.

a̲n̲i̲mals   cha̲nge   clim a̲te   conserv a̲tion   d a̲maged
end a̲ngered   gl a̲ss   n a̲tural   p a̲per   pl a̲nts

/eɪ/	/ɑː/	/æ/	/ə/
			animals

c ▶2.2 Listen again and repeat the words.

d 💬 Choose two questions from 1a that interest you. Discuss your answers to the questions.

e ▶ Now go to Vocabulary Focus 5A on p.154

2 READING

a Read about the Whitley Fund for Nature below and answer the questions.

1 Who do they give money to?
2 How much money do they give?
3 What can winners do with the money?

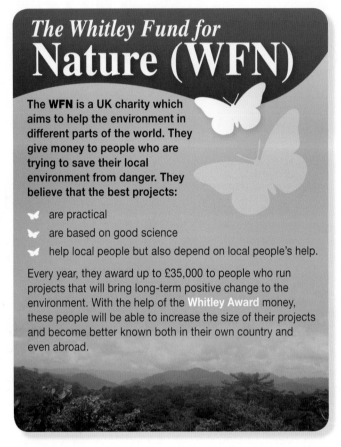

The Whitley Fund for Nature (WFN)

The **WFN is a UK charity** which aims to help the environment in different parts of the world. They give money to people who are trying to save their local environment from danger. They believe that the best projects:

🦋 are practical
🦋 are based on good science
🦋 help local people but also depend on local people's help.

Every year, they award up to £35,000 to people who run projects that will bring long-term positive change to the environment. With the help of the Whitley Award money, these people will be able to increase the size of their projects and become better known both in their own country and even abroad.

b You are going to read about three people who won £35,000 to help their local environments. Look at the photos on p.57. What do you think their projects are?

c Work in groups of three, a, b and c. Read your part of the article on p.57 and answer the questions below.

1 Where does the person work?
2 How did they first get interested in conservation?
3 What wildlife are they trying to protect?
4 Does the person work with local people? What does he/she do?
5 What does the person hope will happen in the future?

d 💬 Work in your group. Use the information in 2c to discuss these questions.

1 What do the people and their projects have in common?
2 Do you think one project is more important than the others?
3 Which project would you like to visit or help? Why?

WFN

WHITLEY FUND FOR NATURE

a Ekwoge Enang Abwe

The Ebo forest in Cameroon covers almost 2,000 km² and is home to a unique mix of 11 primates, including gorillas and the Nigeria-Cameroon chimpanzee, the most endangered of the chimpanzees. These amazing chimps use tools to fish and open fruit. In addition, the spectacular Goliath frog, the largest frog in the world, lives here.

The Cameroon government is considering turning the Ebo forest into a national park with a focus on conservation research and tourism, but there are still threats from local people and large companies who want to use the land for farming.

Ekwoge Enang Abwe grew up in a village in Cameroon, so his love for chimpanzees began at an early age. He has played an important role in the area for almost a decade and, since 2010, he has been managing the Ebo Forest Research Project.

As well as encouraging local communities to be proud of the forest's unique biodiversity, this project has been doing biological research in the forest. The project has regular contact with communities through environmental and conservation education. They hope they will be able to create a safe future for the Ebo forest.

b Dr Aparajita Datta

In 1995, Dr Aparajita Datta arrived at the Pakke Tiger Reserve in north-east India to study the local wildlife. Her attention was captured by a species of beautiful birds called hornbills. These birds are endangered because of hunting and the destruction of their forest home. Aparajita now leads a programme to conserve them.

India's north-eastern region is known for its biological and cultural diversity. The area contains the world's most northerly tropical rainforests with an estimated 7,000–8,000 species of flowering plants, and over 600 bird and 150 mammal species, including tigers and elephants. The region also has small tribal communities and these communities often depend on using the resources from the forest to survive. Aparajita and her team are working with local people and the government. They hope to find a balance between the conservation of wildlife and the needs of the local communities. Aparajita is spreading knowledge of the importance of hornbills to the forest – plants need them to spread their seeds. There is also a nest adoption programme, with money going to villagers who help to protect the birds.

c Çağan Şekercioğlu

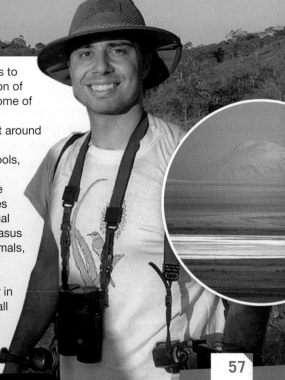

Turkey has a huge variety of natural environments, from Mediterranean forests to coastal mountains. But many of these areas are threatened by the construction of new dams and roads. ÇağanŞekercioğlu has been working hard to protect some of these areas. He is the first conservationist to win two Whitley Gold Awards.

In 2008, he won his first award for his work to protect the natural environment around Lake Kuyucuk, home to over 40,000 birds of 227 species. This work included research into the local wildlife, environmental education programmes for schools, and promoting nature tourism to support the local economy.

He won the award again in 2013 after he persuaded the government to create Turkey's first Wildlife Corridor. Approximately 4.5 million trees will be planted to connect the Sarıkamış-Allahuekber National Park to the forests along the Black Sea coast and the Caucasus mountains in neighbouring Georgia. This will allow large animals, such as the wolf, brown bear and Caucasian lynx, to move freely and safely.

Çağan's interest in conservation began when, as a teenager in Istanbul, a local wetland area where he had played as a small child was destroyed. This early experience inspired his life's work of protecting Turkey's wildlife habitats. For his next mission, he hopes to stop the construction of a dam that could destroy one of the world's most important wetlands.

3 GRAMMAR Future forms

a ▶2.4 Masha is going to Costa Rica to work on an environmental project. Listen to her talking about it. How much does she know about the project?

b ▶2.4 Listen again. Are these sentences true (T) or false (F)?

1 The government in Costa Rica wants to save the rainforests.
2 Masha will find out more about her project soon.
3 She knows exactly who she's going to work with.
4 She promises to send Phil regular emails.

c Match the future verb forms in 1–4 with uses a–d.

1 ☐ It takes quite a long time for forests to recover. **They'll probably get** better, but not immediately.
2 ☐ Tomorrow **I'm meeting** someone who worked on the project.
3 ☐ **I'm going to make** the most of my time in Costa Rica and learn some Spanish too.
4 ☐ **I'll write** regular updates on the blog, and you can follow that.

a to talk about an intention (a future plan)
b to make a prediction about the future
c to make an offer, promise or quick decision to do something in the future
d to talk about something you have arranged to do in the future

d Look at the future forms in **bold** below. Do they sound very sure, or a bit sure? What changes their meaning?

1 **They'll probably get** better, but not immediately.
2 But **I'll definitely be able** to save some turtles!
3 **Perhaps I'll work** with local people, too.
4 **I'm sure you'll have** a good time.

e Underline the best phrases in the blog below.

MY BLOG
Home About me Follow

Welcome to the first entry in my blog! ¹*I'm going / I'll go* to Costa Rica tomorrow for six weeks! It's all arranged. ²*I'll work / I'm working* on a turtle conservation project on the west coast. ³*It will definitely be / It's definitely being* hard work – but so interesting! ⁴*I'm going to work / I'm working* with turtles every day – counting them and collecting their eggs.

⁵*I'm going to have probably / I'm probably going to have* some Spanish lessons while I'm there. Perhaps ⁶*I'll be / I'm being* fluent in a few weeks!

⁷*I'll leave / I'm leaving* tomorrow and I'm back at the beginning of March.

⁸*I'll write / I'm writing* again soon with more details. Probably not tomorrow, because ⁹*I'll be / I'm being* tired after the flight. But definitely as soon as I can.

f ▶ Now go to Grammar Focus 5A on p.140

g Work in pairs. Write six predictions about your partner using the ideas in the box.

travel around the world	get your hair cut
learn another language	get a new job
live in a different country	be famous

1 I think you'll …
2 Perhaps you'll …
3 I'm sure you'll …
4 You'll probably …
5 You probably won't …
6 You definitely won't …

h 💬 Discuss your predictions.

> I'm sure you'll get a good job and become very rich in the next few years.
> I hope so!

4 SPEAKING

a Read predictions 1–6. Do you agree with them? If not, change them so you do.

In the future …

1 people will stop killing endangered animals and cutting down trees.
2 we will lose some animal or plant species for ever.
3 people will discover new wildlife species.
4 pollution will continue to get worse in big cities.
5 more areas of my country will become national parks.
6 people will behave in a more environmentally friendly way (recycle more, use public transport more, etc.).

b 💬 Discuss your ideas. Do you generally agree with each other? Are you optimistic or pessimistic about the future?

> In general, our group is quite hopeful because we think that pollution will get better, not worse. We think that people will recycle more in the future.

5B If you go to the beach, you can see dolphins

(a)

1 LISTENING

a 💬 Look at photos a and b and discuss the questions.

1 What do you think each photo shows?
2 What is the material in photo b used for?
3 What is the connection between the things in the two photos?

b Read the TV guide and check your ideas.

ON **TV** TONIGHT...

Nature knows best, Channel 4, 21:30

In this series, Professor Leslie Cook takes a closer look at common objects which were invented by humans, but inspired by nature.

Professor Cook begins the programme by talking about Velcro: a material we use every day on our shoes, clothes, purses and bags. It was inspired by the 'hook and loop' system that some plants use to move their seeds. In 1948, Swiss engineer George de Mestral was walking with his dog in the countryside when he noticed that little seeds from a plant were sticking to his dog's fur. He studied the plants more closely and saw how the hooks on the plant attach themselves to the loops and curls of an animal's fur. This gave him the idea of making Velcro.

(b)

Watch now ▶   **Record** ⏺

c 💬 Match the things from the natural world (1–3) with the related objects (a–c).

① a thorny dragon lizard

② a spider

③ a typical seashell

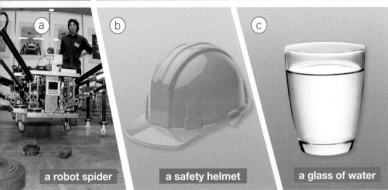

ⓐ a robot spider

ⓑ a safety helmet

ⓒ a glass of water

d ▶2.8 Listen to part of the TV programme and check your ideas.

e ▶2.8 Listen again and complete the summary with one word in each gap.

- One reptile, the thorny dragon lizard, can pull up water through 'pipes' in its [1]_____. It has inspired a device which can [2]_____ water. This will help people who live in very [3]_____ environments.
- Most spiders can move [4]_____ and make themselves very small. This has inspired the invention of a [5]_____ robot which will help people who are trapped in [6]_____ spaces.
- Seashells are very [7]_____ and light. This has inspired the production of material for safety [8]_____ such as gloves and helmets.

f Which of the inventions do you think is most useful? Why?

g 💬 Compare your ideas in 1f. Do you agree about the most useful invention?

2 GRAMMAR Zero and first conditional

a Read the conditional sentences from the TV programme and <u>underline</u> the correct words in rules 1 and 2.

- Zero conditional: *If the lizard puts a foot somewhere wet, its skin pulls the water up and over its whole body.*
- First conditional: *If we are successful, the device will provide water for people who live in very dry environments.*

1 The *zero / first* conditional talks about what will probably happen in the future as a result of something.
2 The *zero / first* conditional talks about what always happens as a result of something.

b <u>Underline</u> the correct words in rules 1 and 2 below.

1 We can use *if / when* to talk about things which will possibly or can happen.
2 We can use *if / when* for things which will definitely happen.

c Complete the text below with the correct form of the verbs in the box.

try   succeed   save   attach   make   fall off

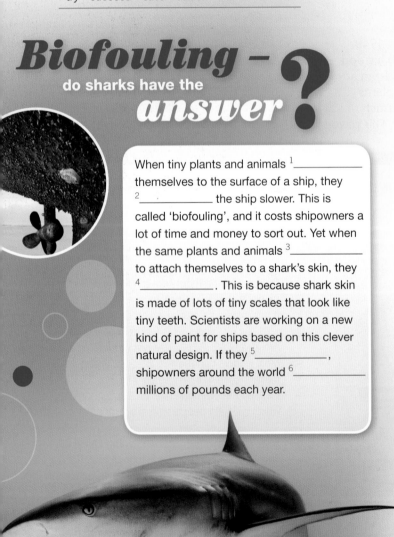

Biofouling –
do sharks have the
answer?

When tiny plants and animals ¹_____ themselves to the surface of a ship, they ²_____ the ship slower. This is called 'biofouling', and it costs shipowners a lot of time and money to sort out. Yet when the same plants and animals ³_____ to attach themselves to a shark's skin, they ⁴_____. This is because shark skin is made of lots of tiny scales that look like tiny teeth. Scientists are working on a new kind of paint for ships based on this clever natural design. If they ⁵_____, shipowners around the world ⁶_____ millions of pounds each year.

d ▶ Now go to Grammar Focus 5B on p.140

e 💬 Complete the sentences so they are true for you. Work in pairs and compare your sentences.

1 When I get a cold, I …
2 When I need to study for an exam, I …
3 If I go to a party where I don't know anyone, I …
4 If it rains today, I …
5 If I'm not too busy this weekend, I …
6 If I get up early tomorrow, I …

3 READING AND VOCABULARY
The natural world

a Look at the photos on p.61. Which animals or plants can you see? Read *Animals have adapted to survive everywhere* quickly and check your answers.

b Look at the words in the box. Which can you see in the photos?

branch   feathers   fur   leaf   paws
petals   scales   skin   tail   web

c Read the article again on p.61 and complete the gaps with the words in 3b.

d ▶2.11 **Pronunciation** Words with several consonants together can sometimes be difficult to pronounce correctly. Listen and practise saying these words, paying attention to the <u>underlined</u> parts.

a<u>dapt</u>   ba<u>ckgr</u>ound   bra<u>nch</u>   de<u>str</u>uction
mu<u>shr</u>oom   <u>scr</u>eam   <u>spl</u>ash   <u>spr</u>eading   <u>thr</u>eatened

e 💬 Which animal or plant on p.61 do you think is the most amazing? Do you know any other animals which can do amazing things?

f 💬 Describe the animals and plants in the box using the words in 3b. Do not say what you are describing. Try to guess your partner's word.

chicken   goldfish   monkey   orang-utan   palm tree
parrot   pine tree   rose   shark   snake   spider

> It's tall, and has short branches. It has little leaves. It doesn't lose its leaves in the winter.

> A pine tree?

g ▶ Now go to Vocabulary Focus 5B on p.155

ANIMALS HAVE
ADAPTED to survive
EVERYWHERE

Polar bears are a good example. They have layers of fat under their [1]_____, which means that they can swim in freezing water. Not only this, but it's very difficult for other animals to see them in the snow. Because they have completely white [2]_____, they can easily run up to other animals and attack with their huge [3]_____.

Another amazing animal is the ptarmigan. This Arctic bird is also white, which helps it hide in the snow. However, when the snow melts, the bird's [4]_____ change colour. From its head to its [5]_____, it turns grey to match the rocky environment.

Plants have adapted, too. This bee orchid looks exactly like it has a real bee resting on its [6]_____. This 'bee' is actually part of the flower, and it's nature's way of attracting real bees to the orchid.

Many fish can change the colour of their [7]_____ instantly to match their background.

At first, you might think that this is a [8]_____. But it's really an Indian leaf butterfly, sitting on the [9]_____ of a tree. Because it doesn't look like a butterfly, it can hide from other animals that would like to eat it.

This Amazon jungle spider also has an inventive way of protecting itself. It creates a [10]_____ which looks like a much larger spider, possibly to frighten other animals.

4 SPEAKING

a You are going to recommend the best place to experience the natural beauty of your country. Make notes on these topics:

- beautiful places
- what you can see there (rivers, forests, beaches, etc.)
- animals or plants you can see
- what you can do
- the best time of year to go

b 💬 Practise talking about the places on your list. Try to use conditional sentences.

> If you go to the beach near here, you will be able to see dolphins.

> If you like forests, you can go to …

c 💬 Work with another pair. Take turns to describe your places.

1 LISTENING

a 💬 Discuss the questions.

1 What hobbies and interests do you have?
2 Could any of your hobbies become a job? Would you like to do those jobs?

b 💬 You are going to watch Rachel and Becky talking about Rachel's job. Discuss the questions.

1 Why do you think Rachel became a florist?
2 What might the advantages of the job be?

c ▶2.14 Watch or listen to Part 1. Do Rachel and Becky mention your ideas?

d ▶2.14 Watch or listen to Part 1 again. Complete each sentence with one or two words.

1 Tina spent the morning _____ .
2 Tina _____ to be in the photos.
3 Becky thinks that being a florist is good because you can be your own _____ .
4 Becky doesn't like dealing with other people's _____ .
5 Rachel suggests that Becky could be a _____ .

2 USEFUL LANGUAGE
Reasons, results and examples

a Complete the sentences with the words/phrases in the box.

for instance   such as   like   because of

1 That's _____ Tina. She spent the morning cleaning up!
2 Oh, lots of things. _____, all I seem to do is deal with other people's problems, _____ issues with their pay or holidays.
3 **Becky** I wish I had a job where I could travel the world, spread my wings, be free!
  Rachel _____?

b ▶2.15 Listen and check your answers.

c Add the words/phrases in the box to the table.

because   for instance   like   as a result   due to
for example   since   because of   so   such as

Giving reasons	Giving results	Giving examples

d Read this conversation and <u>underline</u> the correct words/phrases.

A So, do you still want to be a vet?
B Sure. That's my dream. I've always wanted to work with animals, [1]*for example / due to*, in a zoo or something like that.
A A zoo! Wow, that would be good.
B Well, I need to do lots of things first, [2]*since / like* finding the best college to go to.
A I see. And is it easy to become a vet?
B Not really. It takes years at university [3]*because of / so* all the things you have to study. But that's OK. I really want to do it, [4]*so / for example* I'm sure I won't find it too difficult.
A Well, if there's anything I can do to help, [5]*so / such as* looking at college websites, let me now!

a

b

c

3 LISTENING

a Look at photos a–c above. Which one would be best for Rachel's website?

b ▶2.16 Watch or listen to Part 2. Which photo does Rachel suggest using first? Does Becky agree?

c Answer the questions.
1 What is Rachel looking at on the computer?
2 Do they choose a photo for Rachel's website in the end?

d 💬 Do you think that Becky should give up her job and become a photographer?

4 CONVERSATION SKILLS
Giving yourself time to think

a ▶2.17 Listen and complete the extract.
Becky Rachel, we can't see you in that one.
Rachel OK, _____, I think this one.

b Complete the exchanges with the words in the box.

Just   Let   sure   Well   That's

1 **A** When did you meet Frankie?
   B _____ me see, I think it was in 2004.
2 **A** This thermometer says it's 21° in here.
   B I'm not _____. I think that's wrong.
3 **A** How old were you when you decided to work with animals?
   B _____ a good question … I was about 15, I think.
4 **A** What time does the restaurant open?
   B _____ a second, I'm not sure. I'll check on their website.
5 **A** Why did you decide to resign?
   B _____, I was bored in my job.

c 💬 Ask and answer the questions. Give yourself time to think using phrases from 4b.
1 What's your dream job?
2 What's your favourite natural place? (e.g. the beach, mountains, forest)

> Let me see … I think my dream job involves working with animals …

5 PRONUNCIATION
Voiced and unvoiced consonants

a ▶2.18 Listen to these words from the conversation which begin with the sounds /p/ and /b/.

pay   people   Becky   being

b Repeat the words in 5a. Touch your throat when you try to say them. Then complete the rules with /b/ and /p/.

1 When you say _____, there is a sound in the throat.
2 When you say _____, there is no sound in the throat.

c ▶2.19 Listen and <u>underline</u> the words you hear.
1 pay / bay
2 pie / buy
3 pair / bear
4 rope / robe
5 pride / bride

d ▶2.20 Listen and repeat the words in 5c. Which sounds are voiced in the throat? Which sounds are not voiced?

6 SPEAKING

▶ **Communication 5C** 💬 Student A: Read the information below. Student B: Go to p.128.

Student A
1 You don't like your job and you want to quit. Think about the answers to these questions.
   • Why don't you like it?
   • What are you going to do next? Why?

2 Student B will tell you he/she is going to move to another part of the country. Ask him/her about their decision, including why he/she has decided to do this.

⟳ Unit Progress Test

CHECK YOUR PROGRESS

You can now do the Unit Progress Test.

1 SPEAKING AND LISTENING

a 💬 How much do you know about whales?

b 💬 Look at the Whale File on the right. Which sentence is NOT true? Check your answer on p.127.

c ▶2.21 Liz Kerr is an environmental journalist who is helping whales that have come ashore. Listen to her audio diary and answer the questions.

1 How many whales is Liz looking after?
2 Is she working alone or in a group?
3 What happened in the end?

d ▶2.21 Listen again and complete the suggestions for saving whales that have come ashore. Write one word in each gap.

1 Don't try and do things on your own – talk to the Marine _____ Service.
2 Put on a wetsuit – it can get quite _____.
3 Cover the whale with _____ towels.
4 Pour buckets of water over the whale to keep her _____.
5 Make sure you don't _____ the whale's blowhole.
6 Make a _____ in the sand around the whale to fill with water.
7 When the tide comes in, _____ the whale out to sea again.

THE WHALE FILE TRUE OR FALSE?

1 Whales aren't fish, so they need to come to the surface to breathe.
2 All whales have teeth.
3 Female whales are bigger than male ones.
4 Whales never sleep because they need to breathe.
5 Whales breathe every 15 minutes.
6 Whales can communicate by singing to each other.
7 Whales sometimes swim onto the shore and can't get back to sea.

2 READING

a Read Tomas' essay about water pollution below. In his opinion, who should do something about this kind of pollution?

b Read the essay again. Are the sentences true (T) or false (F)?

1 Tomas suggests that we probably don't complain when people throw rubbish in water.
2 He suggests there's more rubbish in lakes than on beaches.
3 Eating plastic can make animals and birds ill.
4 Forgotten bits of fishing net can kill fish.
5 Tomas thinks water pollution is worse than air pollution.

c 💬 What do you think should be done about water pollution?

Keeping our water clean

1 If you walk down the street and see someone throw a plastic bottle on the ground, you'll probably get annoyed. You might even say something to that person. But do we react in the same way when we see people throwing rubbish into the sea? We all know how rubbish damages the environment on land, but we often forget the effect that it can have on environments like the sea, lakes and rivers, too.

2 First of all, water pollution looks terrible. Beautiful beaches can become covered in rubbish when whatever we have thrown into the water comes ashore. It's just not pleasant to swim in rivers and lakes that have plastic bags floating in them.

3 Secondly, rubbish can hurt animals and birds that live in or by the water. If they see a plastic bottle, they may think it is food. However, when they try and eat the bottle, it can get caught in their mouth or stomach and stop them from eating anything else. Plastic bottles can also stop dolphins from breathing. Sometimes, fishing boats leave bits of fishing net behind in the water. Fish can get caught in this and die.

4 Finally, people forget that plastic contains chemicals which stay in the water. This is very bad for both fish and plants. If you eat fish containing these chemicals, then you can also get sick.

5 In conclusion, I would say that we need to worry about water pollution as much as we care about land or air pollution. We should all look after the seas, lakes and rivers, and remember to take our rubbish away with us.

3 WRITING SKILLS
Organising an essay; signposting language

a How is the essay organised? Tick (✓) 1 or 2.

1 ☐ introduction → a discussion of different points connected to the topic → conclusion
2 ☐ introduction → points in favour of the topic → points against the topic → conclusion

b Look at the sentence below and answer the questions.

First of all, water pollution looks terrible.

1 Which paragraph of the essay does the sentence come from?
2 Does the signposting phrase in **bold** refer to something that has already been mentioned or introduce a new topic?
3 What other signposting phrases in the essay are similar to this one?

c Read the essay again and answer the questions.

1 In the first paragraph, does *you* refer to 'people in general' or 'the reader'?
2 In the first paragraph, what does *we* refer to?
3 Why does Tomas use these two pronouns?
4 In paragraph 5, what phrase does Tomas use to introduce his opinion?

4 WRITING

a Plan an essay on an environmental issue. Choose one of the topics below or your own idea. Make notes about your topic. Try to think of at least three main points with examples.

air pollution   cutting down forests   electric cars
taking too many fish from the sea   wasting food

b 💬 Compare your ideas with a partner.

c Write the essay. Use the structure in 3a. Use signposting expressions to organise your ideas. Make sure you communicate directly with the reader in the introduction and conclusion.

d 💬 Read each other's essays. Do you agree with the other students' opinions?

UNIT 5
Review and extension

1 GRAMMAR

a Underline the correct words.

1 The flowers close when you *will touch / touch* them.
2 They've decided they aren't *building / going to build* a road through the forest.
3 *Shall / Will* I pick the apples or do you want to do it?
4 Unless the government does more to stop hunting, tigers *are dying out / will die out*.
5 If you find a plant that you haven't seen before, *don't / you won't* touch it, please.
6 Don't eat wild mushrooms *unless / if* you know they're safe.

b Complete the sentences with the correct future form of the verbs in brackets. (Sometimes there is more than one possible answer.)

1 This weekend, I _____ (not/do) anything special – just staying at home.
2 _____ (you/carry on) learning English when you _____ (finish) this course?
3 It's very cold. I think it _____ (snow) this evening.
4 If the sky _____ (be) red in the morning, it _____ (rain) later in the day.

2 VOCABULARY

a Underline the correct words.

1 The children jumped across the *stream / river / lake*.
2 A *valley / rainforest / national park* is a tropical, wet place with lots of trees.
3 The sun was shining, but it was completely dark inside the *bay / coast / cave*.
4 We could see the monkey hanging from the *leaf / skin / branch* of a tree.
5 The fish's *scales / feathers / wings* were blue, white and black.
6 Dogs and bears have *webs / shells / paws*.

b Complete the words.

1 The w _ _ d _ _ _ _ e in the national park is amazing – from butterflies to flowers to elephants.
2 The Blue Whale and the Mountain Gorilla are both e _ _ _ _ g _ _ _ _ d s _ _ _ _ _ _ s.
3 Most countries r _ c _ _ _ _ e paper, glass and cardboard.
4 The cl _ _ _ a _ e is changing; some places are getting hotter and some are getting colder.
5 Building new roads d _ m _ _ _ es the environment.
6 They want to c _ t d _ _ _ n the trees so they can use the land for farming.

3 WORDPOWER *problem*

a Match pictures a–f with sentences 1–6.

1 ☐ His shoelaces are undone, but he **isn't aware of** the problem.
2 ☐ Greg's car won't start, but he**'s fixing** the problem.
3 ☐ They**'re facing** a lot of problems. Their bills are huge this month.
4 ☐ Bad weather has **caused** a lot of problems for traffic.
5 ☐ Sally is upset, but her parents are trying to **solve** the problem.
6 ☐ The fire quickly got out of control, but they**'re tackling** the problem.

b Replace the words in **bold** with the correct forms of the verbs in the box. (Sometimes there is more than one possible answer.)

be aware of   cause   tackle   face   fix   solve

1 Most people in my country **know about** the problem of rising sea levels. _____
2 My country is **dealing with** the problem of pollution in big cities. _____
3 I'm good at **finding an answer to** problems with computers. _____
4 I express my opinions strongly and that sometimes **creates** problems. _____
5 Damage to the environment is a problem which everyone can **try to stop**. _____
6 Engineers will soon **end** the problem of people not having enough clean drinking water. _____

c 💬 Do you agree with the sentences in 3b?

♻ REVIEW YOUR PROGRESS

How well did you do in this unit? Write 3, 2 or 1 for each objective.
3 = very well   2 = well   1 = not so well

I CAN ...

talk about the future.	☐
talk about *if* and *when*.	☐
give reasons, results and examples.	☐
write a discussion essay.	☐

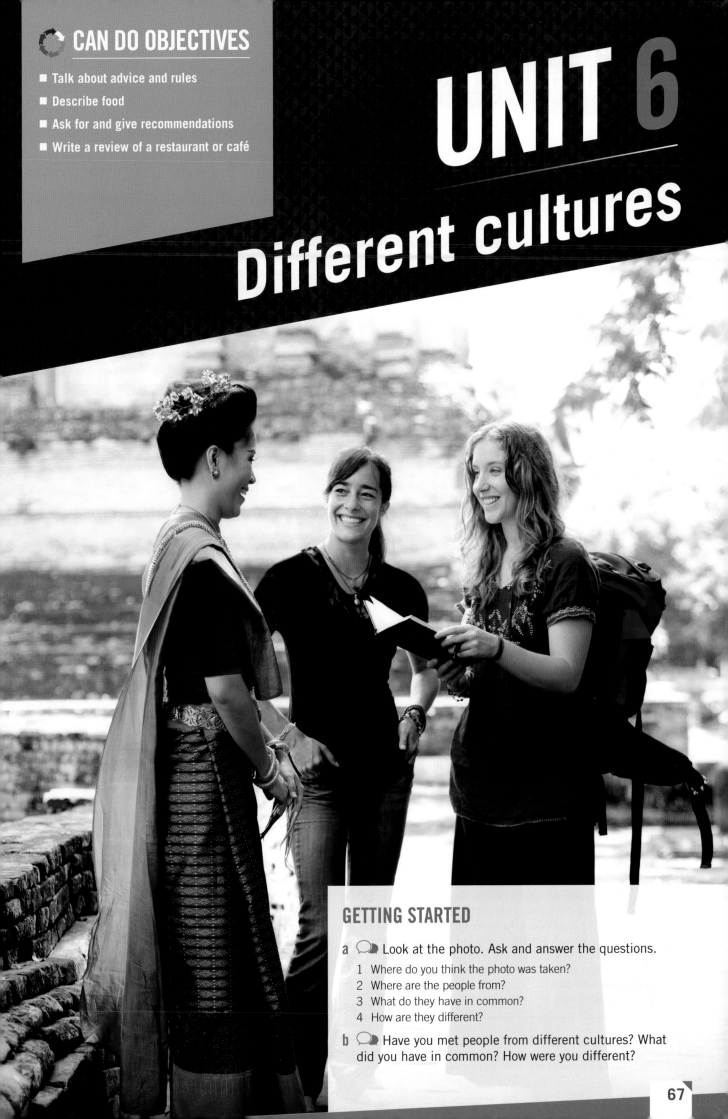

CAN DO OBJECTIVES

- Talk about advice and rules
- Describe food
- Ask for and give recommendations
- Write a review of a restaurant or café

UNIT 6
Different cultures

GETTING STARTED

a 💬 Look at the photo. Ask and answer the questions.

1 Where do you think the photo was taken?
2 Where are the people from?
3 What do they have in common?
4 How are they different?

b 💬 Have you met people from different cultures? What did you have in common? How were you different?

6A You have to use pedestrian crossings

Learn to talk about advice and rules
G Modals of obligation
V Compound nouns; Multi-word verbs

1 READING AND SPEAKING

a 💬 Talk about the jobs that you do or would like to do. Which one is the most difficult?

b 💬 Read *The Toughest Place to be a …* and answer the questions.

1 Which person do you think has the most difficult job?
2 Which British worker do you think will find the change the most difficult? Why?
3 Which episode would you find most interesting? Why?

2 VOCABULARY Compound nouns

a Read about compound nouns, then <u>underline</u> the compound nouns in the article.

> Compound nouns combine two words. Some compound nouns are one word (e.g. *lunchtime*), others are two words (e.g. *swimming pool*). They are usually formed of:
> • noun + noun (e.g. *newspaper*)
> • verb+*ing* + noun (e.g. *washing machine*)
> • noun + verb+*ing* (e.g. *windsurfing*)

b ▶2.22 **Pronunciation** Listen to the compound nouns from the article. Which part is stressed – the first or the second word? Practise saying the words.

c Complete the compound nouns with the words in the box.

air   cycle   hour   jam   pedestrian   traffic

1 _____ crossing   4 _____ lights
2 _____ conditioning   5 traffic _____
3 rush _____   6 _____ lane

d Complete the email with the compound nouns from 2c.

> What a stressful morning! I woke up late and my car didn't start for 30 minutes. By the time I was on the road it was ¹_____ _____ and the roads were very busy. All the ²_____ _____ in the city centre were stuck on red so everything was moving very slowly. The lights at a ³_____ _____ were broken, so lots of people were walking across the roads through the traffic. I sat in the same ⁴_____ _____ for about 45 minutes. To make things worse, the ⁵_____ _____ wasn't working in my car so I was boiling hot! I was just thinking that I really should use public transport instead of my car when suddenly I saw someone waving at me from the ⁶_____ _____. It was you, on your new bike, looking very pleased with yourself!

e 💬 Look at the picture on p.129. How many compound nouns can you find in two minutes?

The TOUGHEST place to be a …

In this TV series, workers from the UK experience what it's like to try doing their jobs in some of the most difficult conditions around the world.

 A London taxi driver tries his job on the busy streets of Mumbai.

 A nurse goes to work in the Emergency Department of a hospital in Ciudad Juárez in Mexico.

 A bus driver tries driving a jeepney in Manila, the Philippines, which is the most densely populated city in the world.

 A firefighter goes to Brazil to fight forest fires with a team in an area of the Amazon the size of England.

As well as the culture shock from moving to a workplace in a completely new country, they often have to deal with tough living conditions. But they get lots of help and support from a local host who looks after them and shows them how to do the job in a very different working environment.

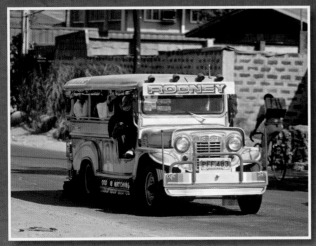

3 LISTENING

a Read about an episode from the TV series *The Toughest Place to be a … .* What do you think Mason will find difficult about working in Mumbai?

In tonight's episode, London taxi driver Mason McQueen works in Mumbai, India for ten days. He is supported by local taxi driver Pradeep, and has driving lessons from a local driving instructor. But how will Mason manage when he has to go out on his own to find passengers in the Mumbai rush hour?

b ▶ **2.23** Listen to three friends talking about *The Toughest Place to be a … Taxi Driver.* Tick (✓) the things that they mention.

1 ☐ The roads in Mumbai were very busy.
2 ☐ The roads were in a bad condition.
3 ☐ Mason had to drive an old car.
4 ☐ There were a lot of traffic jams.
5 ☐ Mason couldn't communicate with the local people.
6 ☐ The taxis that Mason drove had no air conditioning.
7 ☐ There weren't any traffic lights.
8 ☐ The passengers didn't like Mason.
9 ☐ It was difficult to get passengers.

c ▶ **2.23** Listen again and complete the sentences with one word or a number.

1 Mason spent __3__ years studying maps of London.
2 He spent a __week__ learning how to drive in Mumbai.
3 Mason drove __2__ different taxis in Mumbai.
4 People in India call taxis with air conditioning '__cool__ cabs'.
5 The temperature in Mumbai was in the __40__s.
6 Mason used __hand__ signals to indicate left and right.
7 Pradeep works __15½__ hours a day.
8 Pradeep earns about £ __10__ a day.

d 💬 Discuss the questions.

1 Do you think this was a good experience for Mason and Pradeep? Why / Why not?
2 Would you like to watch the programme?
3 Would you like to take part in the programme?

4 VOCABULARY Multi-word verbs

a ▶ **2.24** What are the missing multi-word verbs? Complete the sentences with the correct form of the verbs in the box. Listen and check.

---
get around   pick up   show around
---

1 He got on really well with Pradeep, the guy who _____ him _____ .
2 He learned how to _____ _____ the city pretty quickly.
3 He _____ _____ a few phrases of the local language.

b ▶ Now go to Vocabulary Focus 6A on p.156

5 GRAMMAR
Modals of obligation

a 💬 What do you think people might find difficult when they spend some time in a different culture?

b Read *Culture shock*. Find four things people might find difficult.

c 💬 Have you ever experienced culture shock? When? Where?

d Read the text again. <u>Underline</u> the words or phrases which express obligation and advice (*must, have to,* etc.).

e Complete rules 1–5 with the words in the box.

can can't don't have to have to
must mustn't ought to should

1 We use _____ and _____ to give advice.
2 We use _____ to say that something is not necessary.
3 We use _____ and _____ to say that something is necessary.
4 We use _____ and _____ when we say that something is forbidden/not allowed.
5 We use _____ to talk about a choice to do something.

f ▶ Now go to Grammar Focus 6A on p.142

g Complete these rules about transport in your country. Use the verbs in the box.

must/have to don't have to mustn't
should shouldn't can can't

Buses
1 You _____ buy a ticket in advance.
   You _____ buy a ticket on the bus.

Walking and cycling
2 You _____ use pedestrian crossings when you want to cross the road.
3 You _____ wear a cycle helmet.
4 You _____ cycle on the pavement.
   You _____ use cycle lanes.

Cars
5 Passengers _____ wear a seat belt.
6 You _____ drive with your lights on during the day.

Taxis
7 You _____ stop taxis in the street.
8 You _____ book taxis in advance.
9 You _____ give taxi drivers a tip.

CULTURE SHOCK

Some people choose to live in another country, other people have to move for family or work reasons. If you're going to live in a new place for some time, you ought to be prepared to experience culture shock at some point.

At first, when you're in a very different environment, everything seems exciting and new. Then, the differences start to be annoying. Life feels too fast or too slow, the food tastes strange, you miss your favourite television programmes. Laws are different – there are things you mustn't do here that you can do at home. This is culture shock.

The good news is, you don't have to spoil your experience of living abroad. Culture shock doesn't usually last very long.

h A foreign visitor is coming to live in your country for six months. Prepare to give him/her some advice. Use the ideas in the box and your own ideas to make a list of rules and tips.

roads, pavements and cycle lanes public transport
eating and drinking talking to people who are older than you
going out at night clothes language parks and public spaces

You mustn't eat or drink when walking in the street.
You should always give your seat to an older passenger on the bus.

i 💬 Take turns to read out your rules. Discuss the questions.
1 Which rules are about safety?
2 Which are about being polite to people?
3 Which rules are the most important?

6 SPEAKING

a Read the questions and make notes about your answers.
1 Which foreign country/other area would you like to study/do your job in?
2 Why would you like to live there?

b 💬 Discuss the questions in 6a. Think of anything your partner should/must/mustn't do to prepare. What other advice would you give them?

> I'd like to work in France.

> You should do some French classes before you go.

> Good idea!

6B It's tastier than I expected

Learn to describe food
G Comparatives and superlatives
V Describing food

1 VOCABULARY Describing food

a 💬 Look at photos a–e and discuss the questions.

1 Which food would you most like to eat?
2 What country do you think each dish comes from?
3 What ingredients does each dish contain?
4 Which of the dishes could a vegetarian eat?

b Match descriptions 1–5 with photos a–e.

1 Tasty Moroccan meatballs cooked in a tomato sauce, served with couscous and fresh herbs.
2 Creamy Mexican avocado and tomato dip with crunchy tortilla chips.
3 Japanese noodles with vegetables in a light soup served with a raw egg.
4 White fish cooked in a spicy Thai sauce with hot green chillies.
5 A slice of rich Austrian chocolate cake with a bitter orange filling.

c Which adjectives in 1b could you use to describe a salad, a soup, or a curry?

d ▶ Now go to Vocabulary Focus 6B on p.156

e ▶2.29 **Pronunciation** Listen and repeat these words. Pay attention to the pronunciation of the letters *sh* and *ch*.

/ʃ/	/tʃ/
fre<u>sh</u>	<u>ch</u>ocolate
ma<u>sh</u>	<u>ch</u>op
	ri<u>ch</u>
	crun<u>ch</u>y

f 💬 A visitor has come to your town. You're going to give advice about where to go and what typical dishes to try.

Student A: Give the visitor advice.
Student B: You are the visitor. Listen and ask further questions.

g 💬 Now change roles and have a second conversation.

2 LISTENING

a 💬 Look at the photo on the right and discuss the questions.

1 Do you have vending machines in your country? What do they sell?
2 How often do you use them?

b ▶2.30 Listen to part of a radio programme about vending machines in Japan.

1 What food and drink is mentioned?
2 What are the advantages for customers of vending machines over buying things from a shop?
3 What does the reporter think of the hot meal?

c 💬 Would you buy hot food from vending machines?

3 GRAMMAR
Comparatives and superlatives

a ▶2.31 Complete the sentences with the words in the box. Then listen and check your answers.

as good as   a bit longer than   the best
by far the highest   much better than   much cheaper

1 Japan has _____ number of vending machines per person in the world.
2 It's _____ for sellers to run a vending machine than a shop.
3 But is curry and rice from a machine _____ curry and rice from a restaurant?
4 It's taking _____ I imagined.
5 It's actually _____ I expected.
6 I think it might be _____ vending machine meal I've ever eaten.

b ▶ Now go to Grammar Focus 6B on p.142

c Use the ideas below to write sentences with comparatives, superlatives and (*not*) as … as.

cheap   fun   good for you   healthy
interesting   nice   spicy   sweet   tasty

• dark chocolate / milk chocolate / white chocolate
• street food / food in expensive restaurants / home-made food
• Japanese food / British food / Indian food
• vegetarian food / meat dishes / fish dishes
• food from my country / food from other countries
• eating alone / eating with friends

Dark chocolate isn't as nice as white chocolate.

d 💬 Read out your sentences. Do you agree or disagree with each other?

'Have you eaten?'
May 13th

Singaporeans are my kind of people – they're passionate about food and eating!

People here eat often – they have five or six meals a day. Instead of 'Hello' or 'How are you?' they ask, 'Have you eaten?'. And it's hard to believe just how many different kinds of dishes you can get in this tiny country – Chinese, Indian, Arabic, European and many, many more.

The best meal of the day today was lunch. The main course was *muri ghonto* or fish head curry – far more delicious than it sounds! It's a southern Indian dish. You can have it with rice, but we had it the way that the Chinese do, with a soft bread roll.

Dessert was *cendol* – coconut milk, ice and green noodles. It's a typical south-east Asian dish. It wasn't as sweet as I expected, but the noodles were lovely – a bit like jelly.

There are places to eat here to suit everyone – from food stalls in shopping malls to more upmarket (and more expensive!) restaurants. My plan is to try as many as I can in the short time I'm here.

4 READING

a 💬 Look at the photo on the left. Which country do you think it is?

b Read the blog, *Hungry adventures*. Check your answer to 4a.

c Read the blog again. Find the descriptions of the dishes and match them with the food photos a–d.
1 ☐ chicken satay   3 ☐ cendol
2 ☐ muri ghonto   4 ☐ thosai

d 💬 Discuss the questions.
1 Did the blog writer enjoy the dishes in 4c?
2 Which of the dishes would you like to try?

HUNGRY ADVENTURES

Travelling and eating around the world

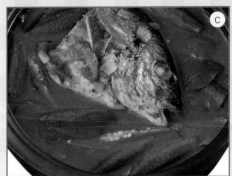

Hawker centres – street food, but not on the streets
May 14th

Singapore is famous for its street food, but it's been illegal to sell cooked food in the streets for many years. So, if you're looking for Singapore's famous street food, hawker centres are the places to go. These are indoor food markets with stalls that sell freshly cooked food. You choose your hawker centre according to what kind of cuisine you fancy – Thai, Malay, Chinese, Indian, Middle Eastern.

I went to the Golden Mile Food Centre – it was amazing to see so many different food stalls under one roof. *Sup tulang* – a Malay-Indian dish of beef bones in a red spicy sauce – looked very tasty. But in the end I wanted something lighter, so I chose *ayam buah keluak*, a Paranakan (Chinese-Malay) dish. It's chicken with Indonesian black nuts, served with steamed rice. A good choice – one of the most unusual dishes I've ever tasted.

Little India, big appetite
May 15th

This part of Singapore was full of the sights and smells of India. I ate *thosai* – crispy Indian pancakes made from rice and lentils. They were served with rich and spicy dips and vegetable curry. The meal was light and fresh – delicious!

Still full from my Indian lunch, I explored the Arab Quarter. There was plenty of great food on offer, but sadly I wasn't hungry! I'll have to come back to Singapore. I haven't had a chance to explore Chinatown either.

By the evening I was hungry again, so I tried some of the barbecued food at Lau Pa Sat, an old market. I went for Malaysian chicken *satay*, pieces of chicken on sticks served with spicy peanut sauce. Absolutely delicious!

---

e Read the blog again and answer the questions.

1 What two habits show that the people in Singapore love food?
2 What did the blog writer eat with her fish head curry?
3 Why can't you buy food on the street in Singapore?
4 Why didn't she have *sup tulang* at the Golden Mile Food Centre?
5 Why didn't she eat anything in the Arab Quarter?
6 Which area of Singapore did she not go to?

f 💬 Imagine you are visiting Singapore. Where will you go? What will you eat?

> I'd really like to go to a big hawker centre, so we can see all the different options.

5 SPEAKING

a You are going to talk about a special meal. Make notes about one of these meals. Use the ideas in the box to help you plan what to say.

- the most special meal that you've ever made
- the most delicious meal you've ever eaten
- a meal you'll never forget

where? when? who with? ingredients?
how was the food cooked? taste, smell, colour?

b 💬 Take turns to describe your meals. Then talk about which of the meals sounds the most delicious.

> The most delicious meal I've ever eaten was in a little restaurant near my grandparents' house. I ate ...

6C Everyday English
Do you think I should take her somewhere special?

Learn to ask for and give recommendations

P Sounding interested
S Asking for and giving recommendations

1 LISTENING

a 💬 Discuss the questions.

1 Which of these do you think is the most romantic?
- flowers
- dinner at a restaurant
- a home-made meal
- a handwritten love letter
- an expensive gift (e.g. jewellery)

2 Have you ever bought/done these things for anyone?

b 💬 Look at the photo below. Where are Tom and Rachel? What are they doing? What do you think they are talking about?

c ▶2.33 Watch or listen to Part 1 and check.

d ▶2.33 Watch or listen again. Are the sentences true (T) or false (F)?

1 Tom isn't going to ask Becky to marry him.
2 Tom is going to take Becky to Paris.
3 Mark asked Rachel to marry him at a special place.
4 Becky and Tom used to work together.

e 💬 Do you agree with Rachel's advice? Where should Tom propose to Becky?

2 USEFUL LANGUAGE
Asking for and giving recommendations

a Look at the phrases in **bold** below. Which ones are asking for recommendations? Which are giving recommendations?

1 **Do you think I should** take her somewhere special?
2 **If I were you, I'd** take her somewhere special.
3 **It's probably worth** asking her where she wants to go.
4 **What would you do** about the ring?
5 **Would you recommend** buying a very expensive ring?
6 **It's much better to** buy something that's her style.
7 **It's not a good idea to** ask her what she likes.

b Complete the conversations with the correct form of the verbs in brackets. Look back at the phrases in 2a to help you.

1
A What do you think I should ^{1}_____ Dad for his birthday? (get)
B If I were you, I ^{2}_____ him what he wants. (ask)
A But that will ruin the surprise.
B It's much better ^{3}_____ him what he wants though. (get)
A True, I suppose.

2
A Where would you recommend ^{1}_____ the party? (have)
B It's probably worth ^{2}_____ Laura if she can recommend a restaurant. She knows lots of great places. (ask)
A And what about the cake? What would you ^{3}_____? (do)
B Get it from a bakery. And it's a good idea ^{4}_____ them as soon as you can. They get very busy. (contact)

3 CONVERSATION SKILLS
Expressing surprise

a Look at the sentences about the next part of the story. Which option do you think is most likely?

1 Rachel advises Tom to buy *a huge diamond* / *something that's Becky's style*.
2 Tom thinks that the rings in the jewellery shop are **very** *expensive* / *cheap*.
3 Rachel and Tom see Becky and *say hello to her* / *hide in the shop*.

b ▶2.34 Watch or listen to Part 2 and check your answers to 3a.

c ▶2.34 Watch or listen to Part 2 again and complete the sentences.

1 **Tom** So, what about the ring? What would you buy? A big diamond, right? So she can show it to her friends?

 Rachel _____? Tom, do you know Becky at all?

2 **Rachel** It's £1500.

 Tom I _____ _____ _____! That's ridiculous.

3 **Rachel** Tom! It's Becky! Over there.

 Tom _____ _____! What should we do?

d 💬 Take it in turns to say the sentences below and express surprise.

1 I'm getting married.
2 I passed all my exams.
3 That coat costs £300.
4 I lost my phone yesterday.

4 PRONUNCIATION
Sounding interested

a ▶2.35 Listen to this extract. Is the intonation flat or not? Underline the correct word in the rule.

 Rachel I am so excited. I still can't believe you're going to ask Becky to marry you.

> Sometimes, intonation is more important than the words we use. If we use *varied* / *flat* intonation, we may sound as if we're bored, or don't care about the subject.

b ▶2.36 Listen to exchanges 1–3. Which of the B speakers sounds bored?

1 **A** I've got a new job.
 B Wow. That's incredible.
2 **A** I've just bought some new shoes.
 B That's amazing.
3 **A** We lost the game last night.
 B That's terrible.

c Practise saying the exchanges in 4b. Try to sound interested.

5 SPEAKING

▶ **Communication 6C** 💬 Student A: Read the instructions below. Student B: Go to p.128

> **Student A**
> 1 You have been offered an amazing job. The salary is very high, and it is a great opportunity. The problem is that you need to move to New York next month! Tell your partner your news and ask for some recommendations what to do.
> 2 Listen to your partner's surprising news and give some recommendations.

I've been offered a new job. It's in New York!

No way! That's great.

Do you think I should take it?

🔄 **Unit Progress Test**

CHECK YOUR PROGRESS

You can now do the Unit Progress Test.

1 SPEAKING AND LISTENING

a Look at situations 1–3. Where would you go for these occasions? Choose from the locations in the box.

1 to meet friends for a chat and a drink
2 a birthday or an anniversary
3 a party at the end of term or the end of a language course

| a café   a cheap restaurant   an expensive restaurant |
| a venue with music or dancing (e.g. a club) |

b 💬 Compare your ideas. Do you agree?

c ▶️ **2.37** Listen to Jeff, Fabio and Carla. Which places in photos 1–3 are they talking about?

d ▶️ **2.37** Listen again and answer the questions.

1 Why doesn't Jeff like the atmosphere at expensive restaurants?
2 What does he say about the food?
3 Does Fabio go to cafés alone, or with friends, or both?
4 Why does he like pavement cafés?
5 What does Carla do before she starts dancing?
6 What kind of music does her favourite place play?

e Think of one place to go out that you really like and one that you don't really like. Make notes about their good and bad points.

f 💬 Discuss your places. If your partner(s) know the two places you chose, do they agree?

2 READING

a Read the four reviews of a café on p.77. The first review gave five stars (= excellent). How many stars do you think the other reviews gave?

b Read reviews a–d again. Underline any words or phrases that are used to describe the things below.

1 the atmosphere
2 the kind of food and drinks they serve
3 the quality of the food
4 the service
5 value for money
6 the location

①

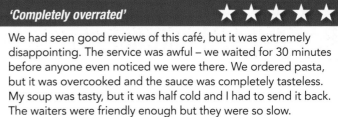

(a) *'Very highly recommended. Would go back again.'* ★ ★ ★ ★ ★

I came here on my birthday. The coffee and cakes were delicious and there was a relaxing atmosphere, with plenty of space. The staff were very friendly and gave us free birthday drinks. I can definitely recommend this café and I'll be going back.'

(b) *'Visited twice in 3 days!'* ★ ★ ★ ★ ★

We had lovely food here. The fish was very fresh and they had delicious salads. It's also a great place to just sit and relax. The second time we went, we just ordered drinks and the waiters were friendly and left us alone. We stayed for three hours! It's right in the town centre, so it's a bit noisy, but it's a convenient place to meet and fairly easy to get to. It's definitely worth a visit!

(c) *'Completely overrated'* ★ ★ ★ ★ ★

We had seen good reviews of this café, but it was extremely disappointing. The service was awful – we waited for 30 minutes before anyone even noticed we were there. We ordered pasta, but it was overcooked and the sauce was completely tasteless. My soup was tasty, but it was half cold and I had to send it back. The waiters were friendly enough but they were so slow.

(d) *'A nice place to meet friends'* ★ ★ ★ ★ ★

This is a bright, friendly café and they also serve good food, although the portions aren't very generous and it's a bit overpriced. I usually go there just for a drink. It's got a fairly pleasant atmosphere and the service is always reasonably friendly and relaxed. I'd recommend it as a place to have a drink with friends, but it might be better to eat somewhere else.

3 WRITING SKILLS
Positive and negative language; adverbs

a Add the adjectives or phrases from the reviews above to the table.

positive	fairly positive
delicious	friendly enough
fairly negative	**negative**
a bit noisy	awful

b 💬 Compare your answers. Did you choose the same adjectives and phrases?

c The two sentences below are similar in meaning. Do you think that in sentence 1 … ?

  a the writer isn't sure what he/she thinks
  b the writer doesn't want to be too negative

  1 The portions weren**'t very generous**.
  2 The portions were **absolutely tiny**.

d Which of the sentences are slightly negative (like sentence 1 in 3c)? Which are very negative (like sentence 2 in 3c)?

  1 It was extremely disappointing.
  2 The bread wasn't very fresh.
  3 The sauce was completely tasteless.
  4 My soup wasn't really hot enough.
  5 The portions were rather small.
  6 The service was awful.

e Do we use these adverbs to make adjectives or phrases stronger or weaker?

> a bit   absolutely   completely   extremely   fairly   not really
> not very   quite   rather   really   reasonably   terribly

f Change the strong comments in the sentences in 3d so that they sound weaker. Change the weaker comments so that they sound stronger.

  1 It was a bit disappointing.   2 The bread was really old.

4 WRITING A review

a Choose two places you know (restaurants, cafés or venues with music). Think of one place you like a lot and one place you don't really like. Make notes about the points below:

  • general atmosphere   • what they serve   • friendliness
  • location   • quality of food   • prices
  • how busy it is   • service   • value for money

b 💬 Compare your ideas with a partner.

c Write two reviews, one for each place.

d Work in pairs. Read your partner's reviews. Check that your partner has done the things below.

  1 covered all the points in 4a
  2 used appropriate adjectives and phrases
  3 used adverbs appropriately

e 💬 Show your reviews to other students. If they know the places, do they agree?

UNIT 6
Review and extension

1 GRAMMAR

a Read the text and <u>underline</u> the best words.

Essaouira is a wonderful place to visit. You ¹*must / should / can* enjoy walking through the streets, shopping at the market or tasting local food. It's often windy in Essaouira, so you ²*don't have to / should / have to* bring warm clothes. The wind means that the beach isn't good for sunbathing but you ³*ought to / shouldn't / must* go kite-surfing – it's really exciting!

If you like history, you ⁴*don't have to / have to / should* explore the old part of town. There are lots of market stalls here. If you want to buy something, discuss the price with the stallholder. You certainly ⁵*shouldn't / ought to / must* pay the first price you hear!

Many people here speak English, Spanish or French, so you ⁶*don't have to / should / mustn't* learn Arabic, although you ⁷*should / must / have to* probably learn a few useful phrases. You ⁸*can't / don't have to / mustn't* stay in expensive hotels; there are other options, including riads, which are hotels that feel like family homes.

b Complete the sentences with the correct form of the words in brackets. Add any extra words you need.

1 A burger in China is _____ (slightly cheap) a burger in Saudi Arabia.
2 Indonesia is _____ (a bit hot) Jamaica.
3 On average, trains in Japan are _____ (much fast) trains in India.
4 Thai food is _____ (by far spicy) I've ever eaten.
5 Travelling on the Rome metro isn't _____ (quite expensive) travelling on the London Underground.

2 VOCABULARY

a Complete each pair of sentences with compound nouns made from the words in the boxes.

air crossing conditioning pedestrian

1 It's safer to use a _____. There's so much traffic.
2 **A** It's so hot!
  B I'll put the _____ on.

hour public rush transport

3 Let's go at ten o'clock when _____ is over.
4 Shall we drive or use _____?

jam lights traffic traffic

5 Sorry I'm late. I got stuck in a _____.
6 Wait for the _____ to change from red to green.

cycle cash lane machine

7 That car shouldn't be in the _____!
8 I need some money. Is there a _____ near here?

b Complete the multi-word verbs.

1 I picked _____ Spanish when I went to Mexico.
2 We'd like to show you _____ our city.
3 I like eating _____, but a lot of restaurants are expensive.
4 I waited for an hour, but Helen didn't turn _____.

3 WORDPOWER *go*

a Match questions 1–6 with responses a–f.

1 ☐ Where does that path **go**?
2 ☐ How did your trip **go**?
3 ☐ This is my new dress. Do these shoes **go** with it?
4 ☐ Where's the milk?
5 ☐ Where's the cake you were making?
6 ☐ Was there food at the party?

a Really well. I met some lovely people.
b No, they're the wrong colour.
c To the beach, I think.
d Yes, but when I got there it had all **gone**.
e It **went** off. I threw it away.
f It **went** wrong. I threw it away.

b Match the phrases with *go* in 3a with these descriptions.
We can use:

* *go* to mean *disappear* _d_
* *go* (*with*) to mean *look similar/look good together* _____
* *go* to mean *go towards* _____
* *go wrong* to mean *develop problems/not succeed* _____
* *go* + adverb to describe how things happen (e.g. *go badly*) _____
* *go* + adjective to describe a change (e.g. *go grey*) _____

c Complete each sentence with the correct form of *go* and a word or phrase from the box, if necessary.

around orange really well with my eyes wrong

1 In the autumn, the leaves _____.
2 I had a job interview yesterday. It _____. I got the job!
3 Don't worry if it _____. Just start again.
4 When I turned to speak to Fred, he had already _____.
5 The road _____ the lake. It's a nice drive.
6 The man in the shop said the scarf _____.

d 💬 Look at what the people are saying. Think of two things that each person might be talking about.

1 It went very well, thanks.
2 It went completely white.
3 It goes very well with cheese.
4 Oh no! It's gone wrong!
5 It goes over the river.
6 It's gone. Good!

♻ REVIEW YOUR PROGRESS

How well did you do in this unit? Write 3, 2 or 1 for each objective.
3 = very well   2 = well   1 = not so well

I CAN ...

talk about advice and rules.	☐
describe food.	☐
ask for and give recommendations.	☐
write a review of a restaurant or café.	☐

CAN DO OBJECTIVES

- Describe a building
- Describe a town or city
- Make offers and ask for permission
- Write a note with useful information

UNIT 7
House and home

GETTING STARTED

a 🗨 Look at the photo and answer the questions.

1 What are the people doing?
2 Do you think they are at home? If not, where are they?
3 Would you like to be in the place in the photo? Why / Why not?

b 🗨 Talk about your ideal home.

1 What would it look like?   3 Where would it be?
2 How big would it be?   4 Who would live there with you?

Learn to describe a building

G Modals of deduction
V Buildings

1 GRAMMAR Modals of deduction

a 💬 Look at photos a–d and discuss the questions.

1 Where do you think the buildings are? Are they in the city or the countryside? Which country? Why?
2 Who do you think lives in each building? A large family? A young couple? Why?

b ▶2.38 Listen to four people talking about photos a–d. Which photo is each person talking about?

Speaker 1 ___   Speaker 3 ___
Speaker 2 ___   Speaker 4 ___

c ▶2.38 Listen again. Where do the speakers think the buildings are? Who do they think lives there? Are their answers the same as yours in 1a?

d Do you like these buildings? Why / Why not?

e Complete each sentence with one word.

1 It's very small, so it _____ belong to a big family.
2 There _____ be much space in there!
3 It _____ belong to a single person or a couple.
4 It _____ be on the outskirts of any big city.
5 It _____ not be a house.
6 Whoever lives there _____ have children.
7 Or it _____ be a holiday home.

f ▶2.38 Listen again and check your answers.

g Match sentences 1–4 with meanings a–c. Two have the same meaning.

1 ☐ It **must** be a holiday home.
2 ☐ It **might** be a holiday home.
3 ☐ It **could** be a holiday home.
4 ☐ It **can't** be a holiday home.

a I think it's a holiday home (but I'm not sure).
b I'm sure it's a holiday home.
c I'm sure it's not a holiday home.

h Look again at the sentences in 1g. What verb form comes after *must*, *might*, *could* and *can't*?

i ▶ Now go to Grammar Focus 7A on p.144

j ▶2.40 **Pronunciation** Listen to the sentences in 1g. Underline the correct words in the rule.

We *pronounce / don't pronounce* the final *t* or *d* in a word when it is followed by a consonant sound.

k ▶2.41 Listen and tick (✓) the sentences where you hear the final *t* or *d*. Practise saying the sentences.

1 ☐ It can'**t** get much sun.
2 ☐ You coul**d** be right.
3 ☐ She mus**t** earn a lot of money.
4 ☐ It migh**t** be very expensive.
5 ☐ You mus**t** enjoy living here!

l 💬 Discuss the questions.

1 What do you think it might be like to live in the homes in 1a?
2 What would you see from the windows?
3 Would you have a lot of space? Are there a lot of rooms?
4 What might the bedrooms be like?

2 VOCABULARY Buildings

I'm [1]*moving house / moving my house* next Friday, so here's my new address: Flat 4c, 82 Buckington Road, Banville, BN1 8UV. I'm [2]*renting / buying* it for six months and if I like it I'll stay longer. It's on the fourth [3]*level / floor* of a modern [4]*house / block* of flats and it's got [5]*views / sights* of the sea!

It's in a good [6]*location / place*. The [7]*neighbour / neighbourhood* is quiet, but there are some nice cafés and shops nearby. You'd like it – you should come and visit. If it's sunny, we can sit on the [8]*upstairs / balcony* and look at the sea!

I've got to move out [9]*of / to* this house on Tuesday, but I can't move [10]*of / into* my new place until Friday, so I'll be staying with my parents for a few days next week. Are you going to be in the area?

a Read Amanda's email and underline the correct words.

b ▶ Now go to Vocabulary Focus 7A on p.158

3 READING

a 💬 Imagine you're going to stay for three nights in a city that you don't know. Discuss the questions.

1 What are the advantages and disadvantages of staying in:
- a hotel?
- a rented apartment?
- a spare room in a local person's house?

2 Where would you prefer to stay? Why?

b Read the introduction of *A more personal place to stay* and choose the best summary.

1 Airbnb is an advertising website for hotels.
2 Airbnb is a website for travellers and people who have rooms to rent.
3 Airbnb is a travel advice website that has reviews of hotels and restaurants.

c 💬 Would you like to stay in someone else's home? What would be good or bad about it?

d Read *What the guests say … .* Answer the questions. Write A (Antonia) or K (Kumi).

1 ☐ Who could swim at the place they stayed?
2 ☐ Who felt 'at home' in the neighbourhood?
3 ☐ Who could easily get around the city?
4 ☐ Who cooked their own food?
5 ☐ Who is going to see their host(s) again?

e 💬 Which of the places would you rather stay in?

A **MORE PERSONAL** PLACE TO STAY

Do you find hotels too cold and unfriendly? Do you want to live like a local when you go on holiday? A new generation of websites, such as Airbnb, can help you find privately owned rooms, apartments and houses to rent.

'Hosts' create profiles of places to rent. 'Guests' can browse the profiles, read reviews written by guests and make reservations online. Prices range from about £25 to £100 per night, depending on the accommodation and the location.

But what's it like to stay at a stranger's house when you're on holiday? And if you're a host, what's it like to open your home to people you don't know? We spoke to some guests and hosts to find out.

WHAT THE **GUESTS** SAY …

Antonia My friend and I stayed in this amazing modern villa in California for ten days. It had eight bedrooms, a pool and the biggest kitchen I've ever seen (in which Jeff, our host, cooked fantastic breakfasts for us!). Jeff was so nice. He gave us lots of information about the local area and invited us to join him for dinner. We ended up becoming good friends – he's going to come and stay in my house when he comes to Italy next year.

Kumi I've stayed in Berlin a few times, but I've always stayed in a hotel. This experience was completely different. I had the whole of the top floor of an old house, and the rent included a bicycle too, which was great for travelling about. The hosts (Karl and Alexandra) were very kind, and we had good conversations every mealtime. They let me use the kitchen, which was great as the restaurants nearby are quite expensive. The shopkeepers in the area knew I was staying at Karl and Alexandra's and they were all very friendly. I felt like a local by the end of the week!

f 💬 What might be the advantages and disadvantages of being an Airbnb host?

g Read *What the hosts say ...* . Do they mention the advantages and disadvantages you talked about?

WHAT THE **HOSTS** SAY ...

Roberto I've been an Airbnb host for three years. In that time I've met some wonderful people – musicians, families, sportspeople, professors, hikers and students – who've needed **accommodation** for different reasons. They've come from different parts of the world and it's been a **pleasure** to get to know them. The only problem is that you have to do so much washing and cleaning!

Lisa Some people worry about **theft**, but I've had more than 100 guests and no one has ever stolen anything from me. Some guests are nicer than others, of course, but on the whole they've been charming and friendly. I usually ask people why they're travelling when they make a **reservation**. It's a good way to get to know a bit about them.

Clara My family has a holiday **cottage** in Scotland. We decided to rent it out when we're not using it. It was easy to set up the profile on the website. You have to trust people to treat your **property** as if it was their own home, but we only accept reservations from guests who have good reviews.

h Read the texts above again and match the words in **bold** with the definitions.

1 a building that someone owns
2 place(s) to stay
3 a small house in the countryside
4 an enjoyable experience
5 the crime of stealing something
6 an arrangement to stay somewhere (e.g. a hotel room)

4 SPEAKING

a 💬 Look at the buildings below and discuss the questions.

1 How old is the building?
2 Where is it?
3 What do you think it's like inside?
4 Would you like to live there?

b 💬 Imagine you are going on holiday with your partner. Discuss which of the houses/flats you would like to stay in. Can you agree on one house/flat to visit?

> I'd like to stay in the New York flat in 'e'. It must be a really great city to visit.

7B There are plenty of things to do

1 LISTENING

a 💬 Where did you grow up – in a big city or a small town? Did you like it? Why / Why not?

b Read *Five reasons why small towns are better than cities*. Do you agree with the reasons in the list? Can you add any more reasons?

c 💬 Think of five reasons why cities are better places to live than small towns. Tell a partner.

d ▶2.44 Listen to Tim and Kate's conversation. Are Tim's reasons the same as yours in 1c?

e ▶2.44 Listen again. Are these statements T (true) or F (false)?
1 Kate grew up in a small town.
2 Tim wouldn't want to live in a small town.
3 Kate thinks small towns are safer.
4 More people have driving accidents in the city than in the country.
5 People who live in the country have a smaller carbon footprint.

f 💬 Discuss the questions.
1 Where do you think it's safer to live in your country – in the city or in the countryside? Think about:
   • driving • crime • hospitals • other ideas
2 Is your (nearest) city designed in a way that's good for the environment? Why / Why not?
3 How could your (nearest) city be better? Think about:
   • public transport • cycle lanes • other ideas

Five reasons
why small towns are better than cities

1 There are no traffic jams. You don't need to spend hours trying to get to work. Fantastic!

2 Everyone knows your name. And who your parents are. And they help you when times are bad.

3 EVERYTHING is cheaper – eating out, buying houses, even going to the cinema.

4 You don't have to queue for the most popular restaurant in town. You probably know the waiter, anyway.

5 You can't get lost. Who cares if you don't have any signal on your phone – you don't need GPS!

2 VOCABULARY Verbs and prepositions

a Complete the sentences with the words in the box.

about (x2)   on   to

1 People care _____ you.
2 It's like you belong _____ one big family.
3 That makes sense if you think _____ it.
4 You can't rely _____ public transport in the countryside like you can in the city.

b ▶️2.45 **Pronunciation** Listen and check your answers to 2a. Then complete the rule.

When we use a verb and a preposition, we *usually* / *don't usually* stress the verb and *stress* / *don't stress* the preposition.

c ▶️2.45 Listen again and practise saying the sentences.

d Match the verbs in the box with the prepositions.

apologise   argue   believe   belong   care
complain   cope   depend   ~~pay~~   ~~rely~~
succeed   ~~think~~   ~~wait~~   worry

1 _____ ----- **with someone**

2 _____ ----- **with something**

think

3 _____
                about something
4 _____

5 _____

pay

wait ----- **for something**

6 _____

7 _____ ----- **in something**

8 _____ ----- **in doing something**

rely

                on someone/something
9 _____

10 _____ ----- **to someone**

e Complete each sentence with the correct form of a verb + preposition from 2d.

1 Do I like living in the countryside? That _____ _____ the weather – when it's warm and sunny, I love it!
2 My friend has just moved from the countryside to the city and she's finding it hard to _____ _____ all the noise.
3 He moved here to look for work, but he hasn't _____ _____ finding a job yet, unfortunately.
4 I'd like to _____ _____ what I said earlier. I didn't mean to be so rude.
5 I _____ _____ the traffic warden about the parking fine for ten minutes, but in the end I had to pay.
6 People _____ _____ the traffic here, but it isn't bad compared to a big city.
7 **A** Do you _____ _____ bad luck?
   B No, not really. I think people are in control of their own lives.
8 All of the land near the river is private – it _____ _____ the university. You can't walk there.

f 💬 Complete the game instructions below with the correct prepositions. Then play the game in teams.

'TWO'   Think of two things for each category. You win a point for each answer that no other team has written.

a ways you can pay _for_ things

   1 _____   2 _____

b things hotel guests often complain _____

   1 _____   2 _____

c ways you can apologise _____ being late

   1 _____   2 _____

d things people often do when they're waiting _____ a bus or train

   1 _____   2 _____

e things that lots of adults worry _____

   1 _____   2 _____

f things that lots of children believe _____

   1 _____   2 _____

3 GRAMMAR Quantifiers

a 💬 Discuss the questions.

1 Are there parks and other green spaces where you live?
2 What activities can people do there?
3 How often do you use them?

b Look at the photo of the High Line Park on p.84 and below. What's unusual about it? Read *The High Line, New York City* and check.

c Read the article again. <u>Underline</u> the correct words.

1 There are *lots of / enough* species of plants in the High Line park.
2 How *much / many* visitors go to the park each year?
3 There is *very little / too much* crime in the park.
4 Jen thinks there are *very few / too many* tourists there.
5 The website contains *lots of / not enough* information.
6 There's *not much / too much* rubbish in the park.

THE HIGH LINE,
NEW YORK CITY

Even the most enthusiastic city lover needs green spaces from time to time. In New York, one of the best places to find some nature is The High Line. Originally a 1930s railway bridge, this park opened in 2006 – ten metres above the street! It has more than 200 species of plants and spectacular views over the Hudson River. The park now attracts 4 million visitors a year, who escape the city streets to take a walk, take photos, and even get something to eat at one of the cafés. The High Line website (www.thehighline.org) is full of useful information about the history of the park and how they built it.

WHAT THE **LOCALS** SAY

I love The High Line. Calm and beautiful. It's safe too – apparently the crime rate is very low. **Pablo**

It used to be a lovely quiet place to go. Now it's full of tourists. Don't go at weekends! But one good thing is that it's quite clean and tidy – they clean up all the rubbish regularly. **Jen**

Make sure that you allow plenty of time. You need about three hours to see it properly. There's a lot to see – and you don't want to miss any of it! **Kira**

d ▶ Now go to Grammar Focus 7B on p.144

e Write sentences about each of the places below. Use quantifiers and the words in the box, and your own ideas. Don't include the name of the place.

- a city area that you know
- a country area that you know

| noise | crime | space | people | flowers | things to do |
| shops | cafés | wildlife | views | pollution | traffic |

f 💬 Read out your sentences. Can your partner guess where the places are?

A lot of people go there at weekends, but there's enough space for everyone. There aren't many shops or cafés.

Is it the beach?

4 SPEAKING

a You are going to talk about the area where you live. Make notes about these questions:

- Is it a healthy or safe place to live? Why / Why not?
- What do people complain about? (e.g. the noise, the roads)

b 💬 Take turns to talk about your areas. Would the places you talk about be good to live in for these people?

- a teenager who likes film and music
- a family with young children
- an elderly couple
- someone who likes sport and outdoor activities

Learn to make offers and ask for permission

P Sounding polite
S Imagining people's feelings

1 LISTENING

a 💬 Discuss the questions.

1 Do you take presents when you visit someone's house? What might you take?
2 What should you do to be polite when visiting someone's house? (e.g. arrive on time, take your shoes off, etc.)

b 💬 Look at the photos on this page. What do you think is happening? How do you think the people feel?

c ▶️2.50 Watch or listen to Part 1 and check your ideas.

d ▶️2.50 Watch or listen again. Are the sentences true (T) or false (F)?

1 Becky hasn't met Tom's parents before.
2 Michael wants to watch a football match.
3 Becky got Charlotte's name wrong.
4 Charlotte is a teacher.
5 Tom tried to tell his parents that Becky is a vegetarian.

e Do you think that Becky has been a good guest? Has she made a good first impression?

2 USEFUL LANGUAGE Offers, requests and asking for permission

a Match questions 1–5 with responses a–e.

1 **Is there anything we can do to help**? `c`
2 **Do you think you could** give me a hand? ☐
3 **Let me** get you something else. ☐
4 **Is it OK if I** just have some bread and butter? ☐
5 **I'll** get you a green salad. ☐

a No, it's fine, really.
b Sure.
c Oh no, it's all under control!
d OK, that would be lovely. Thanks.
e No, we can do better than that.

b What phrases in **bold** in 2a do we use to …

1 offer something politely?
2 ask for help politely?
3 ask for permission?

c Match requests 1–5 with responses a–e.

1 ☐ Do you mind if I borrow some money?
2 ☐ May I sit here?
3 ☐ Do you think I could have a glass of water?
4 ☐ Can I use your phone for a moment?
5 ☐ Would you mind if I opened the window?

a Yes, of course. Let me get you one.
b Not at all. How much do you want?
c Sure. Here it is.
d Not at all. It's hot in here.
e Of course. There's plenty of space.

3 LISTENING

a Look at the photo. What do you think Tom and Michael are talking about?

b ▶ **2.51** Watch or listen to Part 2 and check.

c ▶ **2.51** Watch or listen again. Are the sentences true (T) or false (F)?

1 Tom thinks Becky hasn't made a good impression.
2 Michael doesn't like Becky.

4 CONVERSATION SKILLS
Imagining people's feelings

a ▶ **2.52** What word is missing in each sentence? Listen and check.

1 I _____ you're excited about the match this afternoon.
2 Tom tells me you're an architect. That _____ be very interesting.

b Read the exchanges and <u>underline</u> the phrases we use to imagine what someone else is feeling.

1 **A** I'm doing three part-time jobs at the moment.
   B You must be very tired!
2 **A** I'm going to meet my boyfriend's parents for the first time.
   B I imagine you're a bit nervous!

c 💬 Look at the sentences below. Respond with *must* and an appropriate adjective.

1 I'm planning a holiday to France.
2 I've just broken my tooth!
3 I've lost my smartphone – and I can't remember any of my friends' numbers.
4 I'm learning Japanese at the moment.

> I'm planning a holiday to France.
> > That must be exciting!

d 💬 Tell your partner about some of the things below. Answer with a phrase from 4a or 4b.

- something you're planning on doing soon
- a hobby you have
- a problem you have at school/work

> I go to Spanish lessons at 7.30 in the morning before I go to work.
> > That must be tiring.
> > Yes, but I really enjoy them.

5 PRONUNCIATION Sounding polite

a ▶ **2.53** Listen to these sentences spoken twice. Which sentence sounds more polite, a or b?

1 Do you think you could give me a hand? *a / b*
2 It's lovely to meet you at last. *a / b*

b ▶ **2.54** Listen to three more pairs of sentences. Which sentences sound more polite, a or b?

1 How long are you staying? *a / b*
2 She seems really great. *a / b*
3 I'm really happy to hear that. *a / b*

c 💬 Practise saying the sentences in 5b with polite intonation.

6 SPEAKING

▶ **Communication 7C** 💬 Student A: Read the instructions below. Student B: Go to p.131.

Student A

1 You are staying with Student B in his/her home. During the conversation, ask permission to:
   - use the internet
   - have a shower
   - wash some clothes

2 Student B is a new colleague in your office. Ask him/her how it's going and try to sound interested (e.g. *That must be …*). He/She will ask you permission to do things. Decide whether or not to give permission.

○ Unit Progress Test

CHECK YOUR PROGRESS

You can now do the Unit Progress Test.

1 SPEAKING

💬 Talk about a recent holiday.

1 What kind of activities did you do?
2 Did the people you were with want to do the same things as you or different things?
3 Think of a holiday you would like to go on. What would you do on the holiday?

2 READING AND LISTENING

a 💬 You're going to read about Miami. Before you do, discuss the questions.

1 Where is Miami? Have you ever been there? Do you know anyone who's been there?
2 What is it like, or what do you imagine it's like? Talk about:
   • the weather
   • the people
   • buildings
   • the atmosphere
   • things to see and do

b 💬 Read about the top five things to do in and around Miami. Which would you like to do? Why? Are there any you would <u>not</u> want to do? Why not?

c ▶2.55 Sue is talking to a colleague. Listen to their conversation and answer the questions.

1 How many people are in Sue's family?
2 Where are they staying?
3 Which of the 'top five things' are they going to do?

d ▶2.55 Listen again and make notes in the table.

	Where does he/she want to go?	Why does he/she want to go there?
Sue's daughter		
Sue's son		
Sue's husband		
Sue		

e 💬 Do you think Sue is looking forward to the holiday? Why / Why not?

Top five things to do
... in and around Miami, Florida

1 Admire the architecture of Miami Beach

Wander the streets of Miami Beach and admire the art deco hotels and houses from the 1930s. The movie stars from the 1930s stayed here when they came to Miami. Many of the buildings have been repainted in their original colours.

2 Go to the beach

Miami has endless sandy beaches along the coast. You can find crowds if you want them or you can have a beach to yourself. And the water is always warm.

3 Visit the Everglades

Ninety minutes from Miami are the Everglades, a huge area of natural swamp which is home to alligators, snakes and rare birds. Take a boat through the area and get a close-up view of the wildlife.

4 Spend a day at Disney World

Disney World is just a day's drive away from Miami – a great day trip. You can find all the characters from Disney films and have hours of fun with (or without) your kids.

5 Take a trip to Cape Canaveral

North of Miami is Cape Canaveral, where the USA sends its rockets into space. You can take a tour round the Kennedy Space Center and see where they built the Apollo space rockets.

3 READING

a Read the note below which Sue's cousin left in the apartment in Miami. <u>Underline</u> the correct words.

1 The streets are safe *in the daytime / all the time*.
2 The apartment is *in the centre of / just outside* Miami.
3 The apartment is *right next to / far from* the sea.
4 Jutka will be away for *a week / more than a week*.

b Which adjectives in the box best describe the tone of the note? What words or phrases in the note helped you decide?

friendly   formal   funny   practical

c Match the purposes a–f with sections 1–6 in the note.

a ☐ to explain options for buying food
b ☐ to give information about going to places further away
c ☐ to finish the note
d ☐ to greet the reader and say what the note is about
e ☐ to give safety advice about the area round the apartment
f ☐ to give information about things in the apartment

d What general order are the sections in? Choose the correct answer.

1 things the reader needs to know now → things they need later
2 things which are very important → things which are less important
3 things which are less important → things which are more important

① Welcome to Miami! Hope you have a nice stay in the apartment. Here are a few things you need to know …

② Please make yourselves at home and help yourselves to anything in the kitchen. There's some chicken in the fridge, and lots of fruit and salad, so that should be enough for a couple of meals. I also got a couple of pizzas for the kids – they're in the freezer.

③ After that, you'll need to go shopping. The best place is the Sunshine Center. Go out of the main entrance of the apartment and turn left, and you'll see it about 100 metres down the road. It's got a couple of supermarkets, a good bookshop and a few good places to eat. Otherwise, there's a good place for burgers a bit further down the road. Apart from that, there are some good restaurants by the sea, but they're a bit further away.

④ By the way, if you do go out in the evening, don't walk around late at night – the streets round here are not very safe at night, though they're OK during the daytime.

⑤ Anyway, the car's in the parking lot, so you can use that for any trips. If you're going into Miami, another possibility is to take the train, but you'll find the car easier! You'll also need the car to go to the beach. The nearest one is Golden Beach, about 15 minutes' drive away. Another option is Ocean Beach, about 30 minutes further north, which is usually much less crowded. Alternatively, you could try Miami Beach nearer the centre, but it can be difficult to park.

⑥ Enjoy your stay and see you in a fortnight!

Love,

Jutka

4 WRITING SKILLS   Offering choices

a What do the words in **bold** mean below?

1 The Sunshine Center has got a few good places to eat. **Otherwise**, there's a good place for burgers a bit further down the road.
   a if you don't like that idea
   b however
   c finally

2 The nearest one is Golden Beach, about 15 minutes' drive away. **Another option is** Ocean Beach, about 30 minutes further north.
   a A different direction is
   b A different choice is
   c A much better beach is

b Read the note again and find three more words or phrases that you could use instead of *Otherwise* or *Another option is … .*

c Use words or phrases from 4a and 4b in the second sentences below.

1 If you drive north, you can visit Disney World. You can also go to the Space Center at Cape Canaveral.
   Another option is the Space Center at Cape Canaveral.
2 There are lots of good restaurants at Miami Beach. Or you can try the restaurants at South Beach.
3 To go to the West Coast you can get an inter-city bus. You can also hire a car for a few days.
4 You can drive through the Everglades and stop to look at the birds and alligators. You can also go round them by boat.

5 WRITING   A note with useful information

a You are going to write a note for someone who will be staying in your home while you are away. Think about:

- things in the house/flat
- things he/she can and can't do
- things you want to ask him/her to do
- food and shopping
- things to do in the area.

b 💬 Compare your ideas with a partner.

c Read another student's note and answer the questions.

1 Did you understand all the information?
2 Did he/she put the information in a logical order?
3 Did he/she use words and phrases from 4a or 4b correctly?

d Write a reply.

UNIT 7
Review and extension

1 GRAMMAR

a Underline the correct answer.

1 There are *lots / too many / too much* stairs in this building!
2 There isn't *enough light / light enough / enough of light*. It's always dark.
3 There's too *many / few / much* noise outside.
4 It's got *lots / lots of / much* windows.
5 There are very *little / much / few* buildings in the area.
6 It hasn't got *many / much / little* floors.

b 💬 Discuss the pictures. Use *must, might, could* and *can't*.

1 Is each person a man or a woman?
2 How old are they?
3 Where are they?

2 VOCABULARY

a Complete the text with the words in the box.

block   floor   location   neighbourhood   views

Holiday home swap

This summer, we exchanged homes with the Acuna family from Lisbon. Our home is in a quiet
¹_____ in the Welsh countryside, with
²_____ of the hills in every direction.
The Acunas live on the third ³_____ of a
⁴_____ of flats in the Portuguese capital.
The flat was in a lively ⁵_____ and there were lots of places to visit nearby. Home swapping is a fantastic way to discover new places.

b Complete each sentence with a preposition.

1 Don't worry _____ the neighbours.
2 Who does that house belong _____?
3 You'll have to wait ages _____ a bus.
4 How do you cope _____ the cold winters here?
5 You can't rely _____ public transport here.
6 We succeeded _____ finding a good hotel.
7 Are you going to complain _____ the noise?

3 WORDPOWER *over*

a Match questions 1–6 with responses a–f.

1 ☐ When did you paint the house?
2 ☐ How many people live in Hong Kong?
3 ☐ How long was the meeting?
4 ☐ Can we start the test?
5 ☐ What's the matter?
6 ☐ Was the hotel room nice?

a Yes, we had a view **over** the lake.
b **Over** the summer.
c Yes, turn your papers **over** and begin.
d **Over** 7 million.
e You're getting mud all **over** the floor!
f It started at 2 and it was **over** by 3.15.

b Match the meanings of *over* 1–6 with sentences a–f in 3a.

1 ☐ finished
2 ☐ across / from one side to the other
3 ☐ more than
4 ☐ during (a period of time)
5 ☐ the other way up
6 ☐ covering

c Complete each sentence with *over* and information from the box. One sentence only needs *over*.

16   a lifetime   someone   the last few days
the next few days   the world   your city

1 Where can tourists go to get views _____?
2 What businesses from your country are known all _____?
3 How much work have you done _____?
4 What can you do in your country when you are _____? How about 18?
5 What kind of things do people learn _____?
6 When was the last time you were sad that something was _____?
7 Imagine you spill a drink _____ else in a restaurant. What would you do?
8 What are you going to do _____?

d 💬 Ask and answer the questions.

🔄 REVIEW YOUR PROGRESS

How well did you do in this unit? Write 3, 2 or 1 for each objective.
3 = very well   2 = well   1 = not so well

I CAN ...

describe a building.	☐
describe a town or city.	☐
make offers and ask for permission.	☐
write a note with useful information.	☐

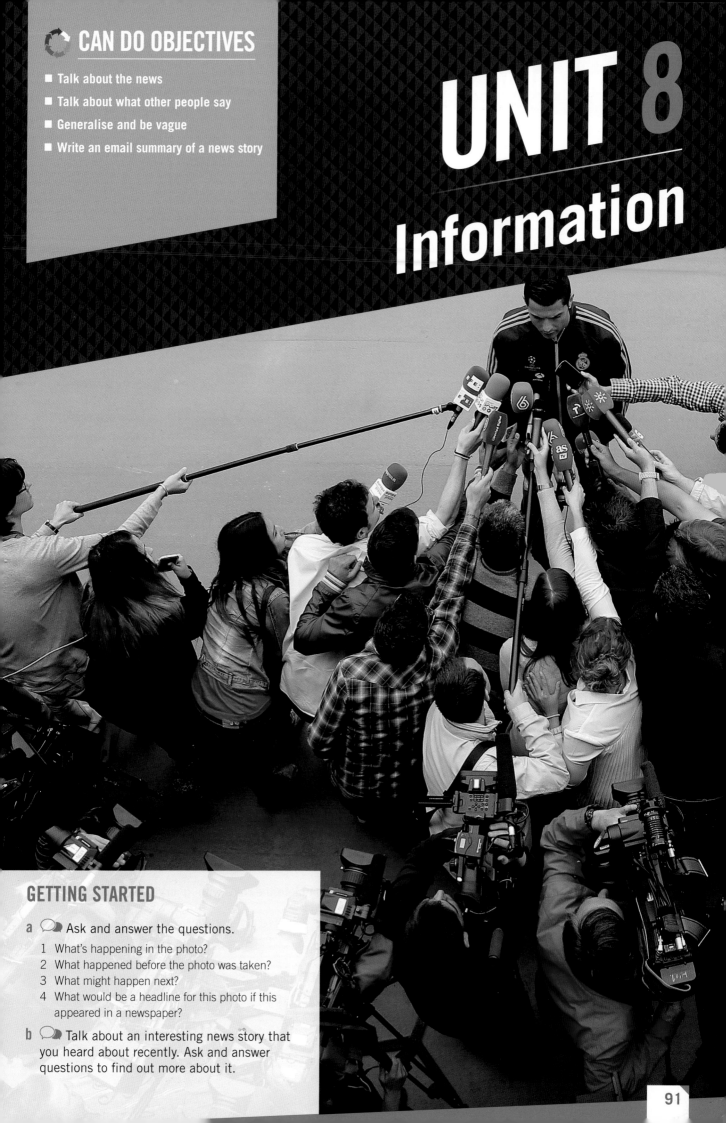

CAN DO OBJECTIVES

- Talk about the news
- Talk about what other people say
- Generalise and be vague
- Write an email summary of a news story

UNIT 8
Information

GETTING STARTED

a 💬 Ask and answer the questions.

1 What's happening in the photo?
2 What happened before the photo was taken?
3 What might happen next?
4 What would be a headline for this photo if this appeared in a newspaper?

b 💬 Talk about an interesting news story that you heard about recently. Ask and answer questions to find out more about it.

8A He said he'd read the news online

1 VOCABULARY The news

a 💬 Discuss the questions.

1 When did you last read a newspaper?
2 How often do you read the news online?
3 Where do you get most of your news from? (TV? / smartphone?)

b Compare your answers in 1a with the information on the right about how people get their news. Did your group have similar results?

c Complete the blog *Too much news* with words in the box.

articles affairs breaking celebrity
news feeds headlines the news

Too much news

The other day a friend said I was addicted to the news. I didn't know what he meant. Me? Well, yes, every day I watch ¹_____ on TV, read a few ²_____ in newspapers and magazines and I subscribe to a couple of ³_____ online. Yes, I'm interested in current ⁴_____ and I always want to keep up to date with ⁵_____ news in my country and abroad. But is it the most important thing in my life? Of course not.

Or is it?

Maybe my friend is right. I quite often go on websites to check the latest ⁶_____ gossip about TV stars and footballers.

And now I think about it, there are screens everywhere – in the streets, on my phone – so I'm surrounded by news. There are dramatic ⁷_____ everywhere I look, and I'm always checking my phone to see what's happening ...

News is everywhere, and it all looks important. I think my friend is right, after all. Maybe it's time to take a break ...

NEWS

d 💬 Discuss the questions.

1 Look at the kinds of news in the box. Which are you interested in? Which are you not interested in? Are you interested in similar things?

business celebrity gossip entertainment
fashion nature and the environment
politics and current affairs
science and technology sport travel weather

2 What makes you read news stories (e.g. interesting headlines, a topic you know about, breaking news)?
3 Are we surrounded by too much news?

e ▶ Now go to Vocabulary Focus 8A on p.159

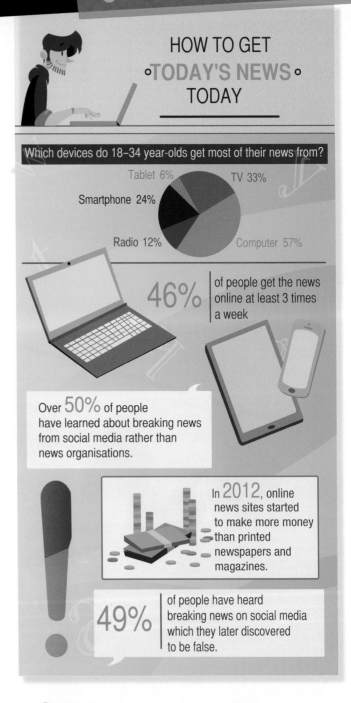

HOW TO GET ∘TODAY'S NEWS∘ TODAY

Which devices do 18–34 year-olds get most of their news from?

Tablet 6% TV 33%
Smartphone 24%
Radio 12% Computer 57%

46% of people get the news online at least 3 times a week

Over **50%** of people have learned about breaking news from social media rather than news organisations.

In **2012**, online news sites started to make more money than printed newspapers and magazines.

49% of people have heard breaking news on social media which they later discovered to be false.

f ▶3.2 **Pronunciation** Listen to the words below. How are the <u>underlined</u> letters *c*, *g* and *k* pronounced?

blogger breaking comments
current gossip organisation

g Complete the rules with /g/ or /k/.

1 When you say _____, there is a sound in the throat.
2 When you say _____, there is no sound in the throat.

h ▶3.2 Listen again and repeat the words.

2 READING

a 💬 Look at the photos of news stories.
Do you know anything about these stories?

b Read *Everyone's a journalist* and answer the questions.

1 What's the connection between social media and the photos?
2 Which news stories not shown in the photos are mentioned in the article?
3 What is the danger of relying on social media to get news?

c Read the article again and answer the questions.

1 How many people died in the Hudson River plane crash?
2 How did people spread images and videos of Chelyabinsk?
3 What did NASA tell people about on Twitter?
4 How did Carel Pedre use social media?
5 What was the problem with some of the photos of Hurricane Sandy?

d Match words in the article with the definitions below.

1 a place where something happens: s_____
2 full of action and excitement: d_____
3 found (for the first time): d_____
4 a very bad situation in which people die or are hurt: d_____
5 a person who sees an event happen: e_____
6 jokes or tricks: h_____
7 things that look real but aren't: f_____

e 💬 Discuss the questions.

1 Have you ever seen breaking news on Facebook or Twitter before it was on TV? What was it? Was it true?
2 Have you ever shared a photo or news story that you later discovered to be false?
3 Do you agree that social media can 'save lives and change the world'? Why / Why not?

EVERYONE'S A JOURNALIST

On 15 January 2009, several interesting things happened. Firstly, a plane crash-landed into the Hudson River, right in the middle of New York City. The pilot, crew and 155 passengers all escaped safely. But then, something else happened …

Jim Hanrahan was nearby and watched the event happen. He immediately tweeted that he had just seen a plane crash in the Hudson. From there the news spread quickly. People contacted him immediately and asked him what was happening, and other people on the street took photos and videos with their phones and posted them online. Ordinary people suddenly became journalists. It was 15 minutes before the news broke on official news channels.

Photos, videos and tweets from ordinary people at the scene of dramatic events now provide the words and images that describe events in the news. When a meteor exploded over the Russian city of Chelyabinsk in 2013, millions of people around the world watched videos and photos of the event on Facebook and YouTube. When NASA discovered ice on Mars, it used Twitter to spread the news. 'Are you ready to celebrate?' they tweeted. 'We have ICE!!!!! Yes, ICE, WATER ICE on Mars!' News from another planet suddenly felt personal.

Social media can also save lives. In January 2010, an earthquake hit the Caribbean island of Haiti. The government said that there had been an earthquake, but they didn't give many details at first. Meanwhile, people living in the disaster area were posting photos and eyewitness accounts on Twitter and Facebook and telling the world that it was an emergency and houses were collapsing. Carel Pedre, a local radio presenter, used this information in his reports to help people find family members, and people even phoned his programme to ask if their relatives were safe.

News travels fast on social media, but false stories spread just as quickly as the truth. Some of these are 'facts' reported in error, others are deliberate hoaxes. When Hurricane Sandy hit the east coast of the USA in 2012, many of the dramatic photos of storms and floods were real. But did you see the photos of stormy skies above the Brooklyn Bridge? Did you see the photos of seals and sharks in the streets? Or the deep-sea diver in the New York subway? These photos were all fakes – either real photos from other events or computer-generated images.

Hoaxes like these remind us that not everything people post and publish is reliable. But social media can change our lives for the better. In the words of Carel Pedre, 'May we continue to use Twitter to save lives and change the world.'

Hudson River crash

Meteor in Chelyabinsk, Russia

3 GRAMMAR Reported speech (statements and questions)

a Read these sentences from the text. Underline the reported speech.

1 He immediately tweeted that <u>he had just seen a plane crash in the Hudson</u>.
2 People contacted him immediately and asked him what was happening.
3 The government said that there had been an earthquake.
4 Meanwhile, people living in the disaster area were posting videos and telling the world that it was an emergency and houses were collapsing.
5 People even phoned his programme to ask if their relatives were safe.

b What do you think they actually said (or tweeted)? Complete the sentences.

1 Jim Hanrahan: 'I _____ a plane crash in the Hudson.'
2 Other people (to Jim Hanrahan): 'What _____?'
3 The government of Haiti: 'There _____ an earthquake.'
4 People in the disaster area: 'It _____ an emergency. Houses _____ collapsing.'
5 Radio listeners: '_____ my relatives safe?'

c Underline the correct words in the rules.

> 1 When we report what someone has said or written, we often change the tense of the direct speech *backwards* / *forwards* in time.
> 2 We use *question order* / *normal sentence order* in reported questions.
> 3 We often don't change the tense when we report things which are *still true* / *no longer true*.

d Write the tense changes in reported speech.

Direct speech	Reported speech
Present simple	_____
Past simple	_____
Present perfect simple	_____
Present perfect continuous	_____
will	_____

e ▶ Now go to Grammar Focus 8A on p.146

f Work in pairs. Write a story using reported speech and questions.

1 Write the first two sentences. Begin like this and continue using reported speech.
   My friend phoned me a few weeks ago with some news. He/She said …
2 Pass your sentences to another pair. Read the sentences you received and add another sentence. Begin:
   I asked him/her …
3 Pass your sentences to another pair. Read the sentences you received and add another sentence. Begin:
   He/She said …
4 Pass your sentences to another pair. Read the sentences and add a final sentence. Check that the reported speech is correct. Then read out the story to the class.

4 SPEAKING

a You're going to talk about a website that you often visit. It should be a news site, a blog, a forum or a social networking site. Make notes about the questions below.

1 What's the website called?
2 What kind of news or information do you get from it (e.g. sport, music, entertainment, current affairs, etc.)?
3 How often do you visit it?
4 Why do you like it? Do you find it useful?
5 What stories or other information have you found out?
6 Have you ever posted a comment there?
7 Have you made any friends through this website?
8 Why would you recommend this website to other people?

b 💬 Take turns to tell each other about your website in 4a. Try to encourage your partner to visit your website. Ask questions to find out more.

I use the MTV website for entertainment news.

Has it got current affairs?

No, not really.

8B I recommended visiting a local restaurant

Learn to talk about what other people say

G Verb patterns
V Shopping; Reporting verbs

1 VOCABULARY Shopping

a 💬 Discuss the questions.

1 Do you prefer browsing online, or in real shops?
2 Do you buy the latest products as soon as they come out?
3 Have you ever returned something or asked for a refund?
4 Where do you look for bargains?
5 What would you like to be able to afford to buy?

b ▶ Now go to Vocabulary Focus 8B on p.159

2 LISTENING

a 💬 Discuss the questions.

1 When was the last time you bought something expensive (e.g. a car, a holiday, a computer, a meal in an expensive restaurant)?
2 How did you decide to buy it? Did you read online reviews or get personal recommendations from people you know?
3 Do you trust online reviews? Why / Why not?
4 Do you ever write reviews?

⭐⭐⭐⭐⭐
'It's worth travelling 100 miles to get there!'

I enjoy going to the country's best restaurants and I've wanted to try this 'restaurant on a boat' for a long time. The location keeps changing depending on the season and making a reservation isn't easy. But we managed to get a table and had an absolutely wonderful evening. You choose your fish from the menu, then a member of staff goes fishing to catch it for you! It's easy to see why this place gets so many five-star reviews.

Dean 56, Bristol, UK

Was the review helpful? ● Yes ● No

b Read the restaurant review above.

1 Where is the restaurant? UK
2 What's unusual about the location? Keeps changing
3 What kind of food does it serve?

c 💬 Would you like to eat at this restaurant? Why / Why not?

d ▶3.6 Listen to the first part of the conversation between Harry and Erica. Why can't they go to the restaurant?

e ▶3.7 Listen to the whole conversation. Are the sentences true (T) or false (F)?

1 The restaurant had excellent reviews.
2 The person who invented Oscar's owned a hotel.
3 His friend's hotel was successful because it got lots of good reviews online.
4 Erica thinks there isn't enough control over online reviews.
5 Fake reviewers often only write one review.

f 💬 Discuss the questions.

1 Which online review websites are common where you live?
2 Which ones do you trust? Why do you trust them?

3 GRAMMAR Verb patterns

a Match the verb patterns in sentences 1–4 with rules a–d.

1 ☐ **Making** a reservation isn't easy.
2 ☐ It's worth **travelling** 100 miles to get there!
3 ☐ I enjoy **going** to the country's best restaurants.
4 ☐ After many attempts, we finally succeeded in **getting** a table.

We use verb + -*ing*:
a after prepositions
b after certain verbs (e.g. *keep*, *mind*, *love*, etc.)
c after some expressions (e.g. *it's worth*, *it's no good*, etc.)
d as the subject of a sentence

b Match the verb patterns in sentences 1–4 with rules a–d.

1 ☐ It's easy **to see** why this place gets so many five-star reviews.
2 ☐ We managed **to get** a table.
3 ☐ A member of staff goes fishing **to catch** it for you!
4 ☐ I didn't know what **to choose** from the menu.

We use *to* + infinitive:
a after question words
b after certain verbs (e.g. *want*, *plan*, *seem*, *decide*, etc.)
c after certain adjectives (e.g. *difficult*, *good*, *important*, etc.)
d to show purpose

c ▶ Now go to Grammar Focus 8B on p.146

d Write the correct form of the verbs in brackets. Then choose an option or add your own idea to make it true for you.

1 I enjoy _____ (shop) *for clothes* / *with friends* / … .
2 I'm planning _____ (get) *a new phone* / *some new shoes* … soon.
3 It's difficult _____ (choose) *clothes* / *music* / … for other people.
4 I know how _____ (write) a good *review* / *blog* / … .
5 I think it's worth _____ (spend) a lot of money on a *meal in a restaurant* / *good haircut* / … .
6 I'm not interested in _____ (hear) about *people's problems* / *new shops and restaurants* / … .
7 I often *walk round the shops* / *look online* / … _____ (see) if there's anything I want _____ (buy).
8 _____ (go) to *language classes* / *the gym* / … is a good way to meet new people.

e 💬 Compare your sentences in 3d. Can you find anyone who has four or more statements which are the same as yours?

> I enjoy shopping for clothes.
> Me too!

4 VOCABULARY Reporting verbs

a ▶ **3.9** Listen and match conversations 1–3 with pictures a–c. Is each customer happy?

b ▶ **3.9** Listen again. Are the sentences true (T) or false (F)?

Conversation 1
a He **suggests** changing the woman's hairstyle. T
b She **warns** him not to cut her hair too short. F
c He **recommends** trying a new hair product. T
d She **agrees** to have the new product on her hair. F

Conversation 2
a He **invites** them to stay another night. F
b He **reminds** them to write a review. T
c They **promise** to write a good review. T
d They **advise** him to advertise the hotel more. F

Conversation 3
a The woman **admits** eating the dessert. T
b The woman **refuses** to pay for the dessert. T
c The woman **threatens** to write a bad review. F
d The waiter **offers** to get the manager. T

c ▶3.10 **Pronunciation** Listen to the sentences below and the words in **bold**. Is the letter *s* pronounced as /s/ or /z/?

1 He **suggested** changing the woman's hairstyle.
2 They **promised** to write a good review.
3 They **advised** him to advertise the hotel more.
4 The woman **refused** to pay for the dessert.

d Practise saying the words in **bold** in 4c.

e Look at pictures 1–8 below. Report what the people said using the reporting verbs from the box.

admitted	advised	offered	~~promised~~
~~refused~~	~~reminded~~	suggested	warned

1 She _reminded_ him to read the label.
2 He _admitted_ writing all the reviews.
3 He _promised_ to delete the reviews.
4 She _advised_ her to make a formal complaint.
5 He _offered_ to pay for lunch.
6 She _warned_ him not to sit down.
7 She _suggested_ asking someone for directions.
8 He _refused_ to ask anyone for help.

5 SPEAKING

a You're going to talk about an experience you've had. Make notes about one of the following:

- a time when you recommended something to someone (e.g. a restaurant or a film) or someone recommended something to you
- a time when someone warned you not to do something
- a time when you admitted making a mistake. What had you done? How did you feel? How did other people react?
- a time when you refused to do something. What did you refuse to do? Why did you refuse to do it?
- a time you or someone else promised to do something, but didn't do it. What was it?

b 💬 Take turns to talk about your experience for at least a minute. Has anyone in your group had a similar experience?

I suggested watching my favourite film to my best friend. I'd kept telling my friend how good it was, but as soon as it started I realised that …

④ If I were you, I'd make a formal complaint.

① Don't forget to read the label

② OK, it's true. I wrote all the reviews.

③ I'll delete them. Really, I will.

⑦ Why don't we ask someone for directions?

⑧ No! I know where we are.

⑤ I'll pay for lunch, if you like.

⑥ Don't sit down!

8C Everyday English
On the whole, I prefer taking action shots

Learn to generalise and be vague
- **P** The sounds /h/ and /w/
- **S** Being vague

1 LISTENING

a 💬 Discuss the questions.

1 Have you had any good news to share recently? Have you been told any good news? What was it?
2 How do you usually share your good news – by text, online, in person?

b 💬 Look at the photo. What do you think is happening? How do you think Becky is feeling?

c ▶3.11 Watch or listen to Part 1. Answer the questions.

1 What does Becky ask questions about in the interview?
2 How does Becky think the interview went?

d ▶3.11 Watch or listen to Part 1 again. Complete each sentence with one or two words.

1 Rachel is worried that there's not enough _____ in the area for two florists.
2 Becky prefers taking _____.
3 The course can include a _____ in a local gallery.
4 There are normally two _____ a year.
5 Becky found her interview more _____ than she was expecting.
6 They will tell her _____ whether she got a place.

e 💬 Discuss the questions.

1 Do you think Rachel is right to be worried about the new florist's in her area? Do you know of an area in your town/city with lots of the same types of shops/ restaurants?
2 Would you like to do the photography course that Becky has applied for? Why / Why not?

2 USEFUL LANGUAGE Generalising

a ▶3.12 Listen and complete the sentences with the phrases in the box.

| generally | on the whole | normally | tends to | typically |

1 But I think, _____, I prefer taking action shots.
2 It _____ either be working at a local gallery on a photography exhibition or working with a professional photographer as an assistant.
3 The placement _____ lasts two weeks.
4 Yes, _____ each class has two opportunities to go on study visits per year.
5 Well, _____ they don't tell you during the interview …

b Underline the phrases for generalising in these sentences.

1 It can be difficult to relax at the end of the day. I find my yoga class really helpful for that.
2 As a rule, I'm not very good at interviews – I get too nervous.
3 I don't usually spend much time worrying about things that haven't happened yet.

c Are the sentences in 2b true for you? If not, change them to make them true.

3 CONVERSATION SKILLS Being vague

a Replace the words in **bold** with the words in the box.

| a couple of | things | sort |

1 I prefer taking action shots – sport and **stuff** like that.
2 You have **a few** portraits in your portfolio.
3 I'm not very good with that **kind** of thing.

b Complete the second sentence in each pair using vague language so that it means the same as the first sentence. More than one answer might be possible.

| a couple of | things/stuff like that | that sort/kind of thing |

1 I like swimming, playing tennis and jogging.
I like swimming and _____.
2 Everything went well except for one or two problems.
Everything went well except for _____ problems.
3 I'm going to the supermarket. I need some milk, eggs, bread and cheese.
I'm going to the supermarket. I need some milk and _____.

4 LISTENING

a 💬 Look at the photos. Discuss the questions.

1 What news do you think Tina has about the new shop?
   a The builders have stopped work.
   b It's going to be a clothes shop.
   c It has closed down.

2 What news do you think Becky might receive?
   a She's got a new job as a photographer.
   b She's got some money to help her do the course.
   c She's got a place on the photography course.

b ▶3.13 Watch or listen to Part 2 and check your ideas.

5 PRONUNCIATION
The sounds /h/ and /w/

a ▶3.14 Listen to these sentences. What sounds do the underlined words begin with?

1 Pretty well, I think, on the <u>whole</u>.
2 <u>What</u> was the question?
3 I was there around two <u>hours</u>.

b ▶3.15 Match the words in the box with the sound each word begins with. Listen and check.

white   honest   hotel   wrap   who   work

- /h/ e.g. *happy*:
- /w/ e.g. *water*:
- first letter silent:

c ▶3.16 Listen to the following sentences. Choose the word you hear.
1 You can *eat / heat* the food up in the microwave.
2 He wrote on the board *invite / in white*.
3 A few weeks ago she lost her *earring / hearing*.
4 The man you are looking for is the one in the *west / vest*.
5 I *hate / ate* the food that my daughter cooked.

6 SPEAKING

💬 Ask your partner for advice on one of these topics:

- a course you would like to do
- a local restaurant for a special occasion
- an area of your town/city to live in

> I'd like to study French at university.

> I've heard that it's quite difficult to get a place. But, on the whole, the teachers are very good.

🔄 **Unit Progress Test**

CHECK YOUR PROGRESS

You can now do the Unit Progress Test.

1 LISTENING AND SPEAKING

a 💬 Look at the three photos of air travel below. What is happening in each photo?

b 💬 Think about the last time you travelled by air. What was the best/worst thing about it?

c 💬 You are going to listen to someone talking about a news story. Some of the key words from the story are in the box. What do you think happened?

> eleven   Manchester   mother   shopping
> airport   security   plane   Rome   complained

d 💬 Compare your stories with other students.

e ▶3.17 Listen to the story. How close was it to your story?

f Do we know if these statements are true? Write true (*T*), false (*F*) or don't know (*DK*).

1 The speaker read the story in a newspaper. F
2 The boy was alone in the shopping centre. F
3 His mother went to the airport to look for him. DK
4 The boy spoke to the children in the other family. F
5 The boy didn't have a boarding pass. T
6 They didn't count the passengers before they took off. F, DK
7 The airline offered the mother free flights in the future. F
8 It's the first time something like this has ever happened. F

g ▶3.17 Listen again and check your answers.

h 💬 Discuss the questions.

1 Do you think something like this could happen in your country?
2 Do you think airport security in your country is:
  a too strict
  b not strict enough
  c about right?

2 READING

a Look at the headline of a similar news story below. What do you think happened? Choose a or b.

1 a He drove the car himself.
  b He was a passenger in the car.
2 a He flew the plane himself.
  b He was a passenger on the plane.

b Read the story quickly and check your answers to 2a.

c Read the story again. Note down things that are the same as in the story you listened to.

13-YEAR-OLD BOY DRIVES TO AIRPORT AND FLIES ACROSS USA

Kenton Weaver is 13 years old and has no photo ID. But that didn't stop him from stealing his father's car in the middle of the night, driving more than 20 miles to a Florida airport and taking two connecting flights to San José, California. 'I really enjoyed it,' said Kenton.

Kenton's mother, Kim Casey, lives just half an hour from San José airport in Fresno, California, but the boy's father, Dean Weaver, thinks it was the journey itself that interested the boy. According to Dean, his son is fascinated by airplanes. 'He'll do anything to go to an airport,' Dean said. 'He wants to be a pilot.'

Kenton did not own a credit card, passport, driver's licence, or photo ID of any kind. Yet he was able somehow to buy a plane ticket, go through airport security, fly to Chicago and catch his connecting flight to San José without any problems. His father said it is possible Kenton used the numbers from one of his own credit cards to buy the ticket online.

3 WRITING SKILLS
Summarising information

a Read a summary of the news story. Which words or phrase in **bold** tell us … ?

   1 that the person is reporting a story he/she read or heard about somewhere

   2 that the person is commenting on what happened

There was an **incredible** story in the newspaper last week. **Apparently**, a boy of 13 stole his father's car, drove it to the airport and then took two flights from Florida to California to see his mother, who lives there. **Amazingly**, he did all this without a credit card, ID or driver's licence. **It seems that** he used his father's credit card number to buy the plane ticket online, and no-one asked him any questions. **Fortunately**, they found the car and everything was all right in the end.

b Look at audioscript 3.17 on p.171. Find more words used to comment on the story.

c Compare the sentences below with the highlighted sentence in the summary in 3a. Answer questions 1–4.

A boy of 13 stole his father's car. The boy drove it to the airport. The boy took two flights from Florida to California. The boy flew there to see his mother. His mother lives in California.

   1 How many sentences are in this part of the summary?
   2 What words are added to join the sentences together in 3a?
   3 What words are left out or changed in the summary in 3a? Why?
   4 Why is the summary in 3a better than the sentences in 3c?

d Here is a different summary of the same news story. Join the sentences together to make four or five sentences. Use the words in the box to help you (you can use the words more than once).

and	before	but	who	with

I read an incredible news story about a boy.
Apparently he flew alone from Florida to California.
He was only 13.
He managed to fly alone across America.
He even changed planes in Chicago.
He bought a ticket online.
He used his father's credit card number.
No one at the airport asked him any questions.
He even took his father's car.
He parked it in the airport car park.
He got on the plane.

e Work in pairs and compare your summaries. Are they the same?

4 WRITING

a Work in pairs. Choose one of the news headlines below or a story in the news at the moment. Discuss and make notes about what happened.

POLICE FIND MISSING GIRL

Tiger escapes from zoo

MAN JUMPS FROM PLANE – AND SURVIVES

SURFER ESCAPES SHARK ATTACK

b Work in pairs. Write an email to a friend, summarising the story in a few sentences. Include words or phrases to comment on the story.

c Work with another pair. Read each other's emails and answer the questions.

   1 Is the information clear and in a logical order?
   2 Is the amount of information right?
   3 Are there too many or too few sentences? Are they connected in the best way?
   4 Can you improve the summary?

d Tell another pair about the news story you read.

UNIT 8
Review and extension

1 GRAMMAR

a Read the text and <u>underline</u> the correct answers.

'Internet users worry about [1]*to lose* / *losing* private information online, but they don't mind [2]*to see* / *seeing* advertisements that are personally directed at them.' That's what the Digital Advertising Alliance discovered when they conducted a survey [3]*to find out* / *finding out* how consumers feel about targeted advertising. Only 4% said they didn't like the idea of [4]*to get* / *getting* targeted advertising.

Consumers seem [5]*to understand* / *understanding* that adverts make it possible [6]*to have* / *having* free websites: 75% of people said that they didn't want [7]*to pay* / *paying* for websites with no advertising on them.

b Complete the reported speech.

1 'I'll never go to that hairdresser again,' you said.
   You said _____ to that hairdresser again.
2 Kate asked John, 'What are you going to buy?'
   Kate asked John _____ to buy.
3 The editor said to me, 'Rewrite this story.'
   The editor told _____ this story.
4 The interviewer asked me, 'Have you ever written a blog?'.
   The interviewer asked me _____ a blog.

2 VOCABULARY

a Replace the words in **bold** with a word or phrase from the box that means the same. There are three words and phrases that you don't need.

article   bargain   browsing   came out   can't afford
current affairs   an editor   a journalist   spread

1 A new version of this software **was first available to buy** six months ago. _____
2 The news will **pass from person to person** very quickly and then everyone will know about it. _____
3 She's training to become **someone who is involved in communicating news to the public**. _____
4 I might buy something, but at the moment I'm just **looking to see what there is**. _____
5 Dan **hasn't got enough money for** a new phone. _____
6 He's interested in **political, social and economic events**.
   _____

b Complete the reporting verbs. Write a sentence with each one.

1 a _ _ i _ _
2 w _ _ n
3 t h _ _ _ _ _ e _
4 r _ c _ _ m _ _ _
5 p _ o _ i _ e

3 WORDPOWER *in/on* + noun

a Look at the phrases in the box and <u>underline</u> the correct words in the rules.

on the label   on a website   in capital letters
in cash   in the photo   in a magazine

1 We use *in* / *on* + flat surfaces like *wall*, *page* and *screen*.
2 We use *in* / *on* + *film*, *photo* and *picture* (when we talk about what they contain).
3 We use *in* / *on* + *the internet*, *the radio*, *TV*, *Facebook* and *Twitter*.
4 We use *in* / *on* + written and printed material (e.g. *the newspaper*, *a sentence*, *an email*, *an attachment*).
5 We use *in* / *on* with sizes (e.g. *39*, *medium*), currencies (e.g. *pounds*, *yen*, *dollars*) and before *stock*.

b Complete the sentences with *in* or *on*.

1 What can you see _____ the picture?
2 I've got some photos of Paul _____ my phone.
3 The answer was _____ the first paragraph.
4 Was it strange to see your name _____ print?
5 The full article is _____ page 4.
6 They were talking about his new film _____ the radio.
7 Did you pay _____ cash?
8 How much is £30 _____ euros?
9 The words 'Not for sale' were _____ the sign.
10 **A** I'm looking for these shoes _____ size 9.
    B I'm afraid we don't have them _____ stock at the moment.
11 Your seat number is _____ the ticket.
12 If you write _____ pencil, it doesn't matter if you make a mistake.

c 💬 Take turns to test each other on the phrases.

> The internet.

> On the internet.

REVIEW YOUR PROGRESS

How well did you do in this unit? Write 3, 2 or 1 for each objective.
3 = very well   2 = well   1 = not so well

I CAN ...

talk about the news.	☐
talk about what other people say.	☐
generalise and be vague.	☐
write an email summary of a news story.	☐

CAN DO OBJECTIVES

- Talk about films and TV
- Give extra information
- Recommend and respond to recommendations
- Write an article

UNIT 9

Entertainment

GETTING STARTED

a 🗨 Look at the photo and answer the questions.

1 Where are these people?
2 What are they doing and why?
3 What do you think the passers-by are thinking?

b ▶ 3.18 Listen and check your answers.

c 🗨 Are there similar street entertainers in your area? Do you like them?

d 🗨 What other kinds of street entertainers can you think of? Which ones do you like best?

1 VOCABULARY Cinema and TV

a 💬 Discuss the questions.

1 What kinds of TV programmes and films do you like? Why?
2 What are the most popular TV shows in your country at the moment? Do you watch them? Why / Why not?

b ▶ Now go to Vocabulary Focus 9A on p.160

2 LISTENING

a 💬 Look at the four film posters and discuss the questions.

1 What do you know about these films?
2 Did they use CGI (computer-generated imagery) and special effects?

b 💬 Look at the information below about a radio programme. What do you think the presenters will say about CGI?

The Big View
Ellie and Nick exchange views on art and entertainment.

Tonight's show
'Has CGI taken the heart out of modern film-making?'

c ▶3.21 Listen to the programme. Do both presenters think there is too much CGI in modern films?

d ▶3.21 Listen again. Are the sentences true (T) or false (F)?

1 Ellie says that directors seem to be more focused on special effects than the story. T
2 *Casablanca* was filmed in Paris. F
3 The fight scene in *Inception* was made using CGI. F
4 Nick thinks that good directors should be able to use technology well. F

e 💬 Discuss the questions.

1 Can you think of other examples of … ?
   • films that have no CGI or special effects
   • films that use CGI and other special effects
2 Have you seen these films? Did you like them?
3 Who do you agree with most – Nick or Ellie? Why?

3 READING

a 💬 Look at the two film posters on the right and discuss the questions.

1 Have you seen these films? If not, would you like to?
2 How are the two films similar? How are they different?

b Read *Film-making has changed a lot in the last 100 years* and check your ideas. Does the writer prefer traditional animated films, or films made with modern technology?

c Read the article again. What do these numbers refer to?

| 33 | 1,500,000 | 4 | 24 | 10,318 | 1937 | 525 | 3 |

d 💬 Discuss the questions.

1 What animated films like this have you seen? What did you think of them?
2 Do you agree with the last sentence of the article?

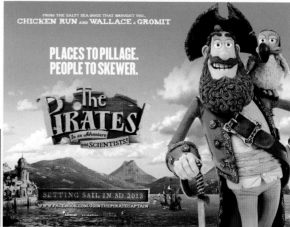

FILM-MAKING
HAS CHANGED A LOT
IN THE LAST 100 YEARS – OR HAS IT ...?

They're slow. They're boring. They don't have any special effects. That's the opinion many people have about old movies. But some film directors continue to use film-making techniques that have not changed in nearly a hundred years, and the results can be charming and fun.

Here, a pin is being used to move the puppet's eyes.

The Pirates! In an Adventure with Scientists!, created by British company Aardman Animations, is one example. It took five years to make this extremely ambitious film, using the 'stop-frame' filming technique. For every second of finished film, the puppets and models in each scene were moved up to 24 times. On average, it took a whole day to make just four seconds of screen action. A total of 525 people – including 33 animators – worked on the production. This kind of film-making requires great attention to detail. For example, pins were used to make tiny changes to the models. In total, 10,318 puppet mouths were used during filming to create realistic face movements.

The puppets in each scene were moved up to 24 times.

However, nearly a hundred years ago, Walt Disney was doing something very similar. Back in 1937, his team made the first ever full-length animated feature film, *Snow White and the Seven Dwarfs*. He also used the stop-frame technique. In this case, each frame was drawn by hand. More than 1,500,000 frames were used in total. The film took three years to make and cost six times more to make than Disney had planned.

Thousands of frames were drawn by hand.

Snow White was hugely successful and it is still loved today by children around the world. There is no doubt that Aardman Animations' films will be enjoyed in the same way for many years to come. Films that use modern technology may be dramatic and exciting, but handmade films will always be more impressive and fun to watch.

4 GRAMMAR The passive

a We use *be* + a past participle to make a passive verb form. Are the <u>underlined</u> verbs active (A) or passive (P)?

1 They <u>don't have</u> any special effects.
2 It <u>took</u> five years to make this extremely ambitious film.
3 Here, a pin <u>is being used</u> to move the puppet's eyes.
4 Thousands of frames <u>were drawn</u> by hand.
5 The film cost six times more to make than Disney <u>had planned</u>.
6 *Snow White* <u>is still loved</u> today by children.
7 Aardman Animations' films <u>will be enjoyed</u> in the same way for many years to come.

b ▶3.22 **Pronunciation** Listen to the passive sentences in 4a. Is the auxiliary verb *be* stressed in these sentences?

c ▶3.22 Listen again to the passive sentences in 4a and practise saying them.

d <u>Underline</u> the correct words in the rules.

> We can use the passive when:
> 1 we *know* / *don't know* who did an action
> 2 it's *obvious* / *not obvious* who did an action
> 3 it's *important* / *not important* who did an action.

> *Thousands of frames were drawn <u>by</u> hand.*
> *Small changes to the puppets were made <u>with</u> a pin.*
>
> 4 We can use *by* / *with* + noun after a passive verb when we say what is used to do the action.
> 5 We can use *by* / *with* + noun after a passive verb when we say what/who does the action.

e ▶ Now go to Grammar Focus 9A on p.148

f ▶ **Communication 9A** 💬 You are going to do a quiz about films. Student A: Look at the questions below. Student B: Look at the questions on p.130.

5 SPEAKING

a You are going to recommend a film or TV show that you like. Make notes on the questions.

- What kind of film or show is it?
- What is it called?
- When and where was it made?
- Who directed it?
- Is it based on a book or a true story?
- Who is in it? Any famous actors or celebrities?
- Does it have special effects or CGI?
- What happens? Who are the main characters?

b Write three reasons why you like this film or TV show.

c 💬 Take turns to recommend your film or TV show. Have you watched the films or TV shows you hear about? If so, do you like them too? If not, would you like to watch them? Why / Why not?

> You've got to watch this new Swedish crime show …

> Oh no! I hate detective shows. They're all the same.

> No, this is different. It's got …

HOW MUCH DO YOU KNOW ABOUT FILMS?

Complete the questions with the correct form of the verbs in brackets. Then test your partner!

❶ Only one of these actors _____ an Oscar. Which one is it: Tom Cruise, Tom Hanks or Johnny Depp? (award) (Tom Hanks)

❷ True or False? 60% of the 2009 science-fiction film *Avatar* _____ with computer graphics. The other 40% showed real people. (make) (True: the director, James Cameron, wanted it to be 100%, but he didn't have enough money.)

❸ Which character from a book _____ in more films: Harry Potter or Dracula? (see) (Dracula. The book, written by Bram Stoker in 1897, is one of the most filmed stories in movie history.)

❹ Which actor _____ the most: Brad Pitt, Robert Downey Jr. or Leonardo di Caprio? (pay) (Robert Downey Jr. According to *Forbes* magazine, he made around $75 million from films like *The Avengers* and *Iron Man 3*.)

❺ In the future, most films _____ with computer graphics. We won't need real actors. (make) (No one knows! What do you think?)

1 VOCABULARY Music

a 💬 What's happening in the photos below? Which words can you use to describe them?

---
audience   choir   DJ   play live
festival   musician   orchestra   perform

b ▶️3.24 Listen to four clips of music and underline the correct words.

1   They are playing *live / in a recording studio*.
2   You can hear a *DJ / musician*.
3   Someone is *performing / enjoying* a piece of music.
4   You can hear *a choir / an orchestra*.

c 💬 Discuss the questions. Check that you understand the words in **bold**.

1   When and where did you last listen to a song?
2   What are your favourite **albums**? And your favourite **tracks**?
3   Do you like making **playlists**?
4   When and where did you last sing or play a musical **instrument**?

2 LISTENING

a 💬 How many different musical experiences can you think of? Write a list.

going to concerts, singing in a choir …

b 💬 Compare your lists. Which of these experiences do you like taking part in or going to? Why?

c ▶️3.25 Listen to three people talk about a music experience which changed their life. Match each speaker with photos a–c.

Annie _____   Jeff _____   Erica _____

d ▶️3.25 Listen again and make notes in the table.

	What sort of music do they talk about?	Where was the event?	How did it change his/her life?
Annie			
Jeff			
Erica			

e 💬 Talk about which of the musical experiences you would like to have. Say why.

3 GRAMMAR
Defining and non-defining relative clauses

a Look at the <u>underlined</u> relative clauses. Circle the noun phrase which each relative clause gives more information about.

1 It was my grandmother <u>who started it</u>.
2 It's a drum <u>you play</u> with your hands.
3 I was sitting next to one of the people <u>who was in my group</u>.
4 It's the kind of place <u>where you could sit and chat all night</u>.

b Look at the two sentences below and <u>underline</u> the correct answer in the rule.

1 It's a drum (which/that) you play with your hands.
2 It was my grandmother who/that started it.

> In defining relative clauses, we *need to /
> don't need to* use *who, which* or *that* when the
> noun is the object of the relative clause.

c ▶ 3.26 **Pronunciation** Listen to the sentences. In which sentence do you hear a pause before and after the relative pronoun in **bold**?

1 People **who** sing a lot always seem happy.
2 Carly, **who**'s a fantastic singer, works in a café during the day.

d ▶ Now go to Grammar Focus 9B on p.148

e ◯▶ Take turns to describe the words in the box using a sentence with a defining relative clause. Say which word your partner is describing.

album	audience	choir	concert	DJ	festival
musician	orchestra	playlist	track	guitarist	

It's something which you can download.

An album?

No, it's something that you can find on an album.

A track!

Yes.

4 READING AND VOCABULARY
Word-building (nouns)

a ◯▶ Discuss the questions.

1 Have you ever been to a music festival?
2 If so, what kind of music was there? Did you enjoy it? Why / Why not?
3 If not, do you know of any music festivals you would like to go to? What are they like?

b Read *The three best music festivals you've probably never heard of*. Which festival would you rather go to? Why?

The three best music festivals you've probably never heard of

Fuji Rock Festival, Japan

Enjoy rock and electronic music at the foot of Mount Fuji

This is Japan's largest outdoor music event. It's held every year at the Naeba Ski Resort. You can enjoy the beauty of the forests and rivers as you walk (often quite a long way!) from one stage to another. This is one of the world's safest and most environmentally friendly festivals, which is probably why everyone's happiness levels are so high!

Past performers include: Radiohead, Coldplay, Massive Attack

Roskilde, Denmark

A rock festival that gives all its profits to charity

Here, you can enjoy rock, punk, heavy metal, hip hop, indie and music from around the world. The organisers donate all the money they make to projects for social and cultural development.
Don't forget that summer days are long in Denmark. It doesn't get dark until 11 pm, and it starts getting light at 3.30 am.

Past performers include: Metallica, Bruce Springsteen, Rihanna

c Read the article again and match the comments with the festivals. Write F (Fuji Rock Festival), R (Roskilde) or C (Coachella).

1 ☐ 'Even the toilet paper is made from recycled cups from last year's festival!'
2 ☐ 'I'm glad I took a good pair of walking boots with me.'
3 ☐ 'The nights were so short!'
4 ☐ 'There was a huge wooden butterfly.'
5 ☐ 'It's really good to know that all the money goes to good causes.'
6 ☐ 'The second weekend was great.'

d Complete the table with words from the article.

adjective	noun	verb
artistic	¹_____ (person)	
beautiful	²_____	
	³_____	celebrate
charitable	⁴_____	
creative	⁵_____	create
cultural	⁶_____	
	⁷_____	develop
happy	⁸_____	
musical	⁹_____ (person)	
organised	¹⁰_____ (person)	organise
	¹¹_____ (person) ¹²_____	perform

e ▶3.28 **Pronunciation** Listen to the words in 4d. Notice how the stress sometimes changes position as we change the form of the word. Mark the stress on each word.

f ▶3.28 Listen again and practise saying the words.

g Write the noun forms of the words. Use one suffix from the box for each pair of words and make spelling changes if necessary.

-ance/-ence -(a)tion -er/-or
-ity -ist -ness -ty

1 loyal, honest: loyalty _____
2 fit, sad: _____ _____
3 able, responsible: _____ _____
4 design, write: _____ _____
5 intelligent, patient: _____ _____
6 piano, guitar: _____ _____
7 locate, relax: _____ _____

h 💬 Talk about which of the qualities in the box are important for the people 1–4. Which qualities are not needed? Say why.

beauty creativity honesty intelligence
kindness musical ability responsibility

1 a pop singer
2 a friend
3 a teacher
4 a politician

5 SPEAKING

a You are going to talk about an interesting or exciting experience in your life which involved music. Make notes on the questions below.

1 What happened?
2 When was it?
3 Who was with you?
4 Why was it important?
5 Why have you remembered it?

b 💬 Take turns to talk about your experiences and ask follow-up questions.

> I went to see a band I've been a fan of for years …

Coachella, California, USA

Music and sculpture in the Californian desert

This annual music and arts festival, which takes place over two long weekends, is a celebration of creativity and culture. Live performances of rock, indie, hip hop and electronic music take place continuously.

As you walk around the grounds, you can also enjoy sculptures and other modern art installations by artists from around the world.

Past performers include: Red Hot Chili Peppers, Florence and the Machine, Kanye West

Learn to recommend and respond to recommendations
P Showing contrast
S Asking someone to wait

1 LISTENING

a 💬 Discuss the questions.

1 How often do you have an evening out with friends? What do you usually do?
2 How easy is it to organise an evening out with your friends? Do you all have the same interests? Do you ever disagree on what you want to do?
3 Which of the activities in the box do you enjoy?

> a meal in a restaurant   a horror film
> a meal at a friend's house   a pop concert
> a play at the theatre

b ▶ 3.29 Watch or listen to Part 1. Which activities are mentioned? What do they decide to do in the end?

c ▶ 3.29 Watch or listen to Part 1 again. Who …

1 suggests going to a jazz club? *Becky / Mark*
2 suggests going to a classical music festival? *Becky / Rachel*
3 doesn't like classical music? *Becky / Tom*
4 suggests a local rock band? *Tom / Rachel*
5 hasn't seen a rock band for 10 years? *Rachel / Mark*

2 USEFUL LANGUAGE
Recommending and responding

a ▶ 3.29 Listen to Part 1 again and tick (✓) the phrases you hear.

1 ☐ That's a great idea!
2 ☐ It's meant to be excellent.
3 ☐ It was highly recommended by …
4 ☐ It's supposed to be really good.
5 ☐ I'm not a big fan of classical music.
6 ☐ Why don't we go and see that local band?
7 ☐ They've had great reviews.
8 ☐ I think you'd love it.
9 ☐ I doubt Mark would be interested.
10 ☐ It sounds really interesting, but …

b Which phrases in 2a … ?

1 give a recommendation or opinion
2 respond to a recommendation

c 💬 Work in groups of three. Use the diagram below to have a conversation.

A   B   C

Suggest going to see a new horror film at the cinema. Say why you recommend it.

Agree.

Say that you don't like horror films.

Suggest going to the theatre instead. Say why you recommend it.

Say that you don't really like the theatre.

You don't really like the idea either.

Suggest going to a new restaurant. Say why you recommend it.

Agree.

Agree.

3 PRONUNCIATION Showing contrast

a ▶3.30 Listen to the following sentence. Which word is stressed?

Tom likes classical music.

b ▶3.31 Listen to these conversations. Decide which word is stressed more in each sentence.

1 **A** You like classical music, don't you?
  B No. Tom likes classical music. I like rock music.
    (= It's Tom who likes classical music, not me.)
2 **A** Does Tom like pop music?
  B No, Tom likes classical music.
    (= It's classical music that Tom likes, not pop.)

> When we want to show a contrast (emphasise that something is different), we stress that word more.

c 💬 Work in pairs. Take it in turns to ask the questions and reply, showing contrast by stressing a word.

1 Did you buy the red shoes? (blue)
2 Did you go to the cinema with John? (theatre)
3 Did you see John? (Chris)

4 CONVERSATION SKILLS
Asking someone to wait

a ▶3.32 Listen to part of the conversation between Rachel and Becky. Complete the sentences.

1 **Rachel** Wait a _____, I'll just ask Mark.
2 **Becky** _____ on, Tom wants to say something.

b Complete the table with the words in the box.

check   hang   please   second   wait

¹ _____ on Just ² _____	a minute / a ³ _____ / a moment.
One moment, ⁴ _____ .	
Let me ⁵ _____ (for you).	

c Which expression is more formal?

d 💬 Work in pairs. Follow the instructions and have a conversation.

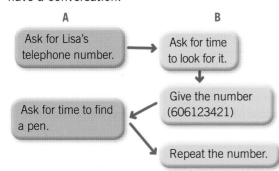

A	B
Ask for Lisa's telephone number. →	Ask for time to look for it.
Ask for time to find a pen. ←	Give the number (606123421)
	Repeat the number.

5 LISTENING

a 💬 Tom told Mark to wear something cool. Look at the clothes below.

Which do you think is the coolest? Which do you think Mark will wear?

b ▶3.33 Watch or listen to Part 2 and check your ideas. What do the others think of Mark's clothes?

c 💬 Discuss the questions.

1 Do you usually spend a lot of time choosing what to wear when you go out? Why / Why not?
2 What kind of clothes do people in your area wear when they go out for the evening (e.g. to a restaurant, to the cinema, to the theatre)?

6 SPEAKING

▶ **Communication 9C** 💬 You're going to have a conversation about what to do today.
Student A: Read the information below. Student B: Go to p.130.

> **Student A**
> • You would like to go to an exhibition of modern art.
> • You've just eaten, so you don't want to go out for a meal.
> • Someone gave you an advert for a photography exhibition. You have the advert in your bag.

> We could go to the modern art exhibition. It's meant to be really interesting.

> That sounds OK, but I'm not a big fan of modern art.

○ Unit Progress Test

CHECK YOUR PROGRESS

You can now do the Unit Progress Test.

1 SPEAKING AND LISTENING

a 💬 Look at photos a–e. If you could win free tickets to go to one of the events, which would you choose? Why?

b ▶3.34 Listen to Anna and her friend, Camila. Answer the questions.

1 Who has tickets to the Kanye West concert?
2 Who doesn't want to go?
3 Why doesn't she want to go?

c Make notes on the positive and negative points of these things:

• live performances (plays, concerts, etc.)
• recorded performances (albums, films, etc.)

d 💬 Do you agree with Camila, or do you like going to live concerts?

2 READING

a Read Julia's blog, *Why I prefer to stay at home*. What is her main point?

1 Films are too expensive and it's cheaper to stay at home.
2 It's more comfortable and convenient to watch films and TV series at home.
3 Films are less satisfying than TV programmes.

b Read the blog again and answer the questions.

1 What annoys Julia about cinema audiences?
2 Why were the couple sitting behind her rude?
3 What does she do if she finds a film boring?
4 Why is the length of a TV series sometimes a good thing?

Why I prefer to stay at home

① What was your last cinema experience like? I remember the expensive tickets, the long queues and the uncomfortable seats. Does this sound familiar? I love going out to see my friends, going to parties or clubs. I like having fun. However, I don't really enjoy going to the cinema any more.

② The other problem for me is the audience at cinemas. Although many people say that seeing a film at a cinema is a good chance to go out and be sociable, I really hate listening to other people's comments. The last time I went to the cinema, there was a couple who commented loudly on everything in the film. They laughed at everything in the film, really loudly – even at things which weren't funny! I politely asked them to be quiet. Despite this, they continued as if they were watching their own TV. If I watch something at home, I can invite my friends and spend time with people I know and like rather than sitting near noisy strangers.

③ Another reason for staying at home is convenience. I like to watch films or TV shows when I want to watch them, not at specific times. In spite of my love of films and TV shows, I don't enjoy all of them. If I'm at home, I can stop the film and watch something else or I can fast-forward through the boring bits. For example, I was really disappointed with a film I saw last night – so I just switched it off!

④ While I watch a lot of films, I also watch a lot of TV shows online now. I really enjoy watching a whole series. It gives characters time to develop in interesting and unexpected ways. In fact, there are so many great TV shows to watch, I've hardly got time to go to the cinema.

⑤ So these days, when my friends invite me to the cinema, I usually say, 'No thanks'. I really do prefer to watch films and TV series at home. I can choose what I want to watch, I can choose the time when I want to watch it and I can choose who I watch it with. The question really is: why should I go out?

3 WRITING SKILLS Contrasting ideas; the structure of an article

a In the example below, *however* introduces a contrast. Find more examples of words used to contrast ideas in the blog in 2a.

I like having fun. **However**, I don't really enjoy going to the cinema any more.

b Complete the rules and examples with the words in the box. Use each word twice.

| although   despite   however   in spite of   while |

- *I enjoy films.* [1]_____, *I think I prefer TV series.*
  We can use [2]_____ at the beginning of a sentence. It contrasts with an idea in the previous sentence.
- [3]_____ / [4]_____ *cinemas have become more comfortable, they're not as comfortable as my sofa.*
  We can use [5]_____ and [6]_____ at the beginning of a sentence to introduce a contrasting idea. They are followed by a clause with a verb.
- *The price of cinema tickets has gone up recently.*
  [7]_____ / [8]_____ *the cost, I still love the movies.*
  We can use [9]_____ and [10]_____ at the beginning of the sentence to introduce a contrasting idea. They are followed by a noun or pronoun.

c Match ideas 1–6 with a contrasting idea a–f. Join the ideas using the words in brackets. Write only one sentence, if possible.

1 ☐ I was given two free tickets to a jazz concert (However)
2 ☐ music is something we normally listen to (Although)
3 ☐ TV screens have got bigger and bigger (Although)
4 ☐ the beat is very important in hip-hop music (While)
5 ☐ the convenience of watching a film at home (In spite of)
6 ☐ my love of special effects (Despite)

a singers still have to know how to sing a tune.
b I don't like that kind of music, so I'll give them away.
c there's nothing like the big screen at the cinema.
d I still want films to have a good story and good acting.
e it's always interesting to watch musicians perform.
f I prefer to see films at a cinema.

d Look at paragraphs 2–4 in the blog on p.112. What is the main idea of each paragraph? Choose a or b.

Paragraph 2:
a cinema audiences   b being polite in cinemas
Paragraph 3:
a boring films   b the convenience of staying at home
Paragraph 4:
a the length of TV series   b an alternative to watching films

e 💬 Discuss the questions.

1 Is the main idea mentioned at the beginning or in the middle of the paragraph?
2 Does the writer sometimes use examples?
3 How does the writer get the reader's attention in paragraph 1, the introduction?
4 In paragraph 5, the conclusion, does the writer introduce new ideas? Why / Why not?

4 WRITING An article

a You are going to write an article about a kind of entertainment you love or hate. Choose one of the topics below or your own idea. Then make notes about questions 1–4.

- music concerts in stadiums or in small clubs
- watching sport in a stadium or live on TV
- classical music or pop music

1 What's your opinion on this topic?
2 What experience do you have of it?
3 What other things do you know about it?
4 What do other people often say about it?

b 💬 Compare your ideas with a partner.

c Plan your article. Follow these instructions:

1 Write down the main ideas of the article.
2 Write down different points for each idea.
3 Think of any examples from your experience.

d Write your article. Make sure you write an introduction and conclusion. Remember to use words or phrases to show contrast.

UNIT 9
Review and extension

1 GRAMMAR

a Read the text and underline the correct words.

Can you imagine a film [1]*who / which* had no music? It would be very boring. Here are two talented film composers [2]*what / that* everyone should know about.

John Williams [3]*sees / is seen* as one of the greatest film composers of all time. He [4]*has nominated / has been nominated* for more awards than anyone else, apart from Walt Disney. Williams, [5]*whose / who* music can be heard in the Harry Potter and *Star Wars* films, is most famous for working with director Steven Spielberg on many of his films.

The music for *Titanic*, *The Amazing Spider-Man* and more than 100 other films was written [6]*with / by* pianist and composer James Horner. In his compositions, Horner often uses Celtic music, [7]*which / that* is traditional music from Western Europe.

b Complete the second sentence so that it means the same as the first sentence (or pair of sentences). Use three words in each gap.

1 The film was based on a book. I loved it when I was a child.
The film was based on a _____ when I was a child.

2 That's the place. The final scene was filmed there.
That's the place _____ scene was filmed.

3 *Catching Fire* is the second film in the *Hunger Games* series. *Catching Fire* came out in 2013.
Catching Fire, _____ in 2013, is the second film in the *Hunger Games* series.

4 People are forgetting many traditional folk songs
Many traditional folk songs _____ .

5 They were recording the concert when I was there.
The concert _____ when I was there.

2 VOCABULARY

a Read the text and underline the correct words.

The epic historical film, *Les Misérables*, is based [1]*on / at* the book in which the different [2]*characters / performers* fight for social change in 19th-century France. [3]*Character / Director* Tom Hooper successfully combines big dramatic [4]*frames / scenes* with quieter moments. What makes the film so powerful is that the songs weren't recorded in a [5]*scene / studio*: all the actors sang [6]*live / tune* as they were filmed. Music played by [7]*an orchestra / a performance* was added after filming had finished.

b Complete the sentences with noun forms of the words in brackets.
1 The festival is a _____ of music from different cultures. (celebrate)
2 We'd like to thank the _____ for all their hard work in preparing the show. (organise)
3 This film shows the _____ of the Pacific Islands. (beautiful)
4 The _____ are preparing for their _____ this evening. (music; perform)

3 WORDPOWER *see, look at, watch, hear, listen to*

a Match questions 1–8 with responses a–h.
1 ☐ Amy! Amy! Why isn't she answering?
2 ☐ What's that noise?
3 ☐ Have you found another painting?
4 ☐ Are they dancing?
5 ☐ What's that light in the sky?
6 ☐ Do you **see** what I mean?
7 ☐ Are you going to **see** the doctor?
8 ☐ Have you **seen** *Iron Man 3*?

a Yes, I've got an appointment tomorrow.
b I can't **see** anything.
c No, I don't understand.
d Yes, I **watched** it with Brendan.
e I can't **hear** anything.
f She's **listening to** music.
g Yes, come and **look at** it! It's amazing!
h Yes, come and **watch**.

b Add the words in **bold** in 3a to the table.

1 _____	pay attention to something because of its appearance (e.g. a photo, a flower)
2 _____	pay attention to something because of the movement (e.g. a film)
3 _____	be able to recognise sights
	go and watch something that's moving
	understand
	visit
4 _____	be able to recognise sounds
5 _____	pay attention to sounds

c Underline the correct words. Then discuss the questions.
1 How often do you *watch / look at* old photos of yourself?
2 When did you last *see / watch* the dentist?
3 What music do you *listen to / hear* when you're in a bad mood?
4 *Watch / Look* out of the window. What can you *see / look at*?
5 *Listen / Hear*. What can you *listen / hear*?
6 If you *listened to / heard* a strange noise in the night, would you go and *watch / see* what it was?
7 What is the worst film you've ever *seen / looked at*?

↻ **CAN DO OBJECTIVES**

- Talk about new things you would like to do
- Talk about imagined past events
- Talk about possible problems and reassure someone
- Write an email with advice

UNIT 10
Opportunities

GETTING STARTED

a 💬 What do you think is happening in the photo?

b 💬 What do you think happens next? Think of three ideas.

c 💬 Ask and answer the questions.

1 What opportunities can studying at university give you?
2 What opportunities have you had in your life? For example, think about education, travel, meeting people, work.
3 Have you ever taken the opportunity to do something very scary or difficult (for example, sky-diving, talking in public or doing a performance)? If not, would you like to have one of those opportunities?

10A If I was fitter, I'd do it!

1 SPEAKING

a 🗨 Look at photos a–c.

1 What is happening (or going to happen) in each photo?
2 How are the people in each photo feeling?

b Add more sports to the lists.

- winter sports: *skiing, …*
- ball sports: *tennis, …*
- water sports: *surfing, …*

c 🗨 Discuss the questions.

1 Which of the sports on your lists in 1b have you tried?
2 Which do you think are the most …?
   - fun
   - dangerous
   - exciting
   - difficult
3 Would you like to try any new sports? Which would you like to try?

2 VOCABULARY Sport

a 🗨 Check that you understand the words in **bold**. Match the sports in the pictures below with sentences 1–5. There is more than one possible answer.

1 It's an **extreme** sport.
2 It's a really good **workout**.
3 You win **points** when your partner **misses** the ball.
4 If you like surfing, you should **have a go** at this.
5 The **training** is very difficult.

b ▶ Now go to Vocabulary Focus 10A on p.161

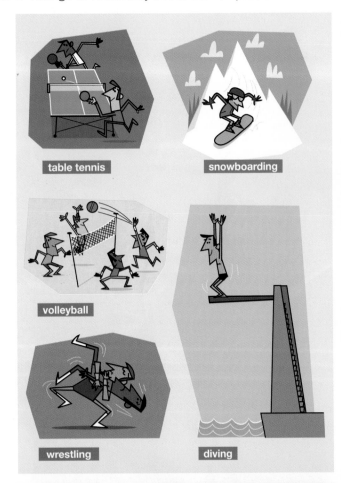

table tennis

snowboarding

volleyball

wrestling

diving

a | ski jumping

b | tennis

c | surfing

3 LISTENING

a 💬 Look at the photos below and discuss the questions.

1 Have you tried these sports, or seen them in action?
2 What do you think looks most fun about them?

b ▶3.36 Listen to Gina and Libby talking about scuba diving and the Colour Run and answer the questions.

1 Why do they like each sport?
2 What do they agree to do at the end?

c 💬 ▶3.36 Listen again and discuss the questions.

1 Where did Gina try scuba diving?
2 How much training did she do?
3 Why was she scared at first?
4 How long is the run that Libby's going to do?
5 Why is it different from normal runs?

d Which of the two sports sounds more exciting/dangerous? Which would you rather try? Why?

e 💬 Write down all the reasons why you like your favourite sport. Work with someone who likes a different sport and tell them why you like yours.

> Of course, football is the greatest game in the world. People in every country love it and …

4 GRAMMAR Second conditional

a Look at these second conditional sentences and answer the questions.

- Was it scary? I think if I went, I'd be terrified!
- If I was a bit fitter, I would definitely do it.

1 When do we use the second conditional? Choose a or b.
   a to talk about things we will probably do in the future
   b to talk about things we imagine, but are not real
2 What verb form do we use after *if*?

b ▶3.37 **Pronunciation** Listen to the pronunciation of *would* in each of the sentences. Is it strong (stressed) or weak (not stressed)? Write S (strong) or W (weak).

1 If you went, you would absolutely love it.
2 I wouldn't do a full marathon – I'm not fit enough.
3 It would be great if there was a big group of us going.
4 Would you like to try?
5 Yes, I would, but …
6 If I was a bit fitter, I would definitely do it.

c ▶3.37 Listen again and repeat the sentences.

d ▶ Now go to Grammar Focus 10A on p.150

e Tick (✓) the sentences that are true for you. Then write second conditional sentences saying what you would or might do if things were different.

☐ I can't run long distances.
☐ I'm not very tall.
☐ I don't live in a country that gets lots of snow.
☐ I can't afford a personal fitness trainer.
☐ I'm scared of heights.
☐ I'm not very fit.
☐ I'm not an Olympic champion.

If I could run long distances, I'd enter a big marathon and raise money for charity.

f 💬 Compare your sentences in 4e.

5 VOCABULARY
Adjectives and prepositions

a Some adjectives are followed by a preposition. Complete each sentence with a preposition.

1 I was a bit worried _____ it before we went into the water for the first time.
2 It sounds perfect _____ me!
3 And it's popular _____ all kinds of people.

b ▶3.39 Listen and check your answers.

c Underline the correct prepositions.

1 I don't like extreme sports – I'm afraid *about / of* hurting myself.
2 I'm not scared *of / to* spiders.
3 I am very proud *of / about* my little sister.
4 I think that having lots of friends is essential *in / for* a happy, healthy life.
5 I'm very interested *in / about* health and fitness.
6 I'm worried *of / about* my football team's performance at the moment.
7 I'll never get tired *in / of* visiting new places.
8 I've found a sport which is right *for / in* me.
9 American football is similar *to / from* rugby.

d Tick (✓) the sentences in 5c that are true for you. Change the others so that they are true for you.

e In adverts a–c below, eight prepositions are missing. Add them in the correct places.

6 SPEAKING

a Make notes about what you would do if you had one of the opportunities below.

> **learn a new skill or sport**
> • What would you learn? Why?

> **a free holiday to anywhere in the world with a friend**
> • Where would you go? Why?
> • Who would you take?

> **meet a famous person**
> • Who would you choose?
> • What would you say or ask?

> **travel in time**
> • What year would you travel to? Why?
> • What would you do when you were there?

b 💬 Compare your ideas. Would you like to do the things your partner would like to do?

ⓐ
DANCE YOURSELF FIT

Are you worried getting unfit, but afraid joining a gym? Fitness is essential good health and happiness – but what can you do if you don't like sport? That's simple – get dancing!

We're very proud our team of qualified dance instructors.

ⓑ
BECOME A GUIDE RUNNER

If you want to keep fit and you're interested helping people too, why not become a guide runner? Running is popular blind people, but many of them need a guide runner for support. Just let us know your level of fitness and where you live. You'll even get automatic entry into any races!

ⓒ
Body Training Adventure Programme

Are you tired the usual exercise classes? Do you need something more exciting and challenging?

Join our intensive fitness training programme for all ages and abilities. It's similar an Army-style Boot Camp but with an added emphasis on fun and team-work.

Activities include rock-climbing, mountain biking and boxing.

10B Making the most of opportunities

1 SPEAKING

a Think of a time when something good happened to you (e.g. you met a friend for the first time, you got a new job, you found a new hobby, etc.). Make notes about the questions.

1 What happened?
2 Why would you describe it as a good experience?
3 Why do you think it happened? Were you lucky, or did you do something to make it happen?

b 💬 Tell each other your stories.

2 READING

a 💬 Look at the photos, which show details of three true stories about good luck. Can you guess what the three stories might be about?

b 💬 Compare your ideas with other students. Are your ideas the same or different?

c Read *Searching for serendipity* quickly. Were your ideas correct in 2a?

Searching for serendipity

HOME   NEWS   YOUR STORIES   LOGIN

Are you making the most of life's opportunities?

ANNA

I had my own business, but needed a website. My friend Wendy gave me the email address of a designer called Mark. Unfortunately, Wendy's handwriting is awful, so I sent the email to the wrong person. Someone called Matt replied. Obviously, there had been a mistake. He said he wasn't actually a designer – he was a primary school teacher – but he could help me if I wanted!

Matt seemed nice. And anyway, I didn't have anyone else to help me, so I decided to write back to him. In the end, Matt worked on my website for free. He did a great job and my business started to go really well. Meanwhile, we got to know each other via email. And ten months later, we met. We fell in love immediately, and a year later, we got married. If Wendy had had better handwriting, my business wouldn't have been such a success, and I certainly wouldn't have met Matt!

Two years ago, Anna Frances had some very good luck when her colleague gave her some wrong information.

So was Anna just lucky? Or did she make her own luck? Why do these lucky accidents seem to happen to some people and not to others? And is there any way to make yourself more lucky? Well, it seems that the secret of happiness is to make the most of the opportunities that life gives us. We need to be open to serendipity – the random events that lead to happy, sometimes life-changing, results.

Dr Stephann Makri is working on a project about serendipity at University College, London. He thinks that serendipity is more than an accident and that we can all have more 'luck' if we learn to pay attention to life's opportunities. He has noticed that many people's good-luck stories share the same basic pattern. First, people notice that there is an opportunity. Then, they take action to make the most of it. For example, if you imagine meeting an old friend in the street who will later introduce you to the love of your life, several things have to happen. First, you have to notice the friend. Then you have to stop and talk to them, even though you might be busy. Finally, you need to be ready to follow up on whatever comes out of the conversation. So, it might be luck that leads you to walk past the friend on the street – but the rest is up to you!

More serendipity stories...

TOM

After university, I didn't have a job. I subscribed to a job website and got lots of emails from them every day. I usually deleted them. One day, I was feeling particularly annoyed by all the emails, so I opened one of them to click on the 'unsubscribe' link. But I spotted an interesting job. It was in the USA and I didn't really have the experience they wanted, but I decided to try. I didn't get the job, but they emailed me two weeks later to say they had another job I could apply for. I got it, and I ended up working in New York City, where I met my girlfriend Paula. None of it would have happened if I had deleted the email.

CARLA

My mum Betty is 71. There's a café in town that I like and I persuaded my mum to come with me, just to get out of the house. She didn't want to come at first, but when we got there she really liked the café. While we were there, she started chatting to some bikers. My mum said she had always wanted to ride a motorbike! I was shocked! Kenny, one of the bikers, offered to take us both out with the rest of the group. To my amazement, my mother said 'yes'! I was really worried, but actually, my mum loved the experience!

---

d Complete the sentences with the names in the box.

Anna   Betty   Carla   Kenny   Matt   Tom

1 _____ failed at first, but was right to take a chance.
2 _____ did an activity she'd always wanted to do.
3 _____ was surprised by someone else's behaviour.
4 _____ did some work for someone, even though it wasn't his job.
5 _____ made contact with the wrong person.
6 _____ did something kind for someone the first time he met her.

e Discuss the questions.

1 Which person do you think was the 'luckiest'?
2 Do you agree that people make their own luck? Why / Why not?
3 Do you think that you are a lucky person? Do you make the most of life's opportunities in a similar way to the people in the stories?

3 VOCABULARY
Expressions with *do*, *make* and *take*

a Underline the correct answers to complete the summary of Dr Makri's ideas.

> Can we [1]*take / make / do* our own luck? Dr Makri has been [2]*doing / making / taking* research into serendipity and he believes we can. The secret lies in [3]*doing / taking / making* advantage of opportunity when it comes our way. If you see an opportunity in a chance event, you should [4]*take / make / do* action and [5]*take / have / make* the most of that opportunity.
>
> Everyone can be 'luckier'. If you get out and meet people you'll have more chance encounters. Be brave and [6]*take / make / do* risks in order to act freely when an opportunity comes your way.

b ▶ Now go to Vocabulary Focus 10B on p.161

4 GRAMMAR Third conditional

a Underline the correct words. Then check your answers in the article on p.120.

If Wendy [1]*had / had had / would have had* better handwriting, my business [2]*wasn't / hadn't been / wouldn't have been* such a success, and I certainly [3]*didn't meet / hadn't met / wouldn't have met* Matt.

b Answer the questions.

1 Did Wendy have good handwriting? Was Anna's business successful? Did she meet Matt?
2 When do we use the third conditional? Choose a or b.
   a to talk about real results of real past events
   b to imagine an alternative to a past event and imagine an alternative result
3 What verb form do we use after *if*? What form of the verb do we use in the other part of the sentence?

c ▶3.40 Listen and match speakers 1–4 with pictures a–d below.

Speaker 1 ☐   Speaker 3 ☐
Speaker 2 ☐   Speaker 4 ☐

d ▶3.41 **Pronunciation** Listen to the sentences below. Which words are stressed in each sentence?

1 I would have won easily if I hadn't hurt my arm.
2 I wouldn't have bought it if I'd known it was in such bad condition.
3 If you hadn't pushed me, that car would have hit me!
4 I wouldn't have discovered the truth if I hadn't read her letters.

e ▶3.41 Listen again and practise saying the sentences.

f ▶ Now go to Grammar Focus 10B on p.150

g Write third conditional sentences about the people in the box from the article on p.120.

| Anna | Wendy | Matt | Tom | Betty | Carla | Kenny |

If Anna's friend had given her the correct email address, she might have fallen in love with a different person instead of Matt.

h 💬 Compare your sentences.

5 SPEAKING

a You're going to tell the story of a past event that made your life better. Make notes about one of these topics:

- a good friend, and how you met him or her
- a sport or hobby, and how you started doing it
- an accident, and how it happened
- a job, and how you got it
- a school, and why you went there
- a big decision, and how you made it

Think about the important events in your story. What were the consequences of what happened? How would your life have been different if you had done something differently?

b 💬 Take turns to tell your stories. Ask each other questions to find out more about what might have happened if things had been different.

> What would have been different if you hadn't gone to that school?

> I wouldn't have met my best friend, Gabriela.

1 LISTENING

a 💬 Discuss the questions.

1 When was the last time you were very nervous?
2 What situations make you nervous (e.g. public speaking, flying, starting a new job)? What do you do to calm down?

b ▶3.43 Watch or listen to Part 1. What do you think Tom and Mark are talking about?

c ▶3.44 Watch or listen to Part 2 to check.

2 USEFUL LANGUAGE
Talking about possible problems and reassuring someone

a ▶3.44 Watch or listen to Part 2 again and complete the sentences.

1 You've got _____ to worry about.
2 I'm _____ it'll be OK.
3 You don't _____ it's a bit boring?
4 I'm still _____ that something will go wrong.
5 What _____ she says no?
6 She's _____ not going to say no.

b Add the sentences in 2a to the table.

Talking about a problem	Reassuring someone
	You've got nothing to worry about.

c 💬 Think of (real or invented) worries you might have about these situations. Talk to your partner. Reassure them about their worries.

- do badly in an exam
- public speaking
- a stressful day at work
- a difficult journey

> I'm worried that I will forget what to say.   You'll be fine!

3 PRONUNCIATION
Sounding sure and unsure

a ▶3.45 Listen to this extract from the conversation. Does Tom sound sure or unsure?

Mark So, where are you taking her?
Tom I've booked a table at *Bella Vita*. It's the place where we went on our first date.

b ▶3.44 Now listen to Part 2 again. Does Tom sound sure or unsure all the way through?

c ▶3.46 Listen to the following sentences. Do you think the speaker is sure or unsure?

1 **A** Do you think Rachel wants to go to a restaurant?
  B I think so, yes.
2 **A** Does Rachel like pizza?
  B I think so, yes.
3 **A** When did you meet her?
  B About two years ago.
4 **A** Where did you go on your first date?
  B We went to *Bella Vita*.

4 LISTENING

a  Tom and Becky are in the restaurant. What might happen? Talk about the ideas below. Which one do you think is most likely? Why?

1 Tom is too nervous and doesn't ask Becky to marry him.
2 Becky asks Tom to marry her before he can ask her.
3 Becky is very surprised and says yes.

b ▶3.47 Watch or listen to Part 3 and check.

c Are the statements true (T) or false (F)?

1 Becky and Tom both think that they went to this restaurant for their first date.
2 Tom tried to phone Becky earlier.
3 Becky wants to talk to Tom about their plans for the weekend.
4 Becky was expecting Tom to ask her to marry him.
5 Becky says she will marry Tom.

5 CONVERSATION SKILLS
Changing the subject

a ▶3.48 Listen and complete the sentences.

1 **Becky** That _____ me, I need to book the restaurant for the office party.
2 **Tom** So, anyway, as I was _____, you've really changed my life.

b Look again at the sentences in 5a. Who is starting a completely new subject, and who is returning to a previous subject?

c Look at the phrases in **bold**. Are they ways to change the subject or return to a previous subject?

1 **Speaking of** cafés, have I told you about the place we found last week?
2 **By the way,** did you see that new comedy programme last night?

d  Work in pairs.

Student A: You want to talk about your weekend. Talk to Student B. Can you keep the conversation on the same subject?

Student B: You don't want to hear about Student A's weekend. Try to change the subject and talk about other things (e.g. a film you've seen recently, someone you saw today, etc.).

> I went to see a film this weekend.

> Oh, speaking of films, did you see that *The Hobbit* is on TV tonight?

6 SPEAKING

▶ Communication 10C  Student A: Read the information below. Student B: Go to p.130.

Student A
You want to talk to Student B about a trip abroad you are going to take (where are you going?).
You are worried because:
- you are scared of flying (what might happen?)
- you are nervous about communicating in a different language (what problems might this cause?)
- you are not very good at trying new food (what food might you have to try?).

Have the conversation. Reassure Student B when he/she tries to talk about a big presentation he/she has to give, but try to bring the conversation back to your trip.

> Anyway, as I was saying, I'm really nervous about what might happen.

○ Unit Progress Test

CHECK YOUR PROGRESS

You can now do the Unit Progress Test.

1 SPEAKING AND READING

a 💬 Read the advert on the right for an organisation called *NowVolunteer* and discuss the questions.

1 What kind of organisation do you think *NowVolunteer* is? What kinds of programmes do you think they offer, and where?

2 What kinds of people do you think do a *NowVolunteer* programme, and why?

3 Do you think volunteers have to pay money to work on a programme?

b Read the web page below quickly and check.

NowVolunteer

Join one of our programmes.
See the world, help other people,
develop new skills.

NowVolunteer

| HOME | PROJECTS | JOIN US |

Volunteering. Adventure. Experience.

Do you want to have the adventure of a lifetime and make new friends from around the world? *NowVolunteer* is a volunteering organisation that gives you everything you need for your gap year between university and settling into a job.

Companies want to know about your experience, not just about your qualifications. So join us to improve your CV.

See our Volunteer profiles to see what people say about their experience.

Unique, award-winning programmes

We organise specialist programmes in 50 countries. You can work with children, help local communities, work on environmental projects, learn a new skill … and at the same time have a great travel experience.

We arrange everything for you

Just choose a programme and we'll take care of the details. All you need to do is raise up to $500 for our programmes before you go. We'll provide free accommodation while you're volunteering.

2 LISTENING AND SPEAKING

a You're going to hear Greg talking about his experience of working with *NowVolunteer*. Look at the photos below. What do you think he might say about his trip?

Greg from Auckland, New Zealand worked on a community health project in Madagascar.

b ▶3.49 Listen to Greg. Does he mention any of your ideas from 2a?

c ▶3.49 Listen again and make notes in the table.

1 What he studied	
2 Reason for going	
3 How he raised money	
4 What he did	
5 What happened next	

d 💬 Discuss the questions.

1 Would you like to do the same programme as Greg? Why / Why not?

2 Do you know anyone who has done volunteer work like this? If so, what was their experience of it?

3 Have you ever worked for no money? If so, did you enjoy it?

3 READING

a Vicky is in her last year at university, studying marketing. She emailed her friends asking for advice. Read her email, and answer the questions.

1 What two programmes is Vicky interested in?
2 What might be a problem for her?

Hi everyone!

I've been thinking about what to do next year, and I thought I'd take a year out and do some voluntary work. It could be my only chance and it would look good on my CV!

There's a site called *NowVolunteer* and they've got some amazing things you can do, like looking after elephants in Thailand or teaching English in China. The only problem is you have to raise about $500 for them first, but then they give you training and they pay for your accommodation.

What do you all think? Am I on to a brilliant idea here or should I just forget it and start looking round for jobs?

Replies please ;-)

Vicky

b 💬 Work in pairs. Student A: Go to p.127 and read Amanda's reply. Student B: Go to p.131 and read Laura's reply. Do they think Vicky should do voluntary work? What reasons do they give?

c 💬 Tell your partner about the reply that you read. Who do you agree with?

4 WRITING SKILLS
Advising a course of action

a Who uses these expressions in their replies to Vicky's email? Write A (Amanda) or L (Laura).

1 ☐ I think you should …
2 ☐ I expect you'd have a good time, but …
3 ☐ I'm pretty sure you'd …
4 ☐ I'm just suggesting that …
5 ☐ It would definitely …
6 ☐ If I were you, I'd …
7 ☐ Maybe it would be better to …

b Answer the questions.

1 Which expressions in 4a … ?
  • only give advice
  • also imagine what would (or wouldn't) happen
2 Compare Amanda's and Laura's emails. Who uses more 'careful' language? Why?
  a because she's advising a friend to do something they want to do
  b because she's advising a friend not to do something they want to do
3 Which of these does Laura use?
  a adverbs to express uncertainty (*maybe, perhaps*)
  b modal verbs to express obligation (*should, must*)
  c modal verbs to express uncertainty (*might, could, would*)
  d expressions of certainty (*I'm sure, definitely*)
  e expressions of uncertainty (*I expect, I'm not sure*)

c Rewrite these sentences using the words in brackets and make any other changes necessary.

1 Write to them and ask where they spend the money. (If I)
2 Look for a job with a marketing company in Thailand. (better)
3 It wouldn't be very interesting. (not sure)
4 You'd meet a lot of interesting people. (expect)
5 Look at other alternatives. (suggesting)

5 WRITING An email with advice

a Think of an alternative to your present lifestyle or job – something you'd like to do for a year. Write an email asking other students if they think it's a good idea.

b Work in pairs. Read your partner's email and write a reply. It can be positive and enthusiastic (like Amanda's) or more careful (like Laura's).

c 💬 Read your partner's reply to your email. Do you think it's good advice? Why / Why not? Does the advice use appropriate expressions?

UNIT 10
Review and extension

1 GRAMMAR

Underline the correct words.

1 **A** We lost so badly.
   B I know. We'd *scored / have scored* a lot more points if we *did / 'd done* more training over the last few weeks.
2 **A** Are you going to accept the offer?
   B I can't decide. What *would / did* you do if you *were / had been* me?
3 **A** If I *didn't miss / hadn't missed* the train, I'd never *met / have met* my wife, Jasmine.
   B That's so romantic!
4 **A** Hey! Was that a golf ball? Where did it come from?
   B I don't know, but you were very lucky. It *could have / could* hit you!
5 **A** James gets so disappointed when he doesn't win.
   B If he *wasn't / couldn't be* such a competitive person, he wouldn't play as well as he does.
6 **A** Why didn't you call me?
   B Well, I *would / wouldn't* have done if my phone *had / hadn't* been broken.

2 VOCABULARY

a Complete the sentences with the words in the box.

beat	lose	net	pass	point	track	workout

1 It's a fun game and a great _____ too.
2 He'll win the match if he scores one more _____!
3 We mustn't _____ this game! We have to win!
4 You must hit the ball over the _____.
5 You won last time, but this time I'm going to _____ you!
6 How many times did you run round the _____?
7 Helen was running behind me, but she didn't _____ me at any point.

b Complete the questions with the correct form of *make*, *do* or *take*.

1 What hobbies do you _____?
2 Do you know anyone who _____ a lot of risks?
3 How often do you _____ a break when you're studying?
4 Do you _____ the most of your free time? Why / Why not?
5 Should scientists _____ more research into medicine or space travel?
6 Have you ever _____ friends with someone from a different country? Who?
7 Have you ever had to _____ an important decision?

c 💬 Ask and answer the questions in 2b.

3 WORDPOWER Easily confused words

a Match the sentence halves.

1 ☐ If you need money, a I can **lend** you some.
2 ☐ If I need money, b please can I **borrow** some?

3 ☐ Go on! You mustn't **miss** a points if you run with the ball.
4 ☐ You'll **lose** b this opportunity! It'll change your life!

5 ☐ **Take** some water a when you come to the gym.
6 ☐ **Bring** some energy drinks b when you go running.

7 ☐ If you want to take part, a **raise** your hands.
8 ☐ If you have work experience, b your chances of getting a job will **rise**.

9 ☐ They **robbed** a the money from a bank.
10 ☐ They **stole** b a bank.

11 ☐ Where are you working? a I'm **currently** working at home.
12 ☐ Do you work at a bank? b **Actually**, I work at a school.

b Underline the correct words.

1 a borrow = *take / give*
   b lend = *take / give*
2 a miss = *not win / not take*
   b lose = *not win / not take*
3 a take = *move to here / move away from here*
   b bring = *move to here / move away from here*
4 a raise = *lift something / go up*
   b rise = *lift something / go up*
5 a rob = *take from a person or place / take something*
   b steal = *take from a person or place / take something*
6 a currently = *at the moment / in fact*
   b actually = *at the moment / in fact*

c Write down three …
- places that can be robbed.
- things that are difficult to steal.
- things that you would only lend to a good friend.
- things you sometimes borrow.
- things you always take with you when you go out.
- things people often bring back from holiday.

d 💬 Compare your answers for c. Are they the same or different?

⟳ REVIEW YOUR PROGRESS

How well did you do in this unit? Write 3, 2 or 1 for each objective.
3 = very well   2 = well   1 = not so well

I CAN …

talk about new things you would like to do.	☐
talk about imagined past events.	☐
talk about possible problems and reassure someone.	☐
write an email with advice.	☐

Communication Plus

1B GRAMMAR Student A

This week's aims: The Present Simple: sports vocabulary

Class trip to Science Museum: Monday 9th July

▶ Now go back to p.13

10D READING Student A

Hi Vicky,

No wonder you don't want to go straight into an office job next year. Looking after elephants in Thailand sounds much more exciting! I think you should definitely go for it. You've got nothing much to lose (except a bit of money) and if it didn't work out you could always come back. But anyway, I'm pretty sure you'd enjoy it and have a great time – you always have been good with animals. It would definitely look good on your CV too. It would show that you're an adventurous person and you're interested in different things, not just studying and jobs. Pity I've got a job already or I'd come with you ;-)

Let me know what you decide.

Love

Amanda

▶ Now go back to p.125

5D SPEAKING AND LISTENING

The wrong statement is: 4 Whales never sleep because they need to breathe.

In fact, whales do sleep. They appear to take turns letting one side of their brain sleep. The other side of the brain stays awake so they remember to breathe.

▶ Now go back to p.64

Results

Research shows that about 70% of the population are extroverts and about 30% of the population are introverts, but not many people are either extreme introverts or extreme extroverts.

Are you a confident introvert? A shy extrovert? Or something else?

How many 'yes' answers did you have?

◀ ⋯⋯⋯⋯⋯⋯⋯⋯⋯⋯⋯⋯⋯⋯⋯⋯⋯⋯⋯⋯⋯⋯⋯⋯⋯⋯ ▶

| 7 | 6 | 5 | 4 | 3 | 2 | 1 | 0 |

Introvert   **Extrovert**

Introverts don't need much external excitement in order to feel happy. They feel alive when they have time to focus on the thoughts and feelings inside them. If you had four or five 'yes' answers, then you're a sociable introvert. You really enjoy spending time with people, but you always need to balance it with time on your own to recharge your batteries.

Extroverts feel happiest when they have lots of external excitement. They get ideas from any kind of conversation and discussion, and they enjoy having people and activity around them. If you had more 'no' answers, then you're probably a quiet extrovert. You don't always say much when you're around other people, but you love the energy you get from their company.

▶ Now go back to p.48

4C SPEAKING Student B

1 Student A wants help. You know quite a bit about computers and you like helping people. But you have your French class on Tuesdays and Thursdays, so you can't go shopping on those days.
2 You need help moving some furniture and you think that Student A has a big car. You would like to move it on Friday. Ask for Student A's help.

▶ Now go back to p.51

5C SPEAKING Student B

1 You are going to move to another part of the country. Think about the answers to these questions.
   • Why are you moving?
   • How do you feel about this?
2 Student A will tell you about his/her job. Ask him/her about what he/she is going to do.

▶ Now go back to p.63

6C SPEAKING Student B

1 Your partner will tell you some surprising news. Listen to the news and give some recommendations.
2 You found an old ring in your house. You think it belonged to your great-grandmother, but you aren't sure. You cleaned it and showed it to a friend, who said it was very valuable. You could sell it for about $1,000,000.

▶ Now go back to p.75

6A VOCABULARY

1 How many compound nouns can you find in the picture in two minutes?

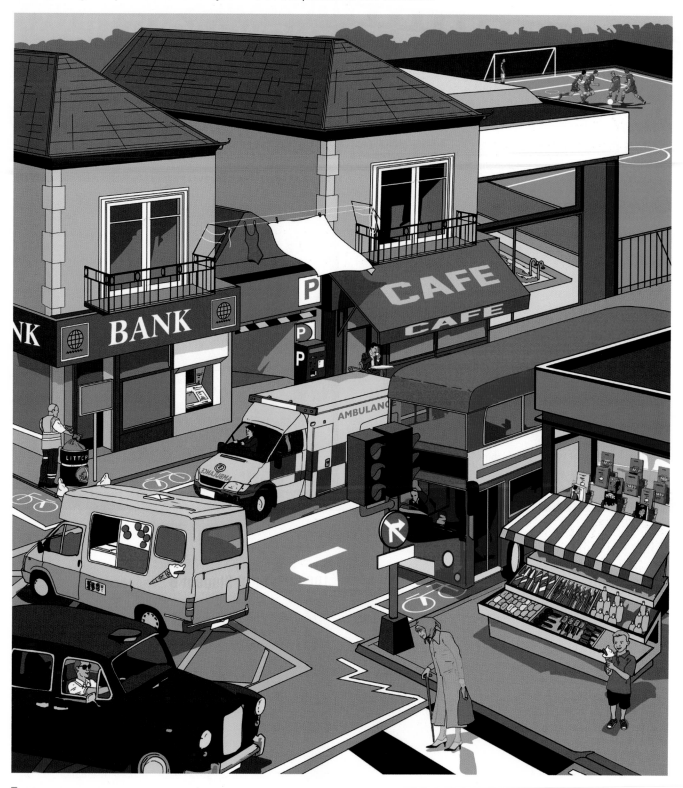

▶ Now go back to p.68

HOW MUCH DO YOU KNOW ABOUT FILMS?

Complete the questions with the correct form of the verbs in brackets. Then test your partner!

❶ Which city _____ in the movies more than any other? (destroy)
(New York. It was attacked by ghosts in *Ghostbusters,* aliens in *Independence Day*, a giant gorilla in *King Kong*, and in many other films.)

❷ True or False? The first *Lord of the Rings* movie _____ in 1978. (make)
(True: it was an animated feature film. It was not very successful – only Part 1 was ever finished.)

❸ In which country _____ most films _____: the US, India or China? (produce)
(India. 'Bollywood' makes nearly 1,000 films every year.)

❹ Which fictional character _____ by more actors than any other: Sherlock Holmes or James Bond? (play)
(Sherlock Holmes. More than 75 different actors have taken on the role of this character in the cinema. Many more versions of Sherlock Holmes have been seen on TV.)

❺ True or False? In the future, most films _____ on the internet, not in cinemas. (watch)
(No one knows! What do you think?)

▶ Now go back to p.106

9C SPEAKING Student B

You want to arrange an afternoon with Student A.
- You don't really like modern art.
- You are hungry. You've heard about a new café that does good food and great coffee. You can't remember what it is called, but you have the details on your phone.
- There is an exhibition of photography on across town, but you don't know where.

▶ Now go back to p.111

10C SPEAKING Student B

You want to talk to Student A about a big presentation you have to do (where? what is it about?).
You're worried because:
- you don't have much time to prepare (when is it?)
- you don't have any experience of public speaking (what problems might you have?)
- you are worried people might ask difficult questions (what might they ask?).
Have the conversation. Reassure Student A when he/she talks about a trip he/she is going on, but try to bring the conversation back to your presentation.

▶ Now go back to p.123

1B GRAMMAR Student B

▶ Now go back to p.13

10D READING Student B

Hi Vicky,

I'm not sure what I think about your idea of doing a gap year abroad. I can see that it might be exciting to go off to somewhere like Thailand or China for a year, but if I were you, I'd think very carefully about it before you make a decision.

I expect you'd have a good time, but you also need to think about getting a job after you come back. While you're away in Thailand everyone else will be going for jobs. Maybe it would be better to do something more closely connected with marketing. I'm not sure experience with elephants would help much in getting you a marketing job!

Anyway, I don't want to sound negative, but I'm just suggesting that you think about it first and make sure it's what you really want to do.

We could meet up and talk about it if you like.

Love,

Laura

▶ Now go back to p.125

7C SPEAKING Student B

1 Student A is staying in your home. He/She will ask you for permission to do things. Decide whether or not to give permission.

2 You have started a new job and Student A is your colleague. Ask permission to:
   • play music at your desk while you're working
   • turn the air conditioning up
   • move your desk closer to the window.

▶ Now go back to p.87

Grammar Focus

1A Subject and object questions

Most questions in English need an auxiliary verb (e.g. *do, be, have* or a modal verb) before the subject. The auxiliary verb can be positive or negative.

▶1.5

Question word	Auxiliary verb or *be*	Subject	Main verb	
	Can	I	borrow	your pen?
	Do	you	have	much homework?
Why	were	you		late?
Who	are	you	waiting	for?
How many people	have	you	invited	to the party?

▶1.6

When we ask about the subject of the verb, we use the same word order in the question as in the statement (subject – verb – object). Don't add an auxiliary verb to subject questions:

*Who **told you the news**? (Stuart **told me the news**.)*
*What **happened yesterday**? (Nothing **happened yesterday**.)*

Question word	Verb	
Who	told	you the news?
What	happened	yesterday?
How many people	are coming	to the party?
Which team	won	the match?

In questions with prepositions, the preposition goes at the end of the question:

A *Who did you go to the cinema **with**?* **B** *My sister.*
A *What's he talking **about**?* **B** *His job.*

💭 Tip

What … like?** and **How … ?
Use *What … like?* to ask for a description of a person:
A *What's your teacher **like**?*
B *She's very friendly.*

Use *How … ?* to ask about a person's health:
A *How's your sister?*
B *She's very well, thanks.*

You can use *What … like?* or *How … ?* to ask for a description of a thing or event:
A *What was your holiday **like**? / **How** was your holiday?*
B *It was excellent.*

1B Present simple and present continuous

▶1.8 Present simple

We use the present simple for:
- facts which are true all the time.
  *The sun **rises** in the east. The bus **doesn't go** past my house.*
- habits and routines.
  *I **study** for about an hour a week. We never **get** much homework.*
- opinions and beliefs.
  *Do you **agree**?   I **don't know** the answer.*

▶1.9 Present continuous

We use the present continuous for:
- actions which are in progress at the moment of speaking.
  *Why **are** you **carrying** an umbrella? It's **not raining**.*
- actions or situations around the moment of speaking.
  *He's **studying** Russian at university.*
- future arrangements (see 5A p.140).
  *I'm **meeting** Andrew **tonight**.*

States and actions

The present continuous is not normally used to describe:
- mental states: *know, agree, understand, believe,* etc.
- likes and preferences: *like, want, love, hate, need, prefer,* etc.
- other states: *be, own, belong, forget, hear, seem, depend,* etc.

Special cases

Some verbs (e.g. *think, see, have*) can be used as states or actions, with different meanings:
State: *I **think** you're wrong.* (= my opinion)
Action: *I'm **thinking** about my birthday.* (= a mental process)
State: *I **see** what you mean.* (= I understand)
Action: *I'm **seeing** the doctor tomorrow.* (= I'm meeting him/her)
State: *I **have** a car / a sister.* (= possession, relationship, etc.)
Action: *I'm **having** a party / a shower / dinner.*

1A Subject and object questions

a Make questions with the words below.

1 listening / why / me / isn't / to / anybody

_____

2 you / question / I / ask / can / a

_____

3 borrow / did / book / whose / you

_____

4 about / are / worrying / what / you

_____

5 has / cake / who / my / eaten

_____

b Correct the mistake in each question.

1 What time you will be here? _____
2 Happened what to your leg? _____
3 To what are you listening? _____
4 Which speaker did gave the best presentation?

_____

5 How's your new friend like? _____

c Write a subject and an object question for each statement. Ask about the information in bold.

1 **400** people have commented on **your photo**.

How many people have commented on your photo?
What have 400 people commented on?

2 **A fire** damaged **the roof**.

_____

_____

3 **Joanna** is afraid of **spiders**.

_____

_____

4 **His brother** told them a joke about **elephants**.

_____

_____

d ▶ Now go back to p.9

1B Present simple and present continuous

a Match the pairs.

1 [b] He drives to work
2 [a] He's driving to work

3 ☐ He wears a red shirt
4 ☐ He's wearing a red shirt

5 ☐ I think
6 ☐ I'm thinking

7 ☐ I have dinner
8 ☐ I'm having dinner

a at the moment, so he can't answer the phone.
b every day.
c every time he goes to a football match.
d so you'll find him easily.
e it's going to be a nice day.
f about what to do at the weekend.
g right now. Can I call you back?
h at a restaurant every week.

b Complete the conversation with the present simple or present continuous form of the verbs in brackets.

A What [1] _are you reading_ (you / read)?
B It's an article about learning languages. It's really interesting!
A Really? [2] _____ (it / have) any good advice?
B Yes, it does. The writer [3] _____ (learn) Japanese.
He [4] _____ (want) to learn ten new words a day.
He [5] _____ (always revise) them again at the end
of each week to check he [6] _____ (still remember)
them. It [7] _____ (not sound) like much, but after a
year, he now [8] _____ (know) over 3,500 new words.
That's a lot!
A Wow, yes, I [9] _____ (see) what you mean. So
[10] _____ (you/think) of trying this technique?
B Yes, maybe. I [11] _____ (try) to learn Russian at the
moment, but I [12] _____ (not make) much progress.
A Really? Why [13] _____ (you/learn) Russian?
B I [14] _____ (go) to Moscow next year for six months.

Yes, I'm studying Russian at the moment. I study about an hour a day but I'm not making much progress... I don't know why.

c ▶ Now go back to p.13

2A Present perfect simple and past simple

▶1.26 Present perfect simple

We use the present perfect simple to talk about:

- experiences in our lifetime, or another unfinished time period.
  Have you ever ***had*** a job interview?
  *I'***ve** never **worked** in an office.*
  We can use adverbs like *ever, never, three times*, etc.
- news and recent events, often with a present result.
  *They'**ve** just **offered** me the job.* (result = I've got a job.)
  *The interviews **have** already **finished** – you're too late.*
  (result = You can't have an interview.)
  *She **hasn't called** me back yet.* (result = I'm still waiting to speak to her.)
  We can use adverbs like *just, already* and *yet*.
- unfinished states (when we want to talk about the duration).
  *I'**ve** only **had** this phone for a week.*
  *We'**ve lived** in London since 2010.*
  We use *for* to give the duration or *since* to give the starting point.

▶1.27 Past simple

We use the past simple for completed past actions in a completed past time period:
*She **didn't get** the job.*
*The interviews **finished** five minutes ago.*
*Why **did** you **miss** the bus?*
We often use past time phrases like *last week, a few days ago, when I was a child*.

▶1.28 Present perfect or past simple?

We often introduce a topic with the present perfect and then change to the past simple in the next sentence to talk about the details:
*I'**ve had** lots of job interviews. The last one **was** about three months ago – it **was** terrible.*
*I'**ve lost** my keys. Maybe I **left** them on the bus this morning.*
*He **hasn't worked** here long. He **started** a few weeks ago.*
Don't use the present perfect when you describe an action that happened at a particular time. Use a past tense instead:
*They **left** yesterday / at four o'clock / ten minutes ago.*

2B Present perfect simple and present perfect continuous

Unfinished actions and states (duration)

- We use the present perfect simple with state verbs:
  *We'**ve owned** this car **for** several years and it has never broken down.*
  *She'**s known** him **since** they were children. They're very good friends.*
- We use the present perfect continuous with action verbs:
  *How long **have** you **been waiting?***
  *I'**ve been working** on my essay **since** 6 o'clock.*
  *He'**s been playing** very well **so far** in this match.*

> 💬 **Tip**
>
> Some verbs (e.g. *work, live*) can be used as action verbs or state verbs with no important change of meaning:
> *How long **have** you **worked** here? / How long **have** you **been working** here?*

Recent past actions with present results

- We use the present perfect simple when completing an action has a result now:
  *I'**ve** just **finished** my essay.* (result of finishing writing = I can relax, I can hand in the work, etc.)
  A *The house looks lovely.*
  B *Thanks! We'**ve** just **painted** it.* (result of finishing painting = the house looks nice)

- We use the present perfect continuous when doing an activity has a result now:
  *I'm tired because I'**ve been writing** an essay.* (result of writing = I'm tired.)
  A *What's that smell?*
  B *We'**ve been painting** the living room.* (result of painting = the house smells of paint)

New habits and repeated actions

- We use the present perfect continuous to describe repeated activities which started recently:
  *I'**ve been doing** a lot of exercise lately.* (In the past, I didn't do much exercise.)
  *She'**s been coming** to the gym with me three times a week.* (She has recently started coming.)

▶1.32 Present perfect continuous

	I / you / we / they	he / she / it
+	*I'**ve been using** a new app.*	*He'**s been using** a new app.*
−	*I **haven't been sleeping** well.*	*She **hasn't been sleeping** well.*
Y/N?	*Have they **been living** abroad? Yes, they **have**. / No, they **haven't**.*	*Has she **been living** abroad? Yes, she **has**. / No, she **hasn't**.*

2A Present perfect simple and past simple

a Find and correct the mistakes.

1 **A** How long do you live here? **B** About two years. — *have you lived*
2 I haven't been to work yesterday – I was ill. — *I didn't go to work yesterday*
3 **A** We need to email the bank this afternoon.
   B Don't worry – I've done it yet. — *I've already done it*
4 On her CV she says she's got lots of experience, but in fact she hasn't never had a job in her life! _____
5 I've wanted to work for your company since I've been a student. _____
6 **A** Have you heard the news? Louise has left her job!
   B Yes, I know. She's told me last week. _____
7 I've worked there for about six months. I've started in January. _____

b Complete the conversation with the present perfect or past simple form of the verbs in brackets.

A There's a really good job advert here in the newspaper. [1] *Have you seen* (you / see) it?
B No, I [2] *haven't read* (not / read) the paper yet. You [3] *have had* (have) it for hours. Can you show me?
A It's this one. Senior Marketing Specialist for a bank. I think you should apply for it.
B Er … no, I don't think so. They want someone with lots of experience in banking, but I [4] *I've never worked* (never / work) in a bank.
A No, but you [5] *'ve worked* (work) for lots of marketing companies, and you [6] *'ve done* (do) lots of projects for banks. Remember? You [7] *worked* (work) on a really big banking project about eight years ago. It [8] *was* (be) really good.
B Yes, but eight years is a long time ago. Everything [9] *has changed* (change) in banking recently. It's a different world now. But what about you? Maybe you should apply. You [10] *told* (tell) me last month that you wanted to try something new.
A Yes, but that [11] *was* (be) last month. I [12] *applied* (apply) for a job at a newspaper last week, and they [13] *'ve just emailed* (just / email) me to offer me the job.
B Wow! Congratulations! [14] *Have you accepted* (you / accept) the offer yet?
A Not yet, no. But I think I will.

c ▶ Now go back to p.21.

2B Present perfect simple and present perfect continuous

a Match the pairs.

1 I've had — [b]
2 I've been having — [a]
   a tennis lessons for a month.
   b this car for a year.

3 I've just read this book. — [ ]
4 I've been reading this book. — [ ]
   c I thought it was amazing.
   d I can't wait to finish it.

5 Have you eaten — [ ]
6 Have you been eating — [ ]
   e properly recently? You look very thin!
   f lunch yet?

b Complete the sentences using the words in brackets and the present perfect continuous.

1 The baby's face is dirty because *she's been eating.* (she / eat)
2 He's tired because _____. (he / cut / the grass)
3 They're stressed because _____. (they / try / to fix the computer)
4 I'm hot because _____. (I / cook)
5 We're all wet because _____. (it / rain)
6 They've got muddy shoes because _____. (they / play / outside)

c Underline the best verb form in each sentence.

1 Angela's on the phone right now – *she's talked / she's been talking* to one of her friends for the last two hours!
2 *I've just found / I've just been finding* my glasses. I'm so happy! I lost them two days ago.
3 *I've known / I've been knowing* Jon for about 15 years.
4 I'm so tired. *I've worked / I've been working* since 7 o'clock this morning.
5 I can't drive, but *I've wanted / I've been wanting* to learn for a long time.
6 *They've studied / They've been studying* every night recently because they have an exam next week.

d ▶ Now go back to p.25

3A Narrative tenses

▶ 1.42 Past simple
We use the past simple to describe the main events of a story in the order they happened:
*We **met** a few years ago. He **offered** to help me fix my car. Later, we **became** good friends.*

▶ 1.43 Past continuous
We use the past continuous:
- to describe the situation at the beginning of a story.
  *That day, I **was driving** home from university for the summer.*
- for longer actions in comparison with shorter actions in the past simple.
  *Where **were** you **going** when I **saw** you by the road?*
  *I **was trying** to get home with some heavy bags when he **stopped** to help me.*
- when actions are interrupted by main events in the past simple.
  *I **was skiing** in the French Alps when I **had** my accident.*

We can connect past simple and past continuous actions with *as*, *while* and *when*:
*Somebody **stole** my bag **while** I **wasn't looking**.*
*Your sister **phoned while** you **were working**.*
*He **looked** out the window **while** the train **was going** through the countryside.*
*The car **broke down as** I **was driving** down the road.*

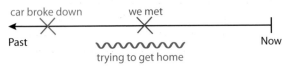

***As** we **were walking** along the road together, we **chatted**.*

Don't use the past continuous for state verbs. Use the past simple instead:
*We met when I **was** a student.*
NOT *... when I was being a student.*

▶ 1.44 Past perfect
We use the past perfect to describe an event that happened before the story started, or earlier in the story than a main event:
*That summer, I **had** just **finished** my second year at university.*
*When we met, my car **had broken** down by the side of the road.*
*I **hadn't taken** my phone with me, so I couldn't phone for help.*

> **Tip**
>
> We can use *by* + a time with the past perfect to show what happened up to a point in the past:
> *I started reading it on Monday and **by Friday I'd read** the whole book.*
> *They were really late for the party. **By the time they arrived**, everyone else **had gone** home.*

3B used to, usually

▶ 1.48
We use *used to* to describe past habits and states:
*When I was at school, I **used to play** football every Saturday.* (past habit)
*The whole family **used to love** animals. We always had two or three pets in the house.* (past state)

The negative forms are *didn't use to* and *never used to*:
*My parents **didn't use to go** out much, so we spent a lot of time together.*
*We **never used to** understand my dad's jokes.*

There is no present tense of *used to*. Use adverbs of frequency instead:
*They **usually go** out to a restaurant once or twice a week.*
*How many times a month **do** you **usually visit** them?*

You can also use adverbs of frequency with the past simple and a past time phrase (e.g. *when I was a child, back then*):
*We **went** abroad for a holiday **quite often back then**.*

We can use the adverbials *not any more* and *not any longer* to say that a past habit or state has now stopped:
*I **don't** play football **any more**. I usually go to the gym instead.*
*They **don't** live in the same house **any longer**.*

We can use the adverb *still* to talk about a past habit or state that has not changed:
*I **still** love board games. I frequently play Chinese Chequers.*
*Do you **still** see him very often?*

Past simple or *used to*?
We use *used to* for situations that were true for a long time (e.g. a few months or years). For shorter periods of time, we usually use the past simple:
*When we were on holiday last week, we **went** swimming every day.*
NOT *... we used to go ...*

We often use *used to* for situations that aren't true now:
*When I was a child I **used to love** ice cream, but now I don't really like it.*

Use the past simple, not *used to*, to describe something that happened once or a specified number of times:
*I **went** to the USA twice when I was a child.*
NOT *I used to go abroad twice ...*

> **Tip**
>
> We often use a mixture of the past simple and *used to* to describe past situations. It sounds unnatural if you use *used to* for every verb.

3A Narrative tenses

a <u>Underline</u> the correct options.

I ¹*meeting* / *met* my friend Alex while I ²*was fixing* / *fixed* my bike last year. The wheel ³*fell* / *had fallen* off and I ⁴*was trying* / *had tried* to put it back on. Alex ⁵*had walked* / *was walking* down the street when he ⁶*saw* / *was seeing* me and he ⁷*was offering* / *offered* to help. After that, we ⁸*became* / *had become* friends.

I ⁹*met* / *had met* my friend Anna in a hospital. I ¹⁰*was being* / *was* there because I ¹¹*was falling* / *had fallen* over and ¹²*had broken* / *was breaking* my arm. Anna ¹³*was* / *had been* there because she ¹⁴*injured* / *had injured* her foot. We ¹⁵*started* / *were starting* talking while we ¹⁶*had waited* / *were waiting* to see the doctor. By the time the doctor ¹⁷*was arriving* / *arrived*, we ¹⁸*had become* / *became* good friends.

b Complete the interview with the most suitable form of the verbs in brackets. Sometimes there is more than one possible answer.

A When ¹_____*did*_____ the accident _____*happen*_____ (happen)?

B It ²___*happened*___ (?) (happen) as I ³___*was driving*___ (drive) along the High Street last night. I ⁴___*saw*___ (see) an old lady. Just as I ⁵___*was turning*___ (turn) left, she ⁶___*fell*___ (fall) over onto the pavement right in front of me. I was pretty sure I could see why. A young man ⁷___*had pushed*___ (push) her over. Straight away I ⁸___*stopped*___ (stop) my car and I ⁹___*jumped*___ (jump) out. I ¹⁰___*ran*___ (run) over to the old lady. She ¹¹___*was lying*___ (lie) on the ground and she ¹²___*was crying*___ (cry).

A ¹³___*Did*___ (you / notice) anything else?

B Yes … a large flowerpot on the pavement. It ¹⁴___*was*___ (be) broken.

A Where ¹⁵___*had it come*___ (it / come) from?

B It ¹⁶___*had fallen*___ (fall) from a window above the street. The young man ¹⁷___*had pushed*___ (push) the old lady out of the way. He ¹⁸___*saved* / *had saved*___ (save) her life!

c ▶ Now go back to p.34

3B used to, usually

a Complete the text with the correct words/phrases.

> ~~used to go~~   use to have   used to be   went
> used to have   usually visit   didn't use to go
> don't go   live   lived   don't live   used to enjoy

When I was a child, I ¹___*used to go*___ to my grandparents' house in the mountains. We ²_____ in a city back then, and we visited them every year. We didn't ³_____ a car at that time, so we travelled by bus. It always took ages! We ⁴_____ in the winter because there was too much snow.

I loved helping my grandfather in his garden (although I usually avoid gardening now!). He never ⁵_____ a lawnmower, so we had to cut the grass by hand. It was hard, but I ⁶_____ it. I still ⁷_____ in the same city, but I ⁸_____ to the mountains any more. My grandparents ⁹_____ there any longer. They ¹⁰_____ to live in a large town five years ago. Now, I ¹¹_____ them in the summer, but it's not as nice as the mountains ¹²_____.

b If possible, change the verbs in **bold** to the correct form of *used to*. If it is not possible, put ✗.

1 I **drank** a lot of cola, but now I don't. ☐ ___*used to drink …*___
2 I **celebrated** New Year with my family last year. ☒
3 She **had** long hair when she was younger. ☐

4 Where **did** you **live** when you were a child? ☐

5 I **went** for a run every day last week. ☐

6 We **didn't wear** the same clothes all the time. ☐

7 In the past, people **spent** more time at work. ☐

8 **Did** you **play** with your sister when you were kids? ☐

9 I **bought** this bag in London – it's my favourite bag. ☐

10 They **weren't** friends in those days. ☐

c ▶ Now go back to p.37

4A Modals and phrases of ability

▶ **1.57** **General ability**

We use *can* / *could* to talk about general abilities:
*I **can** ski, but I **can't** snowboard. I **couldn't do** maths at school.*

We only use *can* in the present tense and *could* in the past tense, so when we need another form we use *be able to*.
We use *be able to*:

- in the present perfect, past perfect and after modal verbs.
  *How long **have** you **been able to drive**?*
  *We hope we**'ll be able to come** on Saturday.*
  *Everyone **should be able to swim**.*
- after other verbs (e.g. *want*, *need*, *like*) or prepositions (e.g. *of*, *about*).
  *The person who gets the job **needs to be able to speak** English.*
  *I **like being able to visit** my parents regularly.*
  *Don't worry **about not being able to understand**. You'll be fine!*

Specific past achievements

Don't use *could* for specific past achievements:
*When I went to France last year, I **was able to** visit the Louvre.*
NOT *I could visit…*

I couldn't play the piano when I was a child but I can play very well now.

In negative sentences about specific past events, we use *couldn't* or *wasn't able to*:
*I went to France last year, but I **couldn't** remember / I **wasn't able to** remember any words in French.*
We can also use *managed to* for specific past achievements, especially to show that something was difficult:
*It was hard work, but I **managed to** finish the project.*

4B Articles

▶ **1.60**

We use *a* / *an*, and *the* with singular countable nouns. We use *the* or no article with plural or uncountable nouns. The choice of article shows:

- if the topic is new.
  *I read **a great book** last week.* (= we haven't discussed this book before)
  *What was **the book** about?* (= the one we discussed earlier)
- if something is the only one.
  *Where are **the car keys**?* (= the only car keys we have.)
- if we are talking about things in general or in particular.
  Cats are clever animals. (= the animal)
  ***The** cats are in the garden.* (= our pets)

Other uses of *a* / *an*

- when you describe something or say what job someone has:
  *That's **a** beautiful photo. / He's **a** doctor.*
- in some frequency expressions:
  *I drink coffee once **a** week / three times **a** day.*

Other uses of *the*

- when the noun is defined by a defining relative clause:
  *I've just met **the** man who lives next door.* (= one specific man)
- before superlatives:
  *Kyoto is **the most beautiful city** in Japan.*
- with certain countries, oceans, rivers, or groups of islands:
  *I went to **the** USA / **the** Pacific / **the** Amazon / **the** Bahamas.*
- with some fixed expressions about:
  time: *all **the** time, most of **the** time, at **the** same time*
  places or seasons: *in **the** countryside / city; in **the** summer*
  free-time activities: *go to **the** cinema / **the** gym; listen to **the** radio (**but** watch TV)*

I've been reading a book.

I've been reading the book you lent me.

Other uses of no article

- in phrases about meals:
  *I **had breakfast** / **lunch** / **dinner** at 7am.*
  NOT *I had a/the breakfast …*
- in some fixed phrases about routines:
  *I usually **go home** / **go to bed** / **go to work** / **go to school** at … o'clock.*
- to talk about most countries, continents, cities, streets, etc.:
  I went to China / Africa / Paris / Bond Street.

> 💬 **Tip**
>
> Be careful with expressions with *next* / *last* + *week* / *month* / *year*:
> *I went there last week.* (= the calendar week before now)
> *I've been there twice in the last week.* (= the seven days before now)
> *We went there in the last week of the holidays.* (= a period of time with no connection to now)

4A Modals and phrases of ability

a Underline the correct option. If both options are possible, underline both of them.

1 I went to India last year but I *cannot /* *could not* take any pictures because my camera was broken.

2 *He's been able to swim / He can swim* since he was a child.

3 When they were children, they *could / were able to* run really fast.

4 She tried to read *War and Peace*, but she *wasn't able to / didn't manage to* finish it.

5 He *managed to / could* climb trees when he was a boy, but he *can't / couldn't* climb them now.

6 Katya needs to *can / be able to* speak Japanese in her new job.

7 You will *can / be able to* find a new person for the job soon, I'm sure.

8 I'm scared of *not being able to / can't* pass my exam tomorrow.

9 They *couldn't / didn't manage to* find a parking place.

10 I think everyone should *manage to / be able to* drive. It's an important skill.

b Complete each gap with a phrase from the box.

> can swim   could all swim   ~~couldn't swim~~   couldn't walk
> didn't manage to   was able to jump   was able to stand
> needed to be able   to be able to   managed to climb

When I was a young child, I [1] _couldn't swim_ – I only learnt to swim when I was about 14. I guess I thought that I didn't need [2] _____ swim, because I never went to swimming pools. But one day I went for a walk on a hill near the sea with my friends – we were about 13 at the time. Part of the path was missing in one place – we [3] _____ along it, so we decided to try to jump across. My friend Andy was quite big, so he [4] _____ across it very easily. But then it was my turn – I was a lot smaller, so I [5] _____ jump across. I fell down the hill and into the sea. My friends [6] _____, so they thought it was really funny to see me in the water, but I was really scared. Luckily, I [7] _____ on a rock under the water and then I [8] _____ out of the water. After that, I knew I [9] _____ to swim, so I started going to swimming lessons every week. And now I [10] _____ really well.

c ▶ Now go back to p.46

4B Articles

a Find the mistakes in these sentences.

1 Do you want to go to a cinema with me?   _Do you want to go to the cinema with me?_

2 Can you give me an advice?   _____

3 I want to buy new shirt.   _____

4 We had a good fun at the beach.   _____

5 I want to go to a countryside.   _____

6 I hope we have good weather at weekend.   _____

7 If you have problem, call me.   _____

8 I was in a shock for a few days.   _____

9 My brother is engineer.   _____

10 Please visit us if you have a time.   _____

b Complete the text with *a / an*, *the* or *Ø* (no article).

I don't like working in [1] _Ø_ groups because I never know what to say when [2] _____ people talk to me. [3] _____ last year I joined [4] _____ language course and [5] _____ teacher made [6] _____ students work in [7] _____ groups for [8] _____ most activities. [9] _____ lessons that we had were good, but I wasn't happy about [10] _____ speaking activities. I know speaking is probably [11] _____ best way to learn to speak [12] _____ language, but I don't really need to speak in my job. [13] _____ only thing I want is to be able to write [14] _____ good emails without making [15] _____ mistakes. One day, after [16] _____ extremely difficult lesson, I decided to speak to [17] _____ teacher about [18] _____ problem. I explained [19] _____ situation and she listened carefully. She explained [20] _____ purpose of working in [21] _____ groups, and that she needs to find [22] _____ right balance for all of [23] _____ students in [24] _____ class. In [25] _____ end, I agreed to try to speak more, and she agreed to give me [26] _____ more time to work quietly.

c ▶ Now go back to p.49

5A Future forms

▶ 2.5 Decisions, plans and arrangements

We use *will* to make a spontaneous decision (= a decision while we are speaking):
OK, I'll come for a run with you.
We use *going to* to talk about future plans (= decisions we made earlier):
We're not going to stay at that hotel again.
We use the present continuous to talk about arrangements (= fixed plans, usually involving other people and specific times and places):
She's travelling to Central America on Sunday.

There is not a big difference in meaning between *going to* and the present continuous to talk about future plans / arrangements. Often both are possible:
I'm visiting / going to visit my sister this weekend.

▶ 2.6 Offers, promises and suggestions

We use *will* to make offers and promises:
I'll help you, if you like.
I'll always be here when you need me.

We use *shall + I / we* in questions to make offers and suggestions:
A Shall I carry that for you?   **B** *Oh, yes, please.*
A Shall we go swimming on Saturday?   **B** *That's a good idea.*

▶ 2.7 Predictions

We use *will* to make predictions based on our opinions:
I'm sure you'll learn a lot when you go travelling.
Don't put that there! It'll fall off.
We use *going to* to make predictions based on concrete facts (= things that we can see or information that we have read, etc.):
We should leave soon. The roads are going to be busy.
It's not going to rain. There isn't a cloud in the sky.

> 🗨 Tip   In negative sentences, say *I don't think + will.*
> **I don't think** the forest **will** recover. NOT ~~I think the forest~~ **won't** ~~recover.~~

5B Zero and first conditional

Conditional sentences have two parts: the *if*-clause describes a possible event and the main clause describes the result of that event. The *if*-clause can come before or after the main clause. When the *if*-clause is first, put a comma between the two parts:
If *the lizard gets scared, it hides.*
The lizard hides **if** *it gets scared.*

▶ 2.9 Zero conditional

The zero conditional describes events and results that happen regularly or are always true. *If* and *when* both mean 'every time': every time the event happens, the same result happens. We use a present tense in both the *if*-clause and the main clause:
If *the lizard* **gets** *scared, it* **hides**.
If I go *to the city centre, I always* **eat** *in that restaurant.*
Anyone **can succeed** *if they* **work** *hard.*
Butter **doesn't burn** *in the pan if you* **add** *a little oil to it.*

▶ 2.10 First conditional

The first conditional describes possible future events and the expected results of those events. We use a present tense in the *if*-clause and a future form in the main clause:
If *the scientists* **succeed**, *many people* **will live** *longer.*
If I don't work *hard, I* **won't be** *successful.*
Will *you* **have to commute** *if you* **get** *the job?*
He'll **cook** *you an amazing meal* **if** *you* **ask** *him to. He loves showing off!*

Imperative conditionals

We can use imperatives in the main clause. The meaning can be present or future:
If you're tired (now), **go** *to bed (now).*
If you're tired when you arrive (this evening), **go** *to bed (then).*

Unless

Unless means 'if not'. We can use it in zero or first conditionals and with imperatives:
We play every Saturday **unless** *it rains.*
It won't hurt you **unless** *you run away.*

> 🗨 Tip
>
> In general, don't use a future form (e.g. *will, going to*) in the *if*-clause (or after *when* or *unless*):
> **If** *the government* **changes** *the law, this area will become a national park.* NOT ~~If the government will change …~~
> *We're going to miss the bus* **unless** *we leave right now.*
> NOT ~~… unless we're going to leave …~~

5A Future forms

a Underline the best option in each sentence.

1 **A** It's a bit hot in here.
   B Yes … *I'll / I'm going to* open a window.
2 I'm going to the shop. *Will / Shall* I get you anything?
3 **A** Why are you carrying those flowers?
   B Because *I'll / I'm going to* ask Sara to marry me!
4 **A** I'm so tired.
   B *I'll / I shall* make you a coffee, if you want.
5 I've got a bad stomach. I think *I'll / I'm going to* be ill …

b Complete the sentences with *will, shall* or *going to* and the verbs in brackets.

1 __Shall I carry__ (I / carry) your bag down the stairs?
2 What time _____ (we / meet)?
3 _____ (you / cook) me a nice meal tonight?
4 I _____ (go) to bed when this programme is finished – I'm tired.
5 I _____ (come) back one day – I promise.
6 I _____ (have) a steak – no, I _____ (have) fish, please.
7 According to the website, she _____ (talk) about some of her trips.
8 I think you _____ (like) my chocolate cake a lot.

c Complete the telephone conversation using the verbs in brackets with *will / shall*, *going to* or the present continuous. Sometimes there is more than one possible answer.

A Hi Dan, it's Tony. Listen, I [1] __'m coming__ (come) to Bristol for a couple of days next week for a big meeting with a client. I [2] _____ (try) to see some of my old friends while I'm there. Do you want to meet up one evening?
B Sounds good. It [3] _____ (be) good to see you again after all these years.
A Yeah, I know. [4] _____ (we / say) Tuesday evening?
B Er … no, that's no good for me. I [5] _____ (take) the kids to the cinema on Tuesday. We've already got tickets.
A OK, no problem. What about Wednesday?
B Yes, that's fine. What time [6] _____ (you / be) free, do you think?
A The meeting [7] _____ (probably / finish) at about 5 o'clock – that's what the client said, anyway.
B OK, so around 7 then? [8] _____ (I / pick) you up at your hotel? Where [9] _____ (you / stay)?
A [10] _____ (I / be) at the King's Hotel. I reserved a room last week.
B Perfect. Listen, I [11] _____ (phone) you before I leave, at about 6.30, to check you're ready.
A Don't worry – I [12] _____ (be) ready.

d ▶ Now go back to p.58

5B Zero and first conditional

a If a pair of sentences has the same meaning, write (S). If they have different meanings, write (D).

1 a I'll send you a text if Petra arrives.
  b I'll send you a text when Petra arrives. ☐ D
2 a If a snail is in danger, it hides in its shell.
  b When a snail is in danger, it hides in its shell. ☐
3 a The animals won't come out if we don't stay quiet.
  b The animals won't come out unless we stay quiet. ☐
4 a If you need some money, I'll lend you some.
  b When you need some money, I'll lend you some. ☐
5 a If you see a bear in the forest, don't run!
  b When you see a bear in the forest, don't run! ☐
6 a Lizards don't bite unless they feel scared.
  b Lizards don't bite if they feel scared. ☐

b Underline the correct options.

1 If I *eat / will eat* too much, I feel sleepy.
2 Simon isn't very talkative when he *wakes up / will wake up*.
3 *I send / I'll send* you some photos if you give me your email address.
4 If we don't leave now, we *don't / won't* get to the airport on time.
5 If you *go / will go* to London, visit the British Museum.
6 I go to the cinema every Friday unless *I'm not / I'm* busy.
7 Karen *will speak / won't speak* to Paul unless he apologises.
8 If someone *phones / is going to phone*, don't tell them I'm here.
9 You can do anything *if / unless* you try hard enough.
10 Will I have to bring anything if I *come / will come* to the party?

c Complete the sentences with the verbs in brackets and a conditional form. Use *will* where possible.

1 You ____'ll feel____ (feel) bad if you ____drink____ (drink) too much coffee.
2 If you _____ (not want) to watch the film, we _____ (do) something else instead.
3 He _____ (not make) any money unless he _____ (start) selling more products.
4 If you _____ (not finish) tonight, you _____ (not have) the weekend free.
5 If you _____ (feel) like going out later, call me.
6 Unless it _____ (be) really cold, we _____ (try) to run tomorrow morning.
7 You _____ (not get) there on time if you _____ (not take) the train.
8 If you _____ (not be) ready in five minutes, we _____ (leave) without you.

d ▶ Now go back to p.60

6A Modals of obligation

▶ 2.25 **must** and **have to**

We use *must* when <u>we</u> make the rules:

*I **must get** a good night's sleep tonight.*

We use *have to* when we talk about other people's rules:

*You **have to buy** a ticket before you get on the train.*

There is no past or future form of *must*. When we talk about rules in the past or future, we always use the correct form of *have to*:

*When you go to India, you**'ll have to** get a visa.*

*I **had to** wear a uniform at school.*

> 💬 **Tip**
>
> Don't use contractions with *have to*:
> *I have to go.* NOT ~~I've to go.~~

> 💬 **Tip**
>
> - Often there is not much difference in meaning between *must* or *have to*. *Have to* is much more common than *must*, especially in spoken English.
> - *have got to* is also used in spoken English and means the same as *have to*.
> - Questions with *must* are very rare.

▶ 2.26 **mustn't**, **can't** and **don't have to**

We use *mustn't* or *can't* to say that something is not allowed. We often use *mustn't* when <u>we</u> make the rules and *can't* to talk about other people's rules:

*I **mustn't** forget to email my mum.*

*We **can't** cross the road yet – the light's still red.*

For things which were not allowed in the past, use *couldn't*:

*I **couldn't** work in India because I only had a tourist visa.*

We use *don't have to* when there is no obligation. It means it's not necessary to do something:

*University students **don't have to wear** a uniform.*

*I **didn't have to** call a taxi. Robert drove me home.*

▶ 2.27 **should** and **ought to**

We use *should* or *ought to* to give advice and recommendations. They have the same meaning, but *should* is much more common:

*We **should see** as much as possible. We **shouldn't waste** time.*

*We **ought to see** as much as possible. We **ought not to waste** time.*

6B Comparatives and superlatives

	Adjectives	Adverbs
One syllable	*rich* → *rich**er**, **the** rich**est***	*fast* → *fast**er**, **the** fast**est***
Two or more syllables	**Ending in -y:** *easy* → *eas**ier**, **the** eas**iest***** *friendly* → *friendl**ier**, the friendl**iest***	**All:** *often* → **more** *often*, **the** **most** *often* *carefully* → **more** *carefully*, **the most** *carefully*
	Other: *careful* → **more** *careful*, **the** **most** *careful*	
Exceptions	*good* → **better, the best** *bad* → **worse, the worst** *far* → **further, the furthest** **more / the most** *bored / tired /* *ill* *clever* → *clever**er** / the* *clever**est***	*well* → **better, the best** *badly* → **worse, the worst** *far* → **further, the furthest** *early* → **earlier, the** **earliest**

*Some two-syllable adjectives can follow the rules for one-syllable adjectives: *clever, narrow, shallow, quiet, simple.*

▶ 2.32 **Comparison**

We can use comparative adjectives and adverbs to compare two things, situations, times, actions, etc. usually with *than*. We can change the degree of comparison with words like *a lot, much, far, even, slightly, a bit, a little*:

*Life's **a lot more interesting than** before.*

*She's **a bit happier than** she used to be.*

*He's speaking **much more slowly than** usual today.*

The opposite of *more* is *less*. We can use it with all adjectives and adverbs:

*The car's **slightly less clean than** it was.*

*I drive **less quickly than** he does.*

as + adjective/adverb + *as* shows that two things are equal; *not as … as* means *less than*:

*They're **as wealthy as** the royal family.*

*She does**n't** listen **as carefully as** she should.*

Some common adverbs can change the degree of the comparison:

*You're **just as pretty as** your sister!* (= exactly equal)

*My brother is**n't nearly as hard-working as** me.*
(= very different)

*She does**n't** sleep **quite as well as** I do.*
(= slightly different)

Extremes

We use superlative adjectives and adverbs to talk about extremes:

*It's **the worst** hotel in the world!*

*I got **the lowest** score possible.*

We often use the present perfect with *ever* with superlatives:

*This is **the best** meal I**'ve ever eaten**.*

*It was **the least interesting** film I**'ve ever seen**.*

We can use the expression *by far* to say an extreme is very different from all others:

*That's **by far the highest** mountain I've ever climbed.*

6A Modals of obligation

a Complete the sentences with the correct form of *must* or *have to*.

1 In my country, you ___have to___ cross the road at a pedestrian crossing – it's illegal to cross anywhere else.
2 When I lived in Moscow, I _____ leave home two hours before work, because the rush hour traffic was so bad.
3 _____ Alex _____ wear a tie to work?
4 I'll tell you a secret, but you _____ tell anyone. I don't want anyone else to know.
5 We took plenty of money, but in the end, we _____ pay – everything was free.
6 The sign says all visitors _____ report to reception
7 If you want to be there on time, you'll _____ leave here very soon.
8 Your brother can borrow my books tonight but he _____ forget to bring them back tomorrow. I need them for my class.

b Look at the signs. Then complete the advice using the verbs in brackets and a modal verb. Sometimes more than one form is possible.

NO PARKING	FREE BUS TO SHOPPING CENTRE	WARNING! Car thieves in this area. LOCK YOUR CAR	Fire exit Emergency only	USE OFFICIAL TAXIS ONLY
You [1] ___mustn't / can't park___ (park) here.	You [2]_____ (pay) for the bus to the shopping centre.	You [3]_____ (leave) your car unlocked. It might get stolen.	You [4]_____ (use) that door – it's for emergencies only.	You [5]_____ (only use) the official taxis.

c ▶ Now go back to p.70

6B Comparatives and superlatives

a Complete the sentences with the comparative or superlative form of the words in brackets. Add *than* or *the* where necessary.

1 Indian food is ___spicier than___ French food. (spicy)
2 This is _____ meal I've ever eaten. (delicious)
3 The weather was _____ I expected. (hot)
4 She's a _____ driver _____ me. (slow)
5 Are you _____ person in your class? (clever)
6 I didn't have a good holiday. The _____ thing was the hotel. It was terrible. (bad)
7 Your English is _____ mine. (good)
8 I'm sorry, I can't come on Friday. That's my _____ day. (busy)

b Complete the sentences so that they mean the same as the sentences in **a**. Use two to five words.

1 French food isn't ___as spicy as Indian food___.
2 I've never eaten a _____ meal than this.
3 I didn't expect the weather to be _____ it was.
4 She drives _____ I do.
5 Is anybody in your class _____ you?
6 I didn't have a good holiday. The hotel was _____ everything else.
7 You speak English _____ I do.
8 I'm sorry, I can't come on Friday. It's _____ the other days.

c Complete the sentences with one word from the box in each space. Use each word once only.

a   as   bit   by   ever   expected   in   just   ~~more~~
most   nearly   one   slightly   than   the

1 Today's lesson was ___a___ lot ___more___ interesting than usual – it was excellent.
2 That's _____ worst joke I've _____ heard!
3 The exam went really well. It wasn't _____ as difficult as I _____.
4 I think she's _____ of the _____ innovative designers in the world.
5 Our holiday was a _____ more expensive _____ we thought, but it was still good value.
6 They started _____ later than usual, but they still finished on time.
7 _____ far the oldest person _____ my family is my great-grandmother.
8 Our new TV is fantastic – the picture quality is _____ as good _____ in the cinema, or maybe even better.

d ▶ Now go back to p.72

7A Modals of deduction

We can use modal verbs to show that we are making a deduction using evidence, not stating a fact:

▶ 2.39

*We **must be** early. Nobody else has arrived yet.*
*They work at the same office so they **may know** each other.*
*She **might not be** in. The lights are all out.*
*That **can't be** Mark's car. He told me his was in the garage.*

Different modal verbs tell us how sure about a deduction we are:

It's cold in that house.	Fact: *I **know** it is.*
It **must** be cold in that house.	Deduction: *I'm **sure** it is.*
It **may / might / could** be cold in that house.	Deduction: *It's **possible** that it is.*
It **may / might not** be cold in that house.	Deduction: *It's **possible** that it isn't.*
It **can't** be cold in that house.	Deduction: *I'm **sure** it isn't.*
It isn't cold in that house.	Fact: *I know it isn't.*

- The opposite of *must* for deductions is *can't*. Don't use *mustn't, can* or *couldn't* for deductions:
  *This bill **can't** be right. I only ordered a salad.*
  NOT ~~This bill couldn't / mustn't be right.~~
  *There **must** be a mistake.*
  NOT ~~There can be a mistake.~~
- There is no difference between *may, might* and *could*. All three mean that something is possible.
- To make deductions about actions happening now, use a modal + *be* + verb + *-ing*:
  *She isn't answering the phone. She **might be listening** to music.*

7B Quantifiers

▶ 2.46 *some, any* and *no*

We usually use *some* in positive statements and *any* in negatives and questions:
*There are **some** nice views from the hotel.*
*He doesn't have **any** good music.*

We can also use *no* in positive sentences to talk about zero quantity:
*There's **no** crime around here.*

To talk about zero quantity, we can use *none of* + plural or *none*:
***None of** my friends could help.*
A *How many holidays have you been on this year?*
B ***None** at all.*

▶ 2.47 Large quantities

We use *lots of / a lot of* in positive sentences, *not many / not much / not a lot of* in negative sentences and *many / much / a lot of* in questions:
*There are quite **a lot of** cars on the roads today.*
*I haven't got **much** money with me.*
*Did **many** people come to the concert?*
*We don't need **a lot of** time to finish this work.*

In positive sentences, we can use *plenty of* to show we are happy with the amount:
*Don't worry – we've got **plenty of** food.*

▶ 2.48 Small quantities

We use *a few / a little* to talk about an amount. We use *few / little* to talk about a negative amount (i.e. there is not a lot):
*We have **a little** time before the show starts.*
*There are **a few** things I need from the shops.*
*I have **very little** time to finish this work.*
*This dish has **very few** ingredients.*

We can say *quite a few / very few / very little* to increase / decrease the amount.

▶ 2.49 *too / not enough*

We use *too much / too many* + noun to say there is more than the right amount. We use *not enough* to say that there is less than the right amount:

*I have **too much furniture**. There isn't **enough room** for all of it!*
*I couldn't move at the concert because there were **too many people**.*

We also use *too* + adjective / adverb and *not* + adjective / adverb *enough*:
*This suitcase is **too heavy**. They won't let you on the plane.*
*You're walking **too quickly**, I can't keep up!*
*The meeting room isn't **big enough** for all of us. There aren't enough chairs.*
*You're **not** walking **fast enough**. Hurry up!*

7A Modals of deduction

a Match the deductions 1–8 with the best sentences a–h.

1 [f] That man must be a doctor.
2 [ ] That man might be a doctor.
3 [ ] That man might not be a doctor.
4 [ ] That man can't be a doctor.
5 [ ] They must be eating dinner now.
6 [ ] They could well be eating dinner now.
7 [ ] They may not be eating dinner now.
8 [ ] They can't be eating dinner now.

a He doesn't know anything about medicine.
b They finished their dinner an hour ago.
c He's wearing a white coat.
d I remember they booked a table at a restaurant for around now.
e Perhaps they've finished.
f Look – he's listening to that man's heart.
g They usually eat around this time.
h It's possible that he's a nurse.

b Complete the sentences using an appropriate modal of deduction. Sometimes more than one modal is possible.

1 It's impossible that she's in the office – she flew to Beijing yesterday.
She _can't be in the office – she flew to Beijing yesterday._

2 I'm sure you're right.
You _____

3 It's possible that they want to sell their flat.
They _____

4 I'm sure he isn't speaking Russian – it sounds more like Spanish to me.
He _____ – it sounds more like Spanish to me.

5 It's possible that you're the perfect person for the job.
You _____

6 There's a possibility that he doesn't know the answer.
He _____

7 I'm sure you don't need that coat today – it's 30 degrees!
It's 30 degrees! You _____

8 They're probably building a new shopping centre.
They _____

c ▶ Now go back to p.80

That can't be right.

No, it must be a mistake

BUILT IN 2012

GUIDE

7B Quantifiers

a Underline the correct quantifier in each sentence.

1 We had *any* / *no* / *none* problems.
2 My parents read *a lot* / *a lot of* / *much* books.
3 I'm not tall *enough* / *too* / *plenty* to be a police officer.
4 There's too *little* / *many* / *much* noise in my block of flats. I can't sleep.
5 You don't go out *little* / *many* / *enough*. You should go out more.
6 I watch *much* / *many* / *a lot of* television.
7 **A** Did you get much work done?
   B Yes, *a lot of* / *a lot* / *none*.
8 **A** Have you got any potatoes left?
   B No, I've got *some* / *any* / *none*.
9 I've been to quite *many* / *few* / *a few* countries.
10 It's *too much* / *too* / *enough* hot in here. Can I open a window?

b Complete the second sentence so that it means the same as the first sentence.

1 **a** I want no visitors for the next 30 minutes.
   b I don't _want any visitors for the next 30 minutes._

2 **a** There aren't enough chairs for everyone.
   b There are too _____

3 **a** I wanted a biscuit, but there weren't any left.
   b I wanted a biscuit, but there were _____

4 **a** Make sure you take plenty of money.
   b Make sure you take a _____

5 **a** They gave us too little information.
   b They didn't _____

6 **a** I didn't see many people.
   b I saw very _____

7 **a** We didn't have any money.
   b We had _____

8 **a** She's got plenty of time tomorrow.
   b She's got a _____

c ▶ Now go back to p.85

8A Reported speech

Reported speech and direct speech

When we talk about what somebody said or thought, we can use direct speech or reported speech:

- *Direct speech:* He said, 'I don't want to talk to you.'
- *Reported speech:* He said he didn't want to talk to me.

▶ 3.3

Direct speech		Reported speech
*'I **don't want** to talk to you.'*	→	*He said he **didn't want** to talk to me.*
*'I'**m planning** to resign.'*	→	*She said she **was planning** to resign.*
*'I'**ve** already **told** you.'*	→	*He said **he had** already **told** me.*
*'I **saw** you break it.'*	→	*I told him I **had seen** him break it.*
*'I'**m going to cook** tonight.'*	→	*You said you **were going to cook** tonight.*
*'I'**ll** see you soon.'*	→	*He said he **would** see me soon.*
*'I **can't** hear you.'*	→	*She said she **could**n't hear me.*
*'You **may** be right.'*	→	*He said I **might** be right.*

Some modal verbs (*would, could, should, might*) stay the same in reported speech:

*I'**d** like to go.* → *He said he'**d** like to go.*
*It **might** be difficult* → *She said it **might** be difficult.*

When I asked him if he **was** going to resign, he said he **didn't want** to talk to me.

▶ 3.4 Reported questions

When you report a *Wh-* question, put the subject before the verb. Don't use the auxiliary *do / does / did*:

*'Where **are you** from?'* → *She asked me where **I was** from.*
*'Why **did she say** that?'* → *He asked me why **you had said** that.*

For *Yes/No* questions, use *if/whether. Whether* is more formal than *if*:

'Are you going to help?' → *We asked them **if** they were going to help.*
'Did you visit the London Eye?' → *She asked us **whether** we had visited the London Eye.*

Other changes

When we report speech, we usually need to change the pronouns (e.g. *I, he*) and possessives (e.g. *my*), depending on who is talking to whom. Time and place words may also need to change:

*'I want **you** to give **this** message to **your** boss **tonight**.'*
→ *She said **she** wanted **me** to give **a / the** message to **my** boss **that night**.*

> 💬 **Tip**
>
> You don't need to change the tense when you want to show that the speaker's words are still true now:
> *I **told** you yesterday that I **don't** want to talk to you.*
> (= I still don't want to talk to you today.)

say and *tell* have different patterns. Always use a person or pronoun after *tell*:

*Tom **said** he had a new car.* NOT ~~Tom said me he had a new car.~~

*Tom **told me** he had a new car.* NOT ~~Tom told he had a new car.~~

8B Verb patterns

▶ 3.8 verb + *-ing* or *to* + infinitive

- Some verbs (e.g. *enjoy, mind, keep, admit, recommend, suggest*) are followed by a verb + *-ing*:
  *She **didn't mind working** late.*
  The negative form is *not* + verb + *-ing*:
  *I **enjoyed not cooking** for a change.*
- Other verbs (e.g. *want, hope, agree, offer, promise, need, refuse, threaten, plan*) are followed by *to* + infinitive:
  *They **threatened to tell** the police.*
  The negative form is *not* + *to* + infinitive:
  *I **promise not to break** anything.*
- Some verbs (e.g. *start, begin, continue*) can be followed by both patterns, with no change of meaning:
  *People **started arriving** an hour ago.*
  *He **started to feel** angry.*
- Some verbs (e.g. *try, forget, remember*) can be followed by both patterns, but the meaning changes:
  *I **tried reading** some reviews online, but they didn't help much.* (= I read them as an experiment)
  *I **tried to read** some reviews online, but my internet connection wasn't working.* (= I attempted to read them)
  *I **remember going** there for the first time.* (= I'm looking back at an earlier experience.)
  *Please **remember to book** a table.* (= keep the plan in your memory)

- Some verbs (e.g. *advise, ask, invite, remind, tell, warn*) need an object before *to* + infinitive:
  *They **warned** me not **to** tell anyone.*
  *I've **invited** your parents **to** visit us.*
  make (= 'force') and *let* (= 'allow') are followed by an object and a bare infinitive:
  *My boss **made me work** late.*
  *He **let me drive** his car.*

Other uses of verb + *-ing*

- When a verb comes after a preposition (e.g. *about, of, by*), the verb is always in the *-ing* form:
  *I'm worried **about** not be**ing** good enough.*
  *They escaped **by** break**ing** a window.*
- When a verb is the subject of a sentence, it is usually in the *-ing* form:
  ***Eating** in a restaurant is more expensive than at home.*

Other uses of *to* + infinitive

- Infinitive of purpose:
  *I went online **to read** the news.*
- adjective + *to* + infinitive:
  *I was relieved **to see** I wasn't late.*
- verb + question word + *to* + infinitive:
  *I don't know where **to go** or who **to ask**.*

8A Reported speech

a Complete the reported speech with the correct verb form. Change the tense where possible.

1 It's going to be a lovely day.
2 I don't want to go out this evening.
3 We're waiting for you.
4 My sister can't drive.
5 I've lost my car keys.
6 Lucy might have a new job.
7 I'll help you with those bags.
8 Mark bought a new car.

He said it _____*was going to be*_____ a lovely day.
She told me she _____ that evening.
They said they _____ for us.
She said her sister _____.
She told me she _____ her car keys.
He said Lucy _____ a new job.
He said he _____ with my bags.
You told me that Mark _____ a new car.

b Read Harry's conversation with Andy. Then choose the best word or phrase to complete Andy's conversation with Harry's sister, Lucy.

> **HARRY** Hi. I'm trying to buy a present for my sister, Lucy. It's her birthday tomorrow.
> **ANDY** What sort of books does she like?
> **HARRY** I'm not sure. She reads a lot of history books.
> **ANDY** This is really good, *A Short History of the World*. I read it a few months ago.
> **HARRY** No, I think she's already read that. She didn't like it. No, I'm going to get her this one, *A History of Amazing Buildings*.

Two days later, Andy sees Lucy in the street …

> **ANDY** Hi Lucy. I met your brother a few days ago – he said it was ¹*my / your / her* birthday ²*tomorrow / the previous day / yesterday*.
> **LUCY** Yes, that's right. Where did you meet him?
> **ANDY** In the bookshop. When I asked him what he was doing ³*here / there / near*, he said ⁴*he was / he's / I'm* looking for a present for ⁵*me / you / her*.
> **LUCY** Really?
> **ANDY** Yes. I asked him what books ⁶*you liked / do you like / does she like*, and he said he wasn't sure. He said ⁷*she reads / you read / I read* history books. So I showed him *A Short History of the World* – I said it was really good. I told him ⁸*you've / I've / I'd* read it a few months ⁹*earlier / ago / later*. But he said ¹⁰*you'd / she's / I'd* already read it, and you hadn't liked it.
> **LUCY** What? I thought it was brilliant!
> **ANDY** Yeah. Anyway, he said ¹¹*I'm / he's / he was* going to get *A History of Amazing Buildings*.
> **LUCY** Yes – and he did. It's really cool.
> **ANDY** Great – I knew ¹²*you'd love it / she'll love that / you'll love that*.

c ▶ Now go back to p.94

8B Verb patterns

a <u>Underline</u> the correct option.

1 I agreed *going / to go* to the hospital.
2 He admitted *to take / taking* the money.
3 Remember *to collect / collecting* the dry cleaning on your way home.
4 We tried *making / to make* some cakes but the oven wasn't working.
5 I made the dog *sit / sitting* down.
6 Maria refused *watching / to watch* the scary film.
7 It's important *making / to make* a reservation in advance.
8 They don't mind *walking / to walk* home tonight.
9 We advised *to have / them to have* a short holiday.
10 My mum always let me *stay / to stay* up late.

b Complete the conversation.

A I want ¹ *to get* (get) my laptop fixed. I don't know where ² to go (go).
B Have you tried ³ looking (look) online? It's easy ⁴ to find (find) repair shops, and you can read reviews ⁵ to see (see) if they're good.
A Er … no. ⁶ check (check) the internet is going to be pretty difficult because my computer's broken.
B Oh yes, sorry, I keep ⁷ forgetting (forget). Listen, I think I know who ⁸ to ask (ask). My neighbour's a computer engineer. I'll phone him now ⁹ to ask (ask) him what ¹⁰ to do (do).

Five minutes later …

B OK, so he says he doesn't mind ¹¹ helping (help) but he's a bit busy. He suggests ¹² trying (switch) it off and back on again ¹³ to see (see) what happens. He says that usually works.
A Yes, I remember ¹⁴ doing (do) that last time I had a problem, and it did work. But now my computer just refuses ¹⁵ to start (start) up.
B Hmmm. I think I know how ¹⁶ to fix (fix) it, but I need ¹⁷ to take (take) the back off. I promise not ¹⁸ to break (break) it …

c ▶ Now go back to p.96

9A The passive

We form the passive using *be* + past participle.

Active	▶ 3.23 Passive
They **make** a lot of films in Hollywood.	A lot of films **are made** in Hollywood.
The scriptwriters **are writing** a new script this week.	A new script **is being written** this week.
The estate agent **sold** the house for £1 million.	The house **has been sold** for £1 million.
There was an accident while they **were building** the bridge.	There was an accident while the bridge **was being built**.
A film studio **will make** a film from the book.	A film **will be made** from the book.
Somebody **stole** our car in the night.	Our car **was stolen** in the night.
An expert **should do** the work.	The work **should be done** by an expert.

We use passive verb forms:
- when the main thing we are talking about is the object of the verb.
  A film **will be made** from the book.
  The work **should be done** by an expert. (We are talking about the work, not the expert.)
- when the agent (the doer) isn't important.
  The house **has been sold** for £1 million. (We don't care about the estate agent.)
- when the agent (the doer) is very obvious.
  A new script **is being written** this week. (by scriptwriters)
- when we don't know who did something / what caused something.
  Our car **was stolen** in the night.

Negatives and questions are made in the same way as other uses of *be*:
Films **aren't** made here. **Is** a film **being** made here?

We use *by* to introduce the person or thing that did the action (the agent):
This frame was drawn **by** one of the animators.
We usually use *with* to introduce a tool, instrument or technique that was used by the agent:
The pirate's beard was controlled **with** a wire.

> 💬 **Tip**
> We can say something was made by hand or by machine:
> *This jumper was made **by hand** in Scotland.*

9B Defining and non-defining relative clauses

▶ 3.27 **Defining and non-defining relative clauses**

Defining relative clauses define a noun or make it more specific. They tell us which particular thing or what kind of thing. In defining relative clauses, we can also use *that* instead of *who* or *which*:
I love **music that makes people dance**.
I hate **books which don't have happy endings**.
My dad met **the woman who reads the news on TV** yesterday!
They're **the couple that I told you about**.

Non-defining relative clauses give extra information about a noun, but they are not necessary for the sentence to make sense:
The DJ was playing hip hop. (This sentence is complete.)
The DJ was playing hip hop, **which is my favourite kind of music**. (This relative clause adds more information.)

In writing, we need a comma before and after a non-defining relative clause. Don't use commas in defining relative clauses:
We visited the market on a **Sunday, when they sell clothes and jewellery**.
I met **Lucy, who was staying with relatives nearby**, for a coffee.

In both types of relative clause, we can use *who*, *which*, *whose*, *where* and *when*:
Have you been to **that restaurant where you cook your own food at the table**?
Did you meet **the girl whose father climbed Mt. Everest**?

Omitting relative pronouns

We can often leave out *who/which/that* or *when* from defining relative clauses:
He likes the cheese (**which/that**) I bought.
(I bought the cheese. *cheese* = object.)

Don't leave out the relative pronoun if it's the subject of the relative clause (*who, which* or *that*):
He likes the cheese **that** comes from Turkey. (The cheese comes from Turkey. *cheese* = subject.)
Never leave out the relative pronoun from a non-defining relative clause:
This cheese, which Greg really likes, comes from Turkey.
NOT ~~This cheese, Greg really likes, ...~~

I think we should buy the chair you are sitting in.

9A The passive

a Complete the passive sentences. Don't include any agents that are inside brackets.

1 James Cameron directed *Avatar*.   *Avatar* _____ *was directed by James Cameron.*
2 (People) still make these shoes by hand.   These shoes _____ *are still made by hand.*
3 (They) will build a new bridge next year.   A new _____
4 My grandfather gave me this watch.   I _____
5 (We)'ve told everybody to be here on time.   Everybody _____
6 (People) will laugh at you if you wear that hat.   You _____
7 A computer program creates the special effects.   The special effects _____
8 My parents are looking after our dog this week.   Our dog _____
9 (They) offered me £1,000 for my painting.   I _____
10 (Somebody) was repairing my car at the time.   My car _____

b Rewrite the sentences as either *Yes/No* questions (?) or negatives (−).

1 We were picked up at the airport.   (−) _____ *We weren't picked up at the airport.* _____
2 The painting's already been sold.   (?) _____ *Has the painting already been sold?* _____
3 The work will be finished by Saturday.   (−) _____
4 The film's being made in Brazil.   (?) _____
5 Tomatoes are grown in Spain.   (?) _____
6 The car was being driven too fast.   (−) _____
7 The costumes were made by hand.   (?) _____
8 The sculpture has been taken to the piazza.   (−) _____

c ▶ Now turn to p.106

9B Defining and non-defining relative clauses

a Complete the sentences with a word from the box.

> which (x3)   who   where   when   whose (x2)

1 I love people _____ can make me laugh.
2 I told Paula my secret, _____ she then told everyone!
3 The film _____ I saw was really good.
4 I usually listen to music _____ I feel sad.
5 This album, _____ came out in 1967, has some great songs.
6 Mark is the person _____ father used to be a singer.
7 The shop _____ I bought this T-shirt has closed now.
8 I met Sara, _____ husband I work with, yesterday.

b Rewrite the sentences adding the information in brackets as a non-defining relative clause. Use relative pronouns which refer to the <u>underlined</u> words.

1 <u>Radiohead</u> performed 'Creep'. (They wrote it in 1992.)
   Radiohead performed 'Creep', which they wrote in 1992.
2 <u>Plácido Domingo</u> studied music in Mexico. (He is a well-known opera singer and conductor.)
   _____
3 We're going to <u>Cuba</u>. (Mambo music comes from there.)
   _____
4 <u>Glastonbury Festival</u> also has theatre, comedy and circus performances. (It's most famous as a music festival.)
   _____
5 My favourite singer is <u>Adele</u>. (Her album '21' is one of the most successful albums of all time.)
   _____
6 The best day of the festival is the <u>last day</u>. (There's a big firework display then.)
   _____

c Rewrite the sentences adding the information in brackets as a defining relative clause. Leave out *who*, *which* or *that* if possible.

1 I like the tune. (You were singing it.)
   I like the tune you were singing.
2 That's the DJ. (He was here two weeks ago.)
   _____
3 We need music. (It makes you want to dance.)
   _____
4 That's the stage. (We're going to perform there.)
   _____
5 I've got a CD. (You'll like it.)
   _____
6 What did you think of the music? (I chose it.)
   _____
7 What's the name of your friend? (You borrowed his CD.)
   _____
8 The song changed my life. (It's playing on the radio.)
   _____

d Are the sentences below correct or incorrect? Put a tick (✓) or a cross (✗). Sometimes both sentences in each pair are correct.

1 a I like music which makes me dance. ✓
   b I like music makes me dance. ✗
2 a It's a drum which you play with your hands.
   b It's a drum you play with your hands.
3 a My father, that is a dentist, looks after my teeth.
   b My father, who is a dentist, looks after my teeth.
4 a This album, I bought last week, is really good.
   b This album, which I bought last week, is really good.

e ▶ Now turn to p.108

10A Second conditional

We use the second conditional to talk about imagined events or states and their consequences. They can be about the unreal present or the unlikely future.

Real present		▶ 3.38 Unreal present and consequence
I don't know the answer.	→	If I **knew** the answer, I**'d tell** you.
Likely future		**Unlikely / imagined future and consequence**
She won't find out that you lied.	→	She **would be** angry **if** she **found** out you had lied.

We usually use the past simple in the *if*-clause and *would* in the main clause.
We can also use *could* or *might* instead of *would*:
You **could afford** to go on holiday if you **were** more careful with your money.
If you **tried** harder, you **might win** a medal.

The verb *be* has a special form in the second conditional. We can use *were* for all persons (*if I were, if you were, if she were,* etc.):
If **I were** taller, I'd be better at basketball.

We use the phrase *If I were you* to give advice:
If I were you, I wouldn't eat that fish. It doesn't smell fresh.

We don't always need to include the *if*-clause if the meaning is clear:
Look at that house! That **would** be a great place to live. (… if I moved there)
I'm sure Jack **would** help you. (… if you asked)

> **Tip**
> When talking about the future, you can usually choose between the first and second conditional. Use the first conditional if you think a future event is likely, use the second conditional if you think it is unlikely.
> - If we **score** one more point, we**'ll** win.
>   (I think there's a good chance of this.)
> - If we **scored** four more points, we**'d** win (but we probably won't.)

> **Tip**
> The contracted form of *would* ('*d*), is the same as the contracted form of *had*.
> You can tell the difference by looking at the verb that comes next.
> - '*d* + past participle: He**'d won** (= had won) *the match.*
> - '*d* + infinitive: He**'d win** (= would win) *the match.*

10B Third conditional

▶ 3.42
We use the third conditional to talk about imagined past events or states and their consequences:
If you**'d told** me about your birthday, I **would have** bought you a present.

We use the past perfect in the *if*-clause and *would have* + past participle in the main clause.

We can also use *could have* or *might have* instead of *would have*:
We **could have saved** some money **if** we**'d known** about the offer.
If I **had done** more work, I **might have passed** the exam.

Common uses of third conditionals
1. Regrets about things that happened or didn't happen in the past:
   If I**'d sold** my house two years ago, I**'d have made** a fortune.
2. Relief about avoiding a past problem:
   I **might have missed** the flight if you **hadn't woken** me up.
3. Surprise about how things were different from expected:
   If you**'d told** me five years ago I'd have my own company one day, I **wouldn't have believed** you.

> **Tip**
> Be especially careful with the contraction '*d*. In the *if*-clause, it's a contraction of *had*. In the main clause, it's a contraction of *would*.

If you'd told me about your birthday, I'd have bought you a present.

10A Second conditional

a Match the sentence beginnings 1–8 with the most logical endings a–h.

1 If I had more money,   [c]
2 I'd be grateful   [ ]
3 If I were you,   [ ]
4 If you asked her again nicely, [ ]
5 I wouldn't be so relaxed   [ ]
6 If he weren't so rude,   [ ]
7 I could get a better job   [ ]
8 Angela would be really sad   [ ]

a she might change her mind.
b more people would like him.
c I could eat in restaurants more often.
d if I spoke better English.
e if we didn't invite her.
f I'd complain to your boss.
g if you didn't tell anybody my secret.
h if I had an exam tomorrow!

b Underline the correct options.

1 *I'd go* / *I went* swimming more if *I'd have* / *I had* time.
2 If *I'd know* / *I knew* his number, *I'd call* / *I called* him.
3 *Would* / *Did* you mind if *I'd ask* / *I asked* you a question?
4 If you *wouldn't* / *didn't* have a car, how *would* / *did* you get around?
5 *You'd be* / *You were* a lot healthier if you *wouldn't* / *didn't* eat so much.
6 If *I'd be* / *I were* you, *I'd get* / *I got* some new shoes.
7 What *would* / *did* you do if *you'd see* / *you saw* a fire?
8 If someone *would treat* / *treated* you like that, how *would* / *did* you feel?

c Decide if the first or second conditional is more suitable for each situation. Then complete the sentences with the correct form of the verbs in brackets.

1 I think I'll probably leave my job soon. But if I _____*leave*_____ (leave) my job, it ____*'ll be*____ (be) difficult to get a new one.
2 I think it's going to be a nice day. We _____ (can) have a picnic if the weather _____ (stay) nice.
3 I'm not very good at football. If I _____ (can) play better, I _____ (join) a football club.
4 If I _____ (win) the lottery, I _____ (buy) a new house. But I know it's never going to happen.
5 I think we're the best team. If we _____ (win) the competition, I _____ (not be) surprised.
6 You drink too much coffee. If you _____ (not drink) so much coffee, you _____ (not be) so stressed.
7 She goes shopping all the time! She _____ (not have) any money left if she _____ (not stop) spending it!
8 I don't like my house in the city. If I _____ (live) in the countryside, I _____ (be) much happier.

d ▶ Now go back to p.117

10B Third conditional

a What does *'d* mean in each sentence? Write *had* or *would*.

1 If you'd (__had__) told me earlier, we'd (__would__) have saved a lot of time.
2 I don't know what I'd (_____) have done if you hadn't helped me.
3 We might have got seriously hurt if you'd (_____) crashed.
4 She'd (_____) have got the job if she'd (_____) applied for it.
5 I'd (_____) have loved to go to the party, but I wasn't invited.

b Write third conditional sentences about the situations.

1 Real past: I didn't win the competition because I made a stupid mistake.
   Unreal past: If *I hadn't made a stupid mistake, I would have won the competition.*
2 Real past: He went to live in Japan. While he was there, he met his wife.
   Unreal past: If he _____
3 Real past: The car was broken so we couldn't go to the concert.
   Unreal past: We _____
4 Real past: I didn't go to see the film because I didn't know it was so good.
   Unreal past: I _____
5 Real past: You didn't take my advice so you got lost.
   Unreal past: If _____
6 Real past: You helped me so much. That's why I was so successful.
   Unreal past: I'd never _____

c Correct the mistakes.

1 If you'd been there too, you ⟨would enjoy⟩ yourself.
   _____*would have enjoyed*_____
2 We couldn't have bought the house if they wouldn't have lent us the money.
   _____
3 If they hadn't noticed the fire, the whole house could burned down.
   _____
4 If I know it was dangerous, I'd never have gone there.
   _____
5 What you would have done if I hadn't helped you?
   _____
6 He could have been an opera singer if he'd have some training.
   _____
7 If they'd arrive a few minutes later, they might have missed you.
   _____

d ▶ Now go back to p.121

1A Communication

a ▶1.3 Listen to the words in **bold**. What do you think they mean?

1 You **argue** with someone when you *agree / don't agree* about something.
2 You **complain** when you're *happy / not happy* about something.
3 You **encourage** someone when you say *good / bad* things about what they want to do.
4 If you **persuade** someone, you make them *agree / forget* to do something.
5 If you **insist** on something, you say that something *must happen / might happen*.
6 You **greet** someone when they *arrive at / leave* a place.

b ▶1.4 Underline the correct words in **a**. Then listen and check.

c 💬 Describe what's happening in pictures 1–4 using the words in **a**.

d 💬 Choose three of these topics to talk about.
- a time when you complained about something in a shop or restaurant
- a time when you insisted on doing something
- a time when you argued about something unimportant
- a time when you encouraged someone who was having problems
- a time when someone persuaded you to do something you didn't want

e ▶ Now go back to p.8

1B Extreme adjectives

a ⏵**1.12** Listen to the extreme adjectives in the box. <u>Underline</u> the stressed syllable in each word.

---
awful /'ɔːfəl/   boiling /'bɔɪlɪŋ/   brilliant /'brɪliənt/   delicious /də'lɪʃəs/   enormous /ɪn'ɔːməs/
filthy /'fɪlθiː/   freezing /'friːzɪŋ/   furious /'fjuːriəs/   miserable /'mɪzərəbəl/   tiny /'taɪni/

---

b ⏵**1.13** Complete the sentences with the extreme adjectives in **a**. Then listen and check.

1 Their house is _____! It's got 12 bedrooms.
2 **A** Was it hot?
    B Yes, it was absolutely _____!
3 Why do you look so _____? I've never seen you looking so sad.
4 We had a _____ holiday. The hotel, the weather, the town – it was all really good.
5 The food was absolutely _____. I'm not going there again!
6 I was _____ when I found out he'd read my private diary!
7 The picture's _____ – I can't see it. Can you make it a bit bigger?
8 **A** It's _____! Why didn't I bring a coat?
    B Here, you can borrow my jacket.
9 Your T-shirt's _____! Put it in the washing machine.
10 That cake is _____! Could I have some more, please?

c 💬 Think of an example of each of the things below. Then work in small groups and compare your answers. Are any of your answers the same?

- someone who earns an enormous amount of money
- something that makes you furious
- a time you felt absolutely miserable
- an awful film or TV show
- something that tastes delicious
- a brilliant website

d 💬 Use extreme adjectives to describe pictures 1–4.

e ▶ Now go back to p.13.

5A Environmental issues

a Match the words in the box with definitions 1–8.

> local /'ləʊkəl/   destroy /dɪ'strɔɪ/   natural /'nætʃrəl/   species /'spiʃiːz/
> survive /sə'vaɪv/   limit /'lɪmɪt/   endangered /in'deɪndʒəd/   creature /'kriːtʃə/

1 found in nature, and not made by people
2 from a small area, especially of a country
3 to control something so that it doesn't become bigger
4 a type of animal or plant
5 to continue living
6 to damage something so badly that it can't be used
7 anything that lives (but is not a plant)
8 used to describe an animal or plant which might disappear because there are not many alive

b ▶2.3 Complete the texts with the correct form of the words in **a**. Sometimes there is more than one possible answer. Then listen and check your answers.

> This is my favourite animal – the orang-utan. Unfortunately, this great ape is ¹_____. It's terrible that people are cutting down the trees in the area where it lives. If we're not careful, its home will be completely ²_____. Fortunately, there are several conservation projects working to save this beautiful ³_____.

> The ice in the Arctic is melting. Some people say that the melting ice is ⁴_____ – that human beings are not causing climate change. But we need to do something about it, and fast. The weather is getting stranger. Some scientists think that many ⁵_____ will not be able to ⁶_____ if the temperature changes too much.

> Pollution is a big problem here. The air is often like a dirty grey fog. You can hardly see what's in front of you! A lot of people are getting ill. The government needs to ⁷_____ the number of cars and factories, but we can't do anything without the support of the ⁸_____ people. The problem is, everyone wants to drive!

c Make notes on your opinions and feelings about one of these topics.
- a favourite animal, plant or natural place
- an environmental problem where you live
- an environmental problem affecting the planet

d 💬 Take turns to talk about your topic.

e ▶ Now go back to p.56.

5B The natural world

a ▶2.12 Match the words in the box with photos 1–8. Then listen and check.

bay /beɪ/   cave /keɪv/   coast /kəʊst/   desert /ˈdezət/
rainforest /ˈreɪnfɒrɪst/   stream /striːm/   valley /ˈvæli/
waterfall /ˈwɔːtəfɔːl/

b ▶2.13 Underline the correct words. Then listen and check.

1 A *park / national park* is a very large area of natural beauty for use by the public.
2 A *river / stream* is a long (and often large) area of water that flows into the sea.
3 There are five *oceans / seas* in the world: the Pacific, the Atlantic, the Indian, the Arctic and the Southern.
4 A *forest / rainforest* is an area of land in a tropical region, where many trees and plants grow together.
5 A *sea / lake* is a large area of water with land all around it.

c 💬 Take turns to describe the animals or plants you can see in photos 1–6 below. Say where they live.

d ▶ Now turn to p.61

6A Multi-word verbs

a Look at the multi-word verbs in **bold**. Match them with definitions a–h.

1 ☐ When I **eat out**, I generally prefer *Chinese / Italian / _____* food.

2 ☐ I try to **pick up** new English vocabulary by *watching TV / reading online newspapers / _____* .

3 ☐ I'd be a good person to **show someone around** *my local neighbourhood / my nearest big city / _____* . I know all the best places to go.

4 ☐ The quickest way to **get around** my home town is *on foot / by bus / _____* .

5 ☐ I was the *first / last / _____* person to **turn up** to class today.

6 ☐ When I get the chance, I really enjoy **looking around** *art galleries / science museums / _____* .

7 ☐ I loved my visit to *the beach / my country's capital city / _____* and I'd like to **go back** soon.

8 ☐ Next time I **go away** with my family, I'd like to go to *Spain / the USA / _____* .

a explore
b arrive (informal)
c give someone a tour
d travel or move from place to place
e have food in a café or restaurant
f learn (a language or skill) by practising, not by having lessons
g leave your home to spend time somewhere else
h return

b Complete the sentences in **a** so they are true for you. Use one of the options given or write your own answer.

c 💬 Talk about your sentences.

d ▶ Now turn to p.70

6B Describing food

a ▶2.28 Label the pictures using the pairs of adjectives in the box. Then listen and check.

creamy /ˈkriːmiː/ / crunchy /ˈkrʌntʃiː/   fresh /freʃ/ / dried /draɪd/
cooked /kʊkt/ / raw /rɔː/   heavy /ˈhevi/ / light /laɪt/   sweet /swiːt/ / sour /ˈsaʊə/

① a _____
① b _____

② a _____
② b _____

③ a _____
③ b _____

④ a _____
④ b _____

⑤ a _____
⑤ b _____

b Complete the two recipes with the words in the box.

add /æd/   chop /tʃɒp/ (x2)   fry /fraɪ/   heat up /hiːt ʌp/
mash /mæʃ/   mix /mɪks/   serve /sɜːv/   squeeze /skwiːz/   stir /stɜː/

Guacamole

1 _____ four chilies, two tomatoes, one onion and a bunch of coriander.

2 _____ three avocados in a bowl.

3 _____ all the ingredients together.

4 _____ the juice of half a lime into the mixture.

5 _____ with tortilla chips.

Meatballs in tomato sauce

1 _____ one onion and two cloves of garlic.

2 _____ 500g minced lamb to the onions, with salt, pepper and spices. Make the mixture into balls.

3 _____ one tablespoon of olive oil in a pan.

4 _____ the meatballs in the oil.

5 Add two tins of tomatoes and 200ml of water. Cook for 30 minutes. _____ occasionally.

c Prepare a simple recipe for a dish you like. Make notes about the ingredients you need and how you make it.

d 💬 Take turns to talk about your recipes. Would you like to eat each other's dishes?

e ▶ Now go back to p.71

7A Describing houses and buildings

a ▶ **2.42** Use the words in the box to label the pictures. Then listen and check.

> attic /ˈætɪk/ balcony /ˈbælkəniː/ basement /ˈbeɪsmənt/ block /blɒk/ of flats doorbell /ˈdɔːbel/ first floor /flɔː/
> flat /flæt/ front /frʌnt/ door ground /ɡraʊnd/ floor landing /ˈlændɪŋ/ lock /lɒk/ steps /steps/ terrace /ˈterəs/

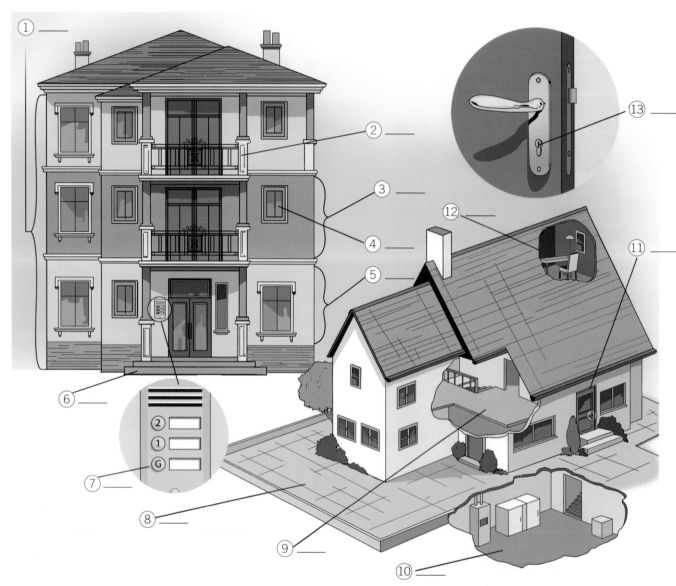

b ▶ **2.43** Complete the sentences with the words in the box. Then listen and check.

> attic balcony floor location /ləʊˈkaɪʃən/ moved
> neighbourhood /ˈneɪbəhʊd/ rent /rent/ view /vjuː/

1 I don't have my own house, so I _____ the house I'm living in.
2 I've _____ house a lot of times, so I've had lots of different addresses.
3 I live in a very busy _____. There are lots of shops, cafés and cars.
4 We don't have a garden or a terrace, but we do have a _____ where we can sit outside.
5 My home is in a good _____ because it's near the train station.
6 I put all the stuff I don't use in the _____.
7 Our flat is on the third _____ of our building.
8 The _____ from my bedroom is nothing special – just a street and more houses.

c 💬 Discuss the sentences in **b** which are true for you.

> The second sentence isn't true for me. I've only moved house once in my life.

d 💬 Imagine you are going to buy or rent a new home. What kind of house or flat would you choose and why? Which of these things are most important?

- price
- views
- location
- number of rooms
- garden
- something else

e ▶ Now turn to p.81

8A The news

a Match headlines 1–4 with the different kinds of news a–d.

1
> # HOSPITALS TO GET MORE NURSES

2
> **THREE BIG BANKS ANNOUNCE PROFITS**

3
> # CAN THIS FILM WIN ANY MORE AWARDS?

4
> ## FOOTBALLER TO MARRY POP STAR

a celebrity news
b current affairs
c entertainment news
d business news

b Complete the sentences with the words in the box.

> bloggers /'blɒgəz/   presenters prɪ'zentəz/
> editors /'edɪtəz/   reporters /rɪ'pɔːtəz/

1 _____ introduce TV and radio shows.
2 _____ write online articles giving their opinions and feelings.
3 _____ often travel to places where events are happening. They conduct interviews and present news stories.
4 _____ make decisions about what appears in magazines and newspapers.

c Underline the correct words.

1 People often express their opinions about news stories on *social* / *sociable* media like Facebook and Twitter.
2 Young adults prefer news websites where they can *post* / *publish* comments about articles.
3 How much do governments influence news *sources* / *organisations* like Sky News and the BBC?
4 Breaking news *posts* / *spreads* quickly online.
5 A *journal* / *journalist* is someone whose job is to collect news and prepare it for the public.

d Discuss the questions below.

1 What blogs do you read?
2 What qualities do you need to be a good journalist or reporter?
3 Do you post comments on news stories or share news stories online?

e ▶ Now go back to p.92

8B Shopping

a Are the phrases in the box talking about things customers do, or talking about products?

> be able to afford /ə'fɔːd/ something
> be in stock /stɒk/
> be on sale /'seɪəl/
> come out
> get a refund /'riːfʌnd/
> good value /'væljuː/ for money
> have a guarantee /gærən'tiː/
> look for a bargain /'bɑːgɪn/
> reasonably priced /'riːzənəbliː praɪst/
> take/send something back

b ▶ 3.5 Underline the correct words. Then listen and check.

A That new game came ¹*out* / *on* last Sunday, so I had to get it for Max, of course!
B Was it very expensive?
A No, it ²*had* / *was* reasonably priced, luckily!

C I've been looking for ³*bargains* / *good value* at the clothes market.
D Did you get anything?
C Well, there were some boots I really liked, but I ⁴*couldn't afford* / *afforded* them. I got these shoes instead. They were very good value ⁵*for* / *in* money – only £17.

E I bought this tablet online six months ago. It's already broken!
F You should ⁶*take* / *send* it back.
E Do you think I'll ⁷*get* / *send* a refund?
F ⁸*Was it on sale* / *Did it have a guarantee* when you bought it?
E Yes.
F That's OK, then. They'll have to give you your money back.

c 💬 Take turns to talk about something:

* you bought recently which was reasonably priced or in a sale
* you would like to buy but cannot afford
* you bought that is good value for money
* you're waiting to come out so that you can buy it.

d ▶ Now go back to p.95

9A Cinema and TV

a **⏵3.19** Match the words in the box with photos 1–12. Then listen and check.

action /ˈækʃn/   animation /ænɪˈmeɪʃn/   chat show /ˈtʃæt ʃəʊ/   comedy /ˈkɒmɪdiː/
documentary /dɒkjuˈmentriː/   drama /ˈdrɑːmə/   game show /ˈɡeɪm ʃəʊ/   horror /ˈhɒrə/
romance /ˈrəʊmæns/   science fiction /saɪəns ˈfɪkʃən/   soap opera /səʊp ɒprə/   thriller /ˈθrɪlə/

1 thriller

2 documentary

3 chat show

4 comedy

5 quiz game show

6 action thriller

7 sci-fi

8 period drama

9 animation

10 drama / soap opera

11 horror

12 romance

b **⏵3.20** Complete the sentences with the words in the box. Then listen and check.

based on /beɪst ɒn/   character /ˈkærəktə/   director /dɪˈrektə/   film /fɪlm/   scene /siːn/   studio /ˈstjuːdiːəʊ/

1 I like Christopher Nolan and Steven Spielberg, but my favourite _____ is Sofia Coppola.
2 The final _____ of the film was amazing – it looked so real!
3 They used some outdoor locations, but most of the filming was done in the _____.
4 I was very surprised when I discovered that this film is _____ a true story.
5 **A** Did you _____ the race?
   B Yes, and I caught the moment when Tom won! I'll show you later.
6 In these films, George Clooney plays a _____ who wants to steal money from a casino.

c Write notes on three of these topics.

- a famous director from your country
- a famous movie scene that many people remember
- a film based on a book
- a popular character from a film
- a big event that was filmed recently

d 💬 Take turns to talk about the topics in **c**. What else do you know about these things or people?

e ▶ Now go back to p.104

10A Sport

a ⏵**3.35** Label the pictures with the words in the box. Then listen and check.

competitor /kɒmˈpetɪtə/   court /kɔːt/   net /net/   opponents /əˈpəʊnənts/   referee /refəˈriː/   track /træk/

① _____   ② _____   ③ _____

④ _____   ⑤ _____   ⑥ _____

b Underline the word in each group which is not possible.

You can …
1 *win* / *lose* / *beat* / *score* a point.
2 *beat* / *attack* / *score* your opponent.
3 win a *game* / *point* / *match* / *competitor*.
4 *compete for* / *win* / *score* a prize.

c 💬 Discuss the questions.

1 When did you last play in a game or sports match? What happened? Did you win?
2 Do you prefer playing in a team or individually?
3 Are you a competitive person?

d Think of a sport and make notes on these questions.

1 Is it a team sport or an individual sport?
2 How do you play it?
3 Do you need a special place or special equipment?
4 Are there any special rules?
5 Is it a popular sport?

e 💬 Describe your sport but do not say its name. Try to guess your partner's sport.

f ▶ Now turn to p.117

10B Expressions with *do*, *make* and *take*

a Write *do*, *make* or *take* for each group of words.

1 _____ money, a decision, a mistake, progress
2 _____ a risk, advantage of something, a chance
3 _____ sense, a difference, the most of something
4 _____ your homework, (some) research
5 _____ well/badly (e.g. in an exam), your best
6 _____ part in something, care of someone, action
7 _____ a break, a nap, it easy
8 _____ a phone call, new friends easily

b Complete the topics with *do*, *make* or *take*. Then choose five topics and write short answers for each one.

When was the last time you … ?
1 _____ a big risk
2 _____ a difficult decision
3 _____ the most of something
4 _____ it easy
5 _____ an important phone call
6 _____ a new friend
7 _____ well in an exam
8 _____ a stupid mistake
9 _____ advantage of something
10 _____ your best at something

c 💬 Take turns to talk about what happened in each situation in **b**.

d ▶ Now go back to p.121

Unit 1

▶ **1.7**

Four generations – and they all prefer communicating in different ways. There are sure to be misunderstandings and other problems, right? Well, there don't have to be.

OK, so I'm a Millennial – I was born in 1990 – and so being able to connect with people is really important to me. I'm constantly trying to learn, grow and change. And, for me, fast on-screen communication is the best way to do this. I love the way that the internet puts you in touch with all kinds of people you wouldn't meet in everyday life.

Generation X, on the other hand, uses communication to build relationships and develop ideas. This sounds pretty good, but they express their feelings and opinions directly, and aren't afraid to say or write how they feel. My boss is Generation X, and she definitely has an opinion on everything!

And, of course, at home I spend time with Baby Boomers and Veterans. My dad is a typical Baby Boomer. They have a lot in common with Generation X – they can be quite direct about what they think. I don't always agree with his opinions, but I do appreciate his honesty – usually! And Baby Boomers definitely prefer face-to-face communication. My dad's really not very good with emails, social networking or anything like that.

My grandparents are in the generation called Veterans. For them, communication is something that keeps people together and traditions alive. Both Veterans and Baby Boomers take time to talk things over that matter to their job or family, but are not that interested in chatting about personal goals and development.

Understanding these different communication styles is really important for improving our relationships, both at work and at home.

So, for example, one really big difference between us Millennials and the other three generations is that we expect people to tell us – gently – how we're doing. So, I used to get a bit annoyed with my boss for not giving me enough feedback about how things are going at work. But then I realised that other generations don't necessarily notice this difference, so I learnt not to be upset if older people didn't praise me all the time, and I also learnt to ask for help if I needed it.

Similarly, some of us Millennials find it difficult when people criticise us or disagree with us. Generation X and Baby Boomers will tell you clearly if they don't like something. Don't take it personally – although that's often easier said than done!

On a practical level, it can help to use different communication styles with different generations. Pick up the phone, write emails, and make time for face-to-face conversation. When you do, pay attention to your writing style. You might think an informal style is friendly, but to an older person it can seem rude.

Finally, understand that communication differences across generations do exist. So talk about them – with people of all ages. This can open the door to other conversations. You can learn a lot by hearing older people's experiences, and in turn you might be able to teach them about life in the modern world.

▶ **1.10**

1 A Are you OK, James?
 B No, I'm not. I'm absolutely exhausted! I've been speaking Spanish all day!
2 C Hi, Linda. Are you learning Russian?
 D I'm trying to, but this book's useless! It teaches you how to say 'my uncle's black trousers', but not how to say 'hello'!
3 E Hey, guess what? I've just read about this girl, and she's only 10 but she's fluent in several different languages.
 F That's fantastic. I can only speak one language – English.
4 G Listen, Olivier: *squirrel*.
 H *Squi… Squill …* It's impossible! I'll never get it right!
 G No, it's not impossible, just difficult. You need to practise. Try again. Listen: *Squirrel*.
 H *Squi…rrel…*
 G Well done!

▶ **1.14** PART 1

RACHEL Really? Oh, no … the bookshop?! Are you sure? Oh, thanks for letting me know. Yes, see you soon, Jo. Bye.

BECKY Excuse me?
R Oh, sorry! I thought you were just looking.
B Um, I want something for a friend's wife. I'm going there for dinner.
R OK. What sort of flowers does she like?
B Oh, I don't know. I haven't met her yet.
R Right, well, in my opinion, roses are always a good option.
B Um, aren't they a bit romantic?
R Yes, I know what you mean. I guess something like tulips might be better.
B Yes, they're lovely. How much are they? … How much are the tulips?
R Oh, they're … sorry.
B It's OK. I'll try somewhere else. Thank you.
R Hello? Yes. Yes, it is.

▶ **1.15** PART 2

MARK Rachel? You OK?
RACHEL Oh, I'm sorry, love. I'm just a bit worried. Jo phoned today and said that the old bookshop is going to be turned into another florist's.
M The bookshop on the corner? I didn't know they'd sold it.
R Me neither. What am I going to do? It's hard enough already to make money, but I think it's going to be impossible with another florist's in the same street.
M Yeah. Was Jo sure about this?
R I don't know. She seemed pretty certain.
M Well, if you ask me, it's not worth worrying about until we know for sure.
R I know, but I can't help it – it's on my mind. I was even rude to a customer today.
M Really? That's not like you. What happened?
R Well I wasn't exactly rude, just not very helpful.
M Hey, don't worry about it. Let's just forget about work. Personally, I need a relaxing evening!
R Me too!
M Anyway, Tom and Becky will be here in a minute. I think we should check on the food.
R Yes. I don't want anything else to go wrong today. So, what's Becky like?
M That'll be them now!

▶ **1.21** PART 3

MARK Hi! Come in! Hello. Come on in. Rachel, this is Tom and Becky.
TOM Hi, Rachel. Good to meet you.

RACHEL Hi, Tom.

BECKY Hi, Rachel. I think we've met before!

R I'm so sorry about earlier! I had something on my mind.

B Don't worry. Um, I was going to bring you some flowers, but I couldn't get any!

R Thank you.

▶ **1.22**

MARIA How's your revision going?

GILBERTO Not so good. I think I can remember most of the grammar, but remembering vocabulary's a bit harder, for me anyway.

M Yes, there are a lot of words to remember.

G What about you?

M For me, it is probably the opposite – I find the grammar hard to get my head around, but the vocabulary is a lot easier. I've been testing myself at home and it's OK.

G How do you manage to remember all the words, though? What's your secret?

M Well, it's no secret! I have this kind of system for learning words that seems to make it easy …

G OK, what?

M Well, when I get home from class, I record all the new words I've learnt onto my phone. And then I might do something like go for a run, and I listen to them when I'm running. And I make up these sentences with the words and say them to myself.

G As you're running?

M Yes, as I'm running – I just say the sentences quietly to myself.

G Do you remember what the words mean?

M Most of the time. If I forget, I check in my notebook when I get home from my run. And sometimes I play the words and write them down. I think the most important thing is to keep repeating them. I don't know why, but remembering the sounds of the words is important for me. Like, last week I learnt the word 'shine' – you know, like 'the sun is shining'. And that 'sh' sound at the beginning of the word makes me think of light that's getting brighter and brighter.

G Interesting. But I don't know if it would work for me. I need to see things written down. I need to look at the word.

M Right – my sister's like that too. She uses vocabulary cards. Have you tried that?

G No. How does that work?

M She has these small cards and writes all the new words on a card with a picture, or a definition and an example – sometimes a translation too. It worked really well … for a while.

G For a while? Why? What happened?

M She left all the cards on a train.

G Oh, yes. That's probably what I would do!

M I felt so sorry for her – after all that work.

G It sounds like a good idea, but it sounds like you have to be quite organised to have a card system.

M Yes, that's true.

G And, to be honest, I think I'm maybe too lazy to write all those cards and keep them with me wherever I go!

Unit 2

▶ **1.29**

You've got good grades and you've been to lots of interviews, but no one's offered you a job yet. Why? Is it because your knowledge and practical skills aren't right for the job?

Well, according to one careers expert, Nancy Maynard, it's probably because you just haven't got the 'likeability factor'. Likeability is the ability to work well with people. It isn't something you can learn easily at school, but employers want it and they're quick to see it in candidates at interview.

Without likeability, Maynard believes, good grades and practical skills are worth very little. In the first 18 months in a job, most of an employee's success is linked to their likeability, not to how well he or she does the job. Likeability is much more important than other abilities, and anyone who's looking for a job should be trying their hardest to improve their own by spending time with other people.

Advice for job hunters goes like this: apply for the jobs that you want, even if you haven't got the right qualifications. If you get an interview, then impress the interviewers with your 'soft skills'. Soft skills are your personal skills – your friendly personality, your positive attitude to work, your ability to communicate with people and your problem-solving skills. It's simple.

Or is it? Is likeability really more important than knowledge and experience? We took to the streets and asked some people for their opinions.

▶ **1.30**

1 People don't realise how important likeability is because employers don't like to talk about it, so they usually give other reasons for not offering someone a job. But let's be honest, if you're paying someone to do a job, you want them to work well with the people around them.

2 Yes, soft skills and likeability are much more important than specific job skills – like being able to use a computer – for the employer and for yourself too. There's no such thing as 'a job for life' any more. Develop your soft skills – be good at working with other people – and you'll always be able to get work.

3 I've been a doctor since I graduated from medical school. I've worked at this hospital for 18 years. My practical skills and my knowledge are all that matters. Without those, I couldn't do my job. I listen to my patients, but I certainly don't believe that I need to be charming and sociable all the time. I've never believed that.

4 I'm afraid it's true and it makes me angry. I'm 23 and I haven't worked since I left college. The only way to develop soft skills is to work with people, but the only way to get work is to have soft skills. It's a no-win situation.

5 When people talk like this, it makes education and hard work sound second best, and that's simply not true. Yes, you need to be able to make a good first impression, but come on, what really matters is that you can offer practical skills and experience to an organisation, not just a friendly face.

▶ **1.33** **PART 1**

RACHEL Oh, hi Becky!

BECKY Oh, hi Rachel.

B Oh no!

R Oh! Oh Becky, I'm so sorry.

B But why? It was me that knocked it over.

R But I distracted you.

B What, by saying hello? Don't worry about it! It was my fault.

R At least let me get you another orange juice!

RACHEL How's the phone?

BECKY Not good. The screen's frozen.

R Oh dear! Have you tried turning it off and on again?

B I was just doing that, but still nothing.

R What about taking the SIM card out and drying it?

B That's worth a try. Thank you. Oh, I hope I haven't lost all my contacts. I haven't saved them anywhere else.

R Oh no, how awful. Could you take it back to the shop?

B Oh, I don't think they'll do anything. I bought it over a year ago.

R Can you claim on your insurance?

B I don't have any. It's just run out. A week ago!

R How annoying! I know, the other day I read about this trick for fixing phones that have got wet.

B Oh yes?

R They said you put the phone in a bag of rice and apparently it dries it out. You could try that.

B That sounds a bit weird.

R I know, but there were lots of comments from people saying that it had worked.

B OK, I'll give it a try. What have I got to lose?

R Exactly, it's cheaper than buying a new phone!

RACHEL Hello. *Fantastic Flowers.*

BECKY Hi Rachel, it's Becky.

R Oh, hi Becky. How are you?

B I'm good and guess what? My phone's working. That rice trick worked.

R That's brilliant! I'm really glad to hear that.

LIN Have you done that presentation yet?

TANIA Yeah, I did it yesterday.

L How did it go?

T Well, you know, the usual thing: I presented my ideas, everyone smiled and thanked me and then said nothing.

L So they didn't even give their opinion?

T No, but I could see they didn't like the idea. The problem with the company I work for is that they're continuing to use the same ideas and aren't thinking enough about new markets. They're not thinking enough about the phone app market at all.

L Isn't that why they employed you?

T That's what I thought. I mean, I've been working there for just over a year now and they haven't said yes to any

of my ideas. When they offered me the job, they said things like, 'Oh yes, we're very interested in your creative thinking and your problem-solving skills', but do they really want to use them? I get the feeling they don't.

L That must be very disappointing.

T I think I've more or less decided. I'm going to look for a new job.

L Really?

T Yeah, it's getting hard to keep having a positive attitude.

L I can understand that. And I thought your app idea was a really good one.

T Thanks. So what do you think about Hong Kong?

L Hong Kong? Why there?

T Well, I'm thinking about making a big change.

L What? Going to live in Hong Kong?

T Yeah, well, you decided to come and live here – maybe I can do the opposite.

L Wow! That's a very big change.

T I want to travel more and I'm really interested in Chinese culture – I'd love to find out more about it.

L Well, yes, everyone says there are plenty of IT jobs in Hong Kong, but it's a bit of a crazy city.

T Well, it could be fun!

Unit 3

CHARLOTTE When people find out I'm a twin, they generally ask the same questions: What's it like? Can you read each other's thoughts? Can people tell you apart? Do you do everything together?

It's true that I often know what Megan is thinking or feeling, but that's because we grew up together and we're very close. We're no different from ordinary sisters.

But if you look at photos of us when we were younger, even I can't say which one is me. We used to look absolutely identical. And Mum says we didn't use to talk much when we were playing together – we seemed to know what each other was thinking.

I guess as we grew up we wanted to create our own unique identities. I remember at school Megan used to dress as differently from me as she could. I went through a phase of wearing lots of black and looking quite messy. So of course, Megan started wearing flowery dresses!

We used to have a lot of arguments as teenagers but now we're really good

friends. We usually speak on the phone two or three times a day, and we get together as often as we can. So, what's it like to have a twin? It's great – you have a best friend for life!

MEGAN Charlotte and I had a wonderful childhood. We did everything together. I had my best friend with me 24/7 and we used to be very close. She had a brilliant imagination and used to invent wonderful stories. Of course, we played the usual twin jokes. At school, we used to swap clothes and confuse the teachers. I'm not sure they even noticed some of the time – we looked so similar that even our parents used to mix us up.

We didn't use to argue much, but in our teenage years we started to grow apart. We were trying to find our own identity, I think, and we each made a different group of friends. Later on, we went to universities in different towns. But it turned out that you can never escape being a twin. After our first year away, we hadn't seen each other for six months. The day we went home, we saw that we'd both cut all our hair off!

These days, I think we have quite different personalities. Charlotte is very kind and caring, but often forgets things and gets lost. I'm a bit more confident and organised. But we still have lots in common – we both love beach holidays, playing football and we both complain about our hair!

PAULA Hi, Mark. Hi, Tom.

MARK Hi, Paula.

TOM Hi!

M We're still meeting at 10, right?

P Yes, we are. We're in meeting room 3, I think. See you in there?

T Yep!

M See you in a minute.

T Coffee?

M Yes, please.

T So, did you have a good weekend?

M It was good, thanks. But you won't believe what I did.

T What?

M Remember I told you my dad wanted a desk for his new office? And I offered to help him find one online?

T Oh yeah?

M Well, I found one. It looked perfect, exactly what I was looking for. It was a fantastic price too.

T Sounds good.

M Exactly, so I ordered it.

T Great!

M And it arrived on Saturday. But, the funny thing is, it was really, really small.

T How small?

M It only came up to my knees!

T Eh?

M It turned out I'd ordered a desk for a child.

T No way!

M Mm-mm! I forgot to check the measurements on the website!

T So, what did you do?

▶ **1.50** PART 2

TOM So, what did you do?

MARK Well, I phoned the company to explain, and luckily they agreed to give me a refund.

T Really? That was very good of them.

M Yeah, it was. But anyway, I still had to find a desk. I was looking everywhere, but I couldn't find anything. In the end, Rachel suggested I try one of those freecycling websites.

T Freecycling? What's that?

M It's where people get rid of stuff they don't want any more. I've never heard of it either. But there are a couple of websites for this area. I found the perfect desk straight away – and the best thing is, it's free.

T It's free?

M Yeah, I think the owner doesn't have enough space for it, so he's just giving it away. So all I have to do is go and pick it up.

T Wow! That's good. And you're sure it's the right size this time?

M Ha-ha. Yeah, I double-checked the measurements this time.

P Guys!

M Oh, sorry, Paula! It's my fault. I was just explaining to Tom about my desk mix-up.

▶ **1.53**

BRYAN It's a shame we don't know much about our grandfather, isn't it? Mom used to love talking about him and Grandma. She always used to tell so many interesting stories about them. But I've got no idea where or when they met.

SUSIE Yeah. Well, I know he was born in England.

B Who, Grandad? Yes, I know. And he wanted to go out and see the world, didn't he? That's why he went to train as a chef – so he could get work on a ship.

S What kind of ship?

B Cruise ships. And that was before the war. Some time in the 1930s.

S Oh, right.

B He loved travelling and that was the best way to see the world if you didn't have a lot of money back then.

S So, how did he meet Gran? She was a nurse, wasn't she? And how did they both end up in Canada?

B I … I don't know. I guess we'll have to do some research!

Unit 4
▶ **1.54**

PRESENTER That was Rimsky-Korsakov's *Flight of the Bumblebee*, a piece which was recently performed to a live audience on TV by a six-year-old boy called Tsung Tsung. Tsung Tsung could play the piano when he was three. At the age of five, an internet clip with him at the piano made him famous. Now, he says, he wants to be able to play like Mozart. Our question today is: Do we have to start young to succeed? We've all heard about kids like Tsung Tsung, bright kids who have a particular ability in, say, music, maths or science. But do they grow up to be successful adults? And if you're over 30 and you haven't achieved your goals yet, is it too late? Ed Bickley's been looking into it for us. Ed, what have you found out?

ED OK, well, clearly some talented children go on to do very well as adults. Take Lionel Messi. He started playing football on the street at the age of five. Soon, he was playing against much older boys – and they couldn't get the ball off him. He was so good that he was able to join the Barcelona junior team when he was 11, and achieved international success at 20. Now he's one of the greatest players in the world!

P A real success story!

E Yes. But what's surprising is that most of these talented children when they grow up don't actually achieve much more than other adults. A recent study followed a group of talented children from 1974 until now. Less than 5% managed to become very successful adults.

P That does seem surprising.

E And now for the good news! If you haven't achieved your goals by the time you're 30, don't give up! Plenty of people have found success much later in life. British fashion designer Vivienne Westwood's first job was in teaching. She always wanted to be a designer, but her successful fashion career didn't begin until she was 30 when she started making clothes for a shop in London called *Let it Rock*. Then there's Andrea Bocelli. He's been able to sing well since he was a child, but he didn't become a famous classical singer until he was

36. At 41, his album became the most successful classical album by a solo artist of all time, with 5 million copies sold around the world.

P So to do well at something, we don't have to be good at it at a young age?

E That's right. In most cases, talent develops with experience. You need to practise, make mistakes, get frustrated, learn from your mistakes, practise more … it's hard work. You need a lot of patience, a lot of determination. Confidence and a positive attitude help, too. Say to yourself, 'I can do it!' And just maybe you will! And don't worry if your 10-year-old child can't play the piano. Maybe they'll be able to do it when they're a bit older.

P Ed, you've given us all hope! Thank you very much.

▶ **1.61** PART 1

BECKY And these are the photos. You haven't seen the ones of our holiday, have you?

RACHEL No, I haven't. Oh, wow! That's a great photo. That's the hotel you stayed in, isn't it?

B Yes. And there's the beach. It was only a few metres from the hotel.

R Wow, Becky, these are really good.

B Thanks. I enjoyed taking them.

R They're amazing. Actually, can I ask a big favour? You know I'm making a new website, don't you? Well, I need some photos of the shop for it. Do you think you could take them?

B Hmm, I'm not sure. I'm not a real photographer. It's just a hobby.

R But I really love your pictures. Will you do it?

B Well, if you're sure. I'd love to.

R Great!

B So, Mark, Tom told me about your internet shopping mistake. You bought a child's desk instead of an adult one, didn't you?

MARK It was an easy mistake to make – could have happened to anyone! Anyway, it all turned out well in the end. Actually, I'm going to get the desk on Saturday.

B Oh, do you need a hand? I'm sure Tom will help.

TOM Oh yeah? You'll need a bit of muscle!

R It would be great if you could, wouldn't it, Mark?

M Yeah, I was wondering how I was going to move it on my own.

T Why not? But could I ask you a favour in return, Rachel?

R Yes, of course. What?

T I'll tell you later.

RACHEL So, what do you need?

TOM Well, I'm going to ask Becky to marry me.

R Wow, that is great news!

T Thanks, but I wondered if you could come with me to buy the ring. I've never done this before and I don't know where to start.

R Yes of course I could. Oh, that is brilliant.

B What are you two gossiping about?

T Oh, nothing!

MARK Go on. Pull it a bit harder.

TOM I can't, it's too heavy!

M We're almost there. Go on.

T No, it's not going to work.

M All right. Put it down.

T What's it made of?

M Metal.

T Let's do it together, both sides. Ready?

M All right. One, two, three … No, put it down, put it down.

T Let's move it across.

M All right. Ready? One, two, three…

T Job done.

SHEENA Last year, I had some free time and a bit of money to spend. I'd always wanted to go walking and climbing in the Himalayas, but I didn't want to go on my own and none of my friends wanted to go. So I found a website called *Travel Groups*, where you can contact other people who want to go to the same places as you, and you can join up and go together as a group. Anyway, I found three other people to go with and we all met in Delhi in north India and we travelled together. It worked out really well. I think websites like this are a good idea because lots of people don't want to travel on their own, and it works as long as everyone's reasonably sociable. I'm quite self-confident and I think I'm an extrovert, so I think I'm quite good at getting on with people and making friends.

ALYA I had a few months off after university, so I looked on the internet for volunteer work and found a really good website for last-minute volunteer jobs called the *Volunteer Community Project*. It was good because you can arrange things straight away and they pay your fares, and you get basic accommodation and food. You don't earn money, but you don't really spend much either. I went to London and worked there with young children from problem families. I didn't have any experience, but that doesn't matter. You just need to be able to get on with kids and understand what they need. I never realised before, but actually, it seems like I've got a natural talent for teaching children. So it was a really great experience and now I've decided to train as a primary school teacher.

BRAD I really needed to earn some money and I couldn't get a proper job. Someone told me about this website called *Short Work*, where people offer short jobs for a few days or a couple of weeks that they need doing, like helping out with things or fixing things for people. I'm quite good at things like that, and I know a bit about electricity and plumbing. I found this advert for a family who've got a large house and needed someone to do some basic work on it. So I went along and chatted to them, and they gave me the job. I think they could see that I was quite serious about it and I was determined to work hard. It was really good – I was only there for two weeks, but in that time I managed to clear their garden, mend their garden fence, I painted three rooms for them, and I got their kitchen light working. So not bad for two weeks' work!

Unit 5

PHIL Are they environmentally friendly in Costa Rica? Do they protect their rainforests and animals?

MASHA Well, yes they do. The government is doing a lot, but it takes quite a long time for forests to recover if they've already been cut down. They'll probably grow back, but not immediately.

P Are you going to work in the rainforests?

M No, no I'm not. I'll be by the sea. I'm going to work on a project that looks after turtles.

P Turtles? That's very cool. But how do you look after turtles, I mean, what do you do?

M Well, to be honest – I don't really know! Tomorrow I'm meeting someone who worked on the project, and she's going to tell me about the kinds of things I'm going to do.

P So, who else works on the project? Just people from overseas or local people too?

M I'm not sure about that either. Perhaps I'll work with local people as well.

P So, you're off to save the world. I think that's great.

M Don't know about saving the world. But I'll definitely be able to save some turtles! And I'm going to make the most of my time in Costa Rica and learn some Spanish too.

P Let me know how things go.

M Sure. Actually, I'm going to keep a blog, so I'll write regular updates on the blog and you can follow that.

P Good idea. I'm sure you'll have a great time.

M Yeah, so am I.

PRESENTER I visited biologist Andrew Parker to find out more about how the natural world has inspired everyday objects. Andrew, hello! What's this little animal you've got here?

ANDREW It's a thorny dragon lizard from the Australian desert. As you can see, it's quite small, about 20cm long. But it's an amazing animal. You see, what I'm really interested in is what this little creature can teach us about collecting water.

P OK.

A So, as I said, this lizard lives in the desert in Australia. And, as you know, it's an incredibly dry place. But this lizard manages to live there very successfully. And we've discovered one of the reasons for this. If the lizard puts a foot somewhere wet – even just a tiny, tiny bit wet – its skin pulls the water up and over its whole body. When the water reaches the lizard's mouth, it drinks it.

P That's very clever!

A Yes. On the lizard's skin, well, in fact, in the skin, we discovered there's like a system of very, very small pipes. So the skin collects the water and these pipes pull it towards the lizard's mouth.

P That sounds really efficient.

A Well, right, yeah. So, you see, we want to copy that system and use it in a device that collects water. If we are successful, the device will provide water for people who live in very dry environments.

P That's fantastic. And what other ideas have we taken from nature?

A Engineers are doing a lot with robots these days. For example, there's the rescue robot. It's just like a spider because it moves on eight legs. And so it can move very quickly and make itself very small. So these rescue robots will be able to help people who are stuck in small spaces, or who are trapped in buildings, for example, if there's an earthquake.

P So they'll be able to help save lives.

A Exactly. And then we're looking at seashells, which are very strong, but, at the same time, they're very light – they don't weigh much at all. Scientists have discovered that seashells are made of lots of tiny blocks that fit together, but this makes them really hard to break. The plan is to copy this material to make safety equipment such as gloves and helmets.

P So this material will protect people like a shell protects a turtle.

A That's right. And again, this could help save lives.

▶ 2.14 PART 1

BECKY Hi!

RACHEL Oh hi, Becky.

B How are you?

R I'm fine, thanks.

B So, are you ready for your photo shoot?

R Ha! I guess so.

B The shop looks great!

R Oh, that's because of Tina. She spent the morning cleaning up!

B Well, she did a great job. So Tina, are you going to be in the photos too?

TINA No! I hate having my photo taken!

B I see! Anyway, if you're ready.

R Make sure you get my good side!

B You look great!

R Thank you! So, how do you want to do this?

B Let me see. I think it would be best if I just take some natural shots of you looking busy with the flowers.

R OK.

B Hmm! That's really good!

R Oh, shall I carry on?

B Yes, that's great. So, why did you become a florist?

R That's a good question. I've always loved flowers, ever since I was a little girl, so it seemed a natural thing for me to do. I think it's really important that you do something that you enjoy.

B Fantastic! Yeah, it must be nice to have a job like yours, the freedom you have, and you can be creative, and you're your own boss.

R You sound like you don't enjoy your job.

B No, not at the moment. Not for a while, actually.

R Really? What's wrong with it?

B Oh, lots of things. For instance, all I seem to do is deal with other people's problems, like issues with their pay or holidays. And I hate being stuck inside an office all day, staring at the clock.

R Oh dear!

B I wish I had a job where I could travel the world, spread my wings, be free!

R Such as?

B I don't know, that's the problem. … Lovely!

R Can I see?

B Sure. Here you go.

R Hmm! That's great.

B Thank you.

R Well, how about becoming a professional photographer? You're really good!

B I don't know. Tina, how about a quick shot of you and Rachel together?

T Do I have to?

B Oh, go on! Just stand by Rachel for a moment.

▶ 2.16 PART 2

RACHEL So, look at this. There are loads of photography courses you can do. Photojournalism, for example, or portrait photography.

BECKY Thanks, that's great, but we're meant to be choosing which photos you want for your website.

R OK, but I just think it's something that you should consider.

B Well, maybe. Let's look at the photos for now.

MARK Hey, Becky. These are great!

B Thank you!

R I think this is the best one.

B Rachel, we can't see you in that one!

R OK, let me see. … I think this one.

▶ 2.21

LIZ I'm on my way to Lane Cove where between 20 and 30 whales have come ashore and can't get back out to sea again. When I get to Lane Cove, I'm meeting Sam Collins from the Marine Life Service. I'm going to help Sam and a team of local people to try and save these whales.

OK, I've just arrived and talked to Sam. It's quite cold, so I think I'll change into my wetsuit before going down on to the beach to work with other people who've come here to help these whales. So far about 50 people have turned up and more are coming. If more people come, we'll have a chance of succeeding.

So, I'm in a team of four people and we're looking after just one poor whale. Sam says it's female, and what we've done is we've covered her with wet towels and we're pouring buckets of water over her to keep her cool. We have to be careful where we put the towels. If we cover her blowhole, she won't be able to breathe. Sam says our whale's in good condition and he thinks she'll survive. The tide's coming in soon. I'm going to help dig up sand around the whale to make a hole. When the water comes in, it'll fill up the hole. Better get going …

Yes! Success! The tide came in and our whale floated again. There were about five of us. We pushed and pushed and she fought back a bit, then she took off. What a great feeling! She's swimming back out to sea. I think she's going to be OK.

Unit 6
▶ 2.23

HARRY Hi, Mel!

MEL Ah, There you are! Hi.

GEMMA We were just talking about that programme last night – that *Toughest Place to Be*… Did you see it?

M No, why?

H It was about this London taxi driver …

G Mason something.

H … and he went to Mumbai. It looks like a nightmare – really, really busy roads, and people and cars all over the place! And people – even little kids – walking through the traffic.

M So, what? Did the guy have to be a taxi driver in Mumbai? I've seen some of that series. It's such a culture shock for the people when they discover how different their job is somewhere else.

G Yeah. This one was good. Mason was a very likeable guy, you know, and he got on really well with Pradeep, the guy who showed him around. You really wanted him to do OK, and he did in the end. He didn't find it easy, though. He'd spent about three years in London learning all the street names and where everything was. And then he only had a week in Mumbai to learn the job. And apart from anything else, it was so hot.

M Yeah, I can imagine.

H He drove two different cars and neither of them were 'cool cabs' – that's what they call the taxis there with air conditioning – and the temperature was over 40°, so he was finding it really difficult. And in the old car he had to use hand signals instead of lights to indicate left and right.

M Bit different from London! And did he manage on his own OK?

H Yes, it was amazing, actually. He learned how to get around the city pretty quickly, and he did all right when he went out on his own. He picked up a few phrases of the local language and of course a lot of people in India speak English.

M Mm-hmm.

H But there's a lot of competition, so he had to work really hard to get passengers.

M I guess that's true for all taxi drivers in Mumbai.

G Well, yeah. It was clear that taxi drivers in Mumbai have to work very hard and don't earn much money. Pradeep works 15 hours a day to support his family and his brother's family, and only earns about £10 a day. When Mason went back to London, he collected money to send to Pradeep and his family.

M Wow, that's really good of him.

H Yeah, so, anyway, I guess we should check out the menu …

▶ **2.30**

PRESENTER Japan has by far the highest number of vending machines per person in the world. In fact it has 5.6 million – that's one vending machine for every 20 people. These machines sell all sorts of things, from coffee to bananas, flowers and umbrellas. In a busy society, they play an important role. It's much cheaper for sellers to run a vending machine than a shop. And customers can buy things more quickly and easily from a machine than in a shop.

And we're not talking here just about drinks and cold snacks. Japan also has vending machines that serve hot food, like instant noodles. Japanese students love curry and rice, it's one of the most popular meals there, and, sure enough, you can get it from a machine. The meal comes out of the machine hot and ready to eat. It's more convenient than cooking at home. But is curry and rice from a machine as good as curry and rice from a restaurant? Our reporter Luke went to central Tokyo to find out.

LUKE OK, I've just put my 300 yen into the vending machine and I'm waiting for my curry and rice to appear. Hmm, it's taking a bit longer than I imagined. OK, so my meal is here. I just have to open the packet of steamed rice. Hmm … the curry smells, well, it smells OK, like a lot of instant curries. Right, let me go and find somewhere to sit down and try it. OK, this will do. Well, this is fine. It's

actually much better than I expected. What can I say? I think it might be the best vending machine meal I've ever eaten – just not the best curry I've ever eaten! For 300 yen – that's less than two pounds – I can't really complain. But I think next time I'll spend a bit more and go to a proper restaurant!

▶ **2.33** PART 1

RACHEL Hi, am I late?

TOM No, you're right on time.

R So, are you ready to go shopping? I am so excited! I still can't believe you're going to ask Becky to marry you.

T Well, I've been thinking about that.

R Oh no! Don't tell me that you've changed your mind!

T Oh no, not at all. I just don't know how to do it.

R What do you mean?

T Well, do you think I should take her somewhere special?

R Um, yes!

T Maybe Paris? I was thinking I could propose at the top of the Eiffel Tower.

R Wow! Just like in the movies!

T Do you think that's too much?

R No, but is it what Becky would really like?

T Um, I just don't know. What do you suggest?

R Well, if I were you, I'd take her somewhere special.

T Exactly, like Paris.

R I mean special for the two of you! Like Mark took me to the place where we first met. It was really romantic, because he'd clearly thought about it. Where did you two first meet?

T At the office where we both worked.

R Oh OK, but there must be somewhere special.

T Hmm, maybe. How about the restaurant where we had our first date?

R Now that sounds like a possibility. Anyway, let's go and look for this ring.

▶ **2.34** PART 2

TOM So what about the ring? What would you buy? A big diamond, right? So she can show it to her friends?

RACHEL Seriously? Tom, do you know Becky at all? It's much better to buy something that's her style. Something that you think she'll like. She doesn't need to show off.

T I'm getting this all wrong!

R That's why I'm here. Come on.

R How about that ring?

T Oh, that's a nice one.

R It's £1500.

T I don't believe it! That's ridiculous.

R Tom! It's Becky! Over there.

T You're kidding! What should we do?

R Quick! Let's go in.

▶ **2.37**

JEFF I like eating out, but I don't really like expensive restaurants. It's not the money so much as the atmosphere. The waiters are often quite unfriendly and you feel you have to talk quietly, or I do anyway. No one seems to be very relaxed. And the food can be good, but you don't often get much on your plate. I'd much rather go somewhere where the food's good and you don't have to pay so much.

FABIO I love going to cafés, either with friends or on my own. I sometimes take a book or a newspaper to read, or I just order a coffee and sit there. I sometimes start talking to someone, in fact I've got quite a good friend who I met in a café. We started talking and then found out we both liked the same kind of music. I like pavement cafés best. You don't have to think about anything, you can just sit and watch the world go by. It's a great way to pass time I think, very relaxing.

CARLA I really love dancing, so I often go out with a group of friends to a club in the evening. It's such a good way to spend the evening. We usually order some food, maybe just some starters and some grilled meat, and something to drink, and then we start dancing. There's a favourite place of mine where they have live music and we all dance Latin American dances like *salsa* or *merengue*. It's quite cheap. You have to pay something to get in, but it's not much and it's always full of people, maybe 200 people all dancing. It's got an amazing atmosphere.

Unit 7

▶ **2.38**

1 Well, it's very small so it can't belong to a big family, maybe a small family or an older couple who live on their own. Where is it? It's somewhere dry and sunny, so it could be Mexico, maybe, or Spain.

2 There can't be much space in there, so I think it must belong to a single person or a couple. And where is it? It could be in any big city, but on the outskirts of the city, I think. It might be somewhere like Tokyo, where land's expensive so you can't build big houses. It might not be a house, it might be two

separate flats. No, they can't be flats, the ground floor one is too small, so it must be a house.

3 You can see tall buildings outside the window, so this flat must be somewhere like Dubai or some modern city. Whoever lives there can't have children, it's much too tidy. It might be someone who works a lot, or someone who doesn't spend much time there.

4 It's a huge house, so a very big family must live there, or maybe two or three different families. Or it might be a holiday home because it's in the mountains somewhere. It could be Switzerland or Austria, or perhaps Slovenia. Somewhere in Europe.

▶ 2.44

TIM What are you reading?

KATE Fran just sent me the link to this list of five reasons why small towns are better than cities.

T Ha-ha!

K What are you laughing at? Small towns are better than cities.

T Yes, if you want to have nothing to do and never meet anyone new!

K Well, I loved growing up in a small town. There's a real sense of community. People care about you. It's like you belong to one big family.

T Yes, I know you liked it. But I've always been a city boy. I love being in the centre of things – there's so much going on here. Cinemas, restaurants, museums. And there are lots more work opportunities in big cities than in a small town.

K But there's also more crime. Life's more dangerous here.

T Actually, research has shown that it's actually safer to live in the city.

K Really? I find that hard to believe.

T Yes, they did a study in the US that compared the number of accidents in country and city areas. And in the country there was a much higher number of accidents than in the city. Car crashes mainly, because people drive more in the countryside.

K That makes sense if you think about it. And hospitals are nearer, I suppose, so you get help quicker.

T Exactly. So it's actually safer to live in the city. And it's better for the environment.

K Really? How do you work that out?

T Well, you can't rely on public transport in the countryside like you can in the city, so you have to drive more. It's been proved that if you live in the city, you

actually have a smaller carbon footprint, especially if you live somewhere with good public transport.

K I've definitely noticed that I walk more now I live in the city. Everything's closer, I guess. And it is nice not to have to get into the car just to go to a supermarket.

T You see! There are a lot of advantages to living in a city. You can't argue with that.

K No, I can't – there are definitely advantages. But I still miss my little home town.

▶ 2.50 PART 1

BECKY Do I look OK, Tom?

TOM You look great! You've got nothing to worry about.

B Oh, I really hope your parents like me.

T Of course they will. You'll be fine! After you, go on. … Dad, this is Becky.

MICHAEL Hello, Becky. I'm Michael. It's very nice to meet you.

B Nice to meet you.

T And this is my mum, Charlotte.

CHARLOTTE Hello! It's lovely to meet you at last!

B Oh, you too!

C Thank you. They're lovely.

M Take a seat, Becky.

B Oh, thank you.

C Would you excuse me for a moment? I just need to check on the food.

B Of course. Is there anything we can do to help?

C Oh no, it's all under control!

B So, Martin …

T Michael!

B Er, Michael. I expect you're excited about the match this afternoon.

M I'm not really a football fan, to be honest. I prefer golf.

B Oh, I see.

C Tom, do you think you could give me a hand in here?

T Sure.

M So, do you play golf?

B No.

B So Caroline, Tom tells me you're an architect. That must be very interesting.

C Oh, er, yes, I really enjoy it. In fact, at the moment, I'm working on –

M Here we go.

B Oh, this looks delicious.

M It's my own recipe.

B What's in it?

M It's chicken and mushroom.

B Oh. Um …

M Is something wrong?

T She's a vegetarian!

B And I'm allergic to mushrooms.

C What? Tom, why didn't you tell us?

T I sent you an email yesterday. Didn't you see it?

M Oh no, we didn't!

C I'm really sorry, Becky. Let me get you something else.

B Oh no, Caroline, it's fine, really. Is it OK if I just have some bread and butter?

C No, we can do better than that. I'll get you a green salad.

B Oh OK, that would be lovely. Thanks.

T Becky, my mum's name is Charlotte, not Caroline!

B Oh no! How embarrassing!

▶ 2.51 PART 2

TOM Listen, I know today hasn't gone very well.

MICHAEL What do you mean?

T Well, Becky kept getting your names wrong. And she didn't eat the food you made.

M Oh, don't worry about that. It wasn't her fault. Becky seems really great.

T You really think so?

M Yes, of course.

T Well, I'm really happy to hear that, because, well, I'm thinking of asking her to marry me.

M Really? But that's great!

▶ 2.55

JON So you're going to Florida, Sue. Lucky you! It must be nice and warm – not like here.

SUE Yes, it's about 30°, I think.

J I'm so jealous! Where are you staying? In a hotel?

S No, we've got an apartment near Miami Beach, with a swimming pool. It actually belongs to my cousin, but she's going to New York so she said we can use it while she's away. And her car.

J And her car? Wow, she must like you a lot!

S Well, yes, it's really generous of her. It means we're just paying for the flight. We couldn't afford it otherwise, not with the four of us.

J So, what are you going to do? Are you going to travel around?

S Well, it depends on the weather. It's hurricane season so it might be quite windy. But we'll probably go to the beach for a start – we all like swimming. Then Mia, my daughter, she's really into wildlife, so she wants to go to the Everglades and see the alligators, so we'll definitely do that. And of course we're going to have to go to Disney World for a day. I don't really want to, but Mark – that's my son – he wants to go there, and he wants to go on all the rides.

J Oh, come on, it might be fun. You'll enjoy it.

S Yes, I might.

J Sounds like you're going to be busy, anyway.

S Yeah. Oh, and my husband says we've got to go to Cape Canaveral – he wants to see the Apollo space rockets, so I guess we'll spend a couple of days doing that. I don't really want to go there. It's so far away, I'm not sure I can cope with so much driving. But there's no point in arguing with him about it. Once he gets an idea in his head …

J So, you're doing everything your family wants. What about you? What do you want to do?

S Me? Oh, I'd just like to relax and do nothing – sit by the pool and read a few books.

J Well, it sounds like you're going to be too busy. You won't have time for that.

S No …

Unit 8

▶ 3.7

ERICA How do you like the sound of this restaurant, Harry? Have a look at the reviews.

HARRY Hmm. *Oscar's* restaurant, mostly five stars, 'One of the best places to eat in Britain', 'Magical place' …

E Sounds pretty good, doesn't it?

H Yeah? Why?

E There's only one problem. It doesn't exist! Lots of people read those reviews and wanted to go there. But when they tried to book a table, there was no response.

H Uh?

E People even went there to see if they could find it. But all they found was an empty street full of rubbish bins. Because the whole thing is a joke, a hoax, and there is actually no restaurant at all.

H So someone made it up, made the whole restaurant up, and then wrote reviews about it?

E Yeah, exactly.

H But why would someone do that, go to all that trouble?

E Well, apparently it was this businessman. He had a friend who owned a hotel. Another hotel owner wrote lots of bad reviews about the friend's hotel, and the hotel lost a lot of business and had financial problems because of the fake reviews. So this businessman wanted to make a point about online reviews.

H About how they can damage people's businesses?

E Exactly. He wanted to show that, really, anyone can write their opinion about anything online and a lot of people will believe it.

H Wow! I never knew these review sites had so much power.

E Yeah, they do. And I think this guy made a really good point. There should be much more control over which reviews are posted. People shouldn't just be able to write anything they like.

H Actually now I read these reviews again, they're not very realistic, are they? And all these fake reviewers have only written one review on the website. So yes, of course, they're all fake reviewers. Yes, it's obvious. I would have spotted that if I'd had more time to look at them.

E Ahem. Yes, of course.

▶ 3.9

1 HAIRDRESSER So I was thinking, maybe we could go for a much shorter style this time? What do you think? Something very different, really short.

WOMAN Yes, yes, really short! Do it!

H If you like, I can use this new product on your hair this time. It's very good. It'll make the cut a bit more expensive, though.

W Oh, no. No thanks.

2 WOMAN Here are the keys. It's been fantastic. Thank you.

RECEPTIONIST That's good to hear. Don't forget to write a review on our website when you get home!

W Yes, we will. We'll give you excellent feedback, don't worry!

3 WAITER Here's your bill.

WOMAN I'm sorry, but I'm not going to pay for the dessert. It was terrible.

WA But you ate it, madam.

WO Well yes, but …

WA Then you have to pay for it, madam.

WO But it wasn't …

WA Would you like me to get the manager?

▶ 3.11 PART 1

MARK Hi!

RACHEL Hi! What are you doing here?

M I left work a bit early, so I brought you some cakes.

R Really? Thank you! I was just getting hungry, actually. I haven't even had lunch yet. We've been really busy today.

M Well, that's good.

R Yes, yes it is.

M Are you still worried about that new florist's opening up down the road?

R Yes, kind of. I just don't know whether there's enough business around here for two places.

M Hmm. And have you heard anything from Becky? She's got her interview today, right?

R Yes, she should be there right now. I hope it goes well – she really wants a place on that course.

BEN And finally, what kind of photos do you enjoy taking the most? You have a couple of portraits in your portfolio.

BECKY Well, taking portraits can be really rewarding, especially if the person likes the final photo. But I think, on the whole, I prefer taking action shots – sport and that sort of thing. It's so satisfying when you manage to take the photo at just the right moment.

BEN OK, well that's all the questions I have. Do you have any questions for me?

B Actually, yes, I do. The course description mentions a work placement. Could you tell me a little more about that?

BEN Of course. It tends to either be working at a local gallery on a photography exhibition or working with a professional photographer as an assistant. The placement generally lasts two weeks and normally happens during the holidays.

B OK, and there are trips abroad too, aren't there?

BEN Yes, typically each class has two opportunities to go on study visits per year. Last year they went to Paris and Berlin to see exhibitions. In Berlin, they even had a private question and answer session with the photographer.

B That sounds fantastic.

TOM So, how did it go?

B Yeah. Pretty well I think, on the whole. But it was much more difficult than I thought it was going to be. I was there around two hours.

T Wow.

B Yeah. There was one question I didn't know how to answer, but otherwise, yeah, pretty well.

T What was the question?

B Oh, it was something about my opinion of a famous photographer. I'm not very good with that sort of thing.

T Don't worry. Surely that's what the course is for. Did you find out much about the course?

B Yeah, he told me quite a lot about it. It looks great. There's a job placement where we get to work with professional photographers. And the university itself seems really nice.

T When will you find out if you have a place?

B Well, normally they don't tell you during the interview, but the tutor said they'd be in touch this week.

▶ 3.13 PART 2

MARK Hi Tina, how are you?

TINA Hi Mark, I'm good, thanks. Listen, I just saw Sam from the newsagent's. Apparently that new shop's not going to be a florist's. It's going to be a clothes shop.

RACHEL Really?

TINA Really!

M That's brilliant.

R Yes, that's fantastic news. Though of course we'd have had no problem with a bit of competition!

BECKY Thank you. I've got an email from the university. Tom, I've got a place. They've accepted me on the course.

TOM Wow, that's fantastic. I knew they would!

B Oh, I'm so excited, I can't wait to start.

T We should celebrate!

B We should, but first I have to phone Rachel. After all, it was all her idea in the first place.

B Hi, Rachel. I've got some fantastic news!

R So have I! You first!

▶ 3.17

People were commenting online recently about an 11-year-old boy from Manchester in England, who flew to Rome on his own. He was out shopping with his mother at a shopping centre near Manchester Airport, and while she was busy looking at something, he slipped away and walked into the airport. Of course he had no money or anything, he was only 11 years old, but he followed a family who were going on holiday and no one noticed him – everyone thought he was part of that family.

Incredibly, he managed to get through security. It seems that no one noticed he didn't have a boarding pass, and they even let him get on the plane. Normally, of course, they check your boarding pass when you get on, but I guess they just thought he was with the family. Anyway, they let him on and he found an empty seat somewhere. They normally count the passengers to make sure they've got the right number, but it seems either they didn't do it this time or they didn't do it properly, so the plane took off and he flew to Rome. Then luckily, when he got to Rome they found out he was on his own without a passport and they put him on the next flight back to Manchester. Naturally, his mother was extremely worried about him and she complained about it. Both the airline and the airport admitted it was their fault straight

away and they promised to look at their security. And they even offered her a free flight.

It's incredible that he managed to get through all the airport security controls without them noticing. But apparently, it happens quite often, and it's nearly always boys of about that age, between 11 and 14, who want to go on a plane.

Unit 9

▶ 3.21

ELLIE Nick, it's time to talk about cinema.

NICK OK.

E Yeah, the thing is I have a bit of a problem with films these days.

N What's that?

E Well, I'm getting a bit sick and tired of all the CGI. You know, I go to watch a drama, or an action film – and it just doesn't look real. It's the directors! They just seem to focus so much on cool special effects – they forget about the story. Think about classic films like *Casablanca*. They had absolutely no special effects. Just good story-telling, good characters, good acting.

N But Ellie, even *Casablanca* has special effects. You know those scenes where they're driving through the streets of Paris – well, that wasn't Paris – it was all filmed in a studio in California! I think CGI is a fantastic tool for directors. Nowadays we can tell stories that wouldn't have been possible 50 years ago. *The Hobbit*, *The Life of Pi*, even *Star Wars*. You couldn't make any of them without special effects.

E But still … I really think special effects are used so much more than necessary. Take Christopher Nolan …

N Christopher Nolan who made the Batman films? And *Inception*? He uses loads of special effects!

E Yes, but he only uses them when he really has to. When he was making *Inception*, he filmed in six different countries to get the different scenes he needed. And remember that fight scene in the room that was moving and turning?

N Oh yes, I do.

E Well, that wasn't done with special effects. They made a room that actually moved around. Leonardo DiCaprio and Joseph Gordon-Levitt had to fight in it.

N Wow, I didn't know that.

E Impressive, right?

N OK, yes, that's clever. But I think that just shows that good directors can have good actors and a good story and they can also use modern technology.

And when the technology is used with imagination and creativity, the results can be amazing. Really spectacular.

▶ 3.25

ANNIE Well, my music experience sort of started when I was seven. It was my grandmother who started it. She gave me a CD of samba music. I loved the rhythms. I played it constantly. My mum says I was always dancing to it. Samba music is Brazilian music with African rhythms and it's very loud, very energetic. Eventually, I decided I wanted to play the music, not just listen to it, so I saved up and bought a drum. It was an *atabaque* … it's a drum you play with your hands. I taught myself to play it. And this year, I played in my first street carnival. We were playing in the street, and people around us were dancing, and it was like my whole body was part of the rhythm. It was incredible, the best thing I've ever done! So now I've decided that I want to be a music teacher.

JEFF Yeah, well, my music experience was going to the opera. I was travelling through Italy with a group from university. We got to Verona and there was this opera festival on. I wasn't really interested in opera, but my friends persuaded me to go. To be honest, it was a bit boring at first. But then it started to get dark. It was a clear night and you could see the stars. I was sitting next to one of the people who was in my group, Laura, and it was, you know, romantic, sitting under the stars, listening to this amazing music. And, well, we've been together ever since! We even went back to Verona for our honeymoon. Although we didn't go to the opera!

ERICA My friend Mark was living in Budapest, in Hungary, and I went to visit him. Mark knew a lot of places in the city and he took me to an old boat on the river, where you can hear bands practising. The atmosphere was great. It's the kind of place where you could sit and chat all night. Anyway, this band was amazing. They were playing folk music from Transylvania. I particularly remember the violinist. I'll never forget the way he played – so fast, but so relaxed. So there I was, in the middle of a freezing, icy river, listening to this amazing music. And I realised this is where I want to be. So a few months later, I quit my job, and Mark helped me find a job in Budapest. And I stayed there for nearly 10 years.

RACHEL Hi, Becky.

BECKY Hi, Rachel!

R How are you?

B I'm good, thanks. Listen, Tom and I were thinking about going to see a band tomorrow night. Would you guys like to come?

R Oh, that's a great idea. Who were you planning to see?

B Well, we thought about going to that jazz club in town. They have live music every Friday and it's meant to be excellent.

R Wait a sec, I'll just ask Mark. … Mark, it's Becky. She wants to know if we'd like to go to a jazz club tomorrow evening. … Ah, sorry, Becky. Mark says he's not that keen on jazz. How about going to the classical music festival at the university? It's supposed to be really good.

B Hmm, I'm not a big fan of classical music. I'm sure Tom would like it, but not me. Hang on. Tom wants to say something.

TOM Why don't we go and see that local band, The Snowmen? They're playing at the Empire tomorrow and they've had great reviews.

B Did you hear what Tom said?

R Yes, but I'm not sure Mark would be interested. What kind of music do they play?

B What kind of music is it, Tom?

T It's rock, but it's a bit retro. They sound quite 1980s, so Mark should like it!

B Tom says it's rock, but a bit retro. 80s' music.

R I doubt Mark would be interested. He hasn't seen a rock band for about 10 years. Wait a moment, I'll ask him. Tom's suggesting an 80s' rock band.

MARK Um, yeah! Sounds good. Let's do it!

R Really?

M Yeah, why not? Something a bit different.

R Um, Becky, are you still there?

B Yeah.

R Mark says yes! So what time does it start?

B Hang on a moment. I'll pass you over to Tom. What time does it start?

T Hi, Rach. It starts at 8, so shall we meet outside at half past seven?

R Great. See you there.

T Oh, and tell Mark to wear something cool.

BECKY Oh, there they are.

TOM What's he wearing?

B I don't know.

RACHEL Hi, guys.

B Hi.

T Mark, what are you wearing?

MARK It's my 'going out' jacket! Don't you like it?

T Er, not really!

ANNA I got two free tickets to the Kanye West concert. I mean, I couldn't believe it! Kanye West, one of the biggest hip-hop stars, for free! So I invited my friend Camila and she said 'no thanks'. And I said 'What? Are you crazy? The ticket costs nothing'. But then she tells me she doesn't like live music. She'd prefer to stay at home and listen to music on her computer. I find that very strange because, for me, music is something full of … full of the singer's feelings, and if you can watch a singer perform, you can see what they're feeling and experience the music much more. But Camila thinks recorded music is better because you can hear everything more clearly. The quality's better, and you don't have crowds around you, and it's just easier to enjoy it. For me, it's more important to see the song come to life when the singer or band connects with the audience. And the other thing I love at the concert is the music is really loud. Anyway, Camila won't be coming with me, but lots of other people will want to.

CAMILA My friend Anna invited me to go to the Kanye West concert next month. She managed to get hold of two free tickets – she's very lucky. She asked me to go with her, but I said no. She thinks I must be mad, saying no to free tickets! I mean, I really like Kanye West and I've got all his albums, but I just don't like going to live concerts. I really prefer listening to music at home or through headphones. In a concert, singers and musicians always make mistakes. They get the rhythm a bit wrong or play notes that are wrong or something. And you see, mistakes can be fixed in recording. Well, that's part of it. The other thing is, but I didn't tell Anna this, I hate the crowds and there are usually so many people that you can only see the singer on the big screen. So what's the point? I know lots of friends who will want the ticket. It was very kind of Anna, but no.

Unit 10

LIBBY So, how are you, Gina? How was your holiday?

GINA Oh, it was great. Really good. Thailand was beautiful. And the food was amazing. But the best bit was when we went scuba diving.

L Scuba diving? I didn't realise you were going to do that!

G Neither did we! But we went to this gorgeous island called Koh Tao, and it turned out it's famous for its diving. Everyone there told us how amazing it is to dive there, so we decided to have a go.

L Wow. So did you have do some training before you went in the sea?

G Yes, we did a three-day course – PADI, it's called. We had to do a few sessions in a classroom and in a pool, but by the second day we were already diving in the open water.

L Was it scary? I think if I went, I'd be terrified!

G I was a bit worried about it before we went into the water for the first time. You start imagining sharks, and running out of oxygen, and all kinds of things! But once we got in, I relaxed really quickly. There were so many amazing fish to see – the colours were fantastic. In fact, I got so excited that I was moving around too much and using up all my oxygen. The instructor told me off. Apparently, diving is a sport for lazy people. You're not supposed to move around too much!

L Oh really? It sounds perfect for me!

G And on the third day we went to Shark Island. Luckily, it turns out that the name comes from the shape of the island – it looks like a fin – not the local wildlife! The coral there was just so beautiful – all these gorgeous colours.

L It all sounds so amazing.

G It really was. If you get the chance, you should definitely go scuba diving. If you went, you would absolutely love it.

L OK, well, if I ever go to somewhere like Thailand, I might try it.

G So, how are you? What's been happening here?

L Not much, really. Oh, I've just signed up for my first ever public run!

G Oh, great! I was wondering if you were still going running. A marathon?!

L No, not quite! I wouldn't do a full marathon – I'm not fit enough! It's only five kilometres, and it's not a timed race, or anything. It's just for fun, really. It's called the Colour Run, because every kilometre they cover you in coloured powder paint. So, by the end, you're all covered in different colours.

G Ha-ha, that sounds like fun.

L Yes, I think it'll be a bit more relaxed than a proper race – not quite so competitive. And at the end of the race, there's a big party, with music – and loads more powder paint. And it's popular with all kinds of people.

G Excellent!

L You should do it too! It would be great if there was a big group of us going. Would you like to try?

G Hmm, yes, I would, but I don't know. If I was a bit fitter, I would definitely do it. When is it?

L It's not for a couple of months. You've got time to prepare. And five kilometres is not very far.

G Hmm, OK then. I'll give it a try!

▶ **3.40**

1 A How did the match go?

B Oh, I lost 5–1.

A Oh dear.

B Well, I wasn't playing my best. Of course I would have won easily if I hadn't hurt my arm.

A Oh, of course.

2 C It's no good. I can't start the engine.

D Oh great. This car's nothing but trouble.

C I know. I wouldn't have bought it if I'd known it was in such bad condition.

D Well, what did you expect for such a cheap price?

3 E Careful! Are you OK?

F Yes, thank you, I'm fine. Thank you. If you hadn't pushed me, that car would have hit me!

E Yes, I know. Some people just don't look.

F Yes. Thank you so much anyway.

E That's all right. You be careful, though.

4 G We found out that he was lying all the time. He had a daughter living in Hong Kong and he was sending her all the money.

H Ah, that explains why his bank account was empty.

G Yes, exactly. I wouldn't have discovered the truth if I hadn't read her letters. I found them in a box in his attic.

H Well done. Good work.

▶ **3.43** **PART 1**

MARK Thanks Tom. So have you …?

TOM Not yet.

M Right.

T I'm going to ask her tonight.

M Oh! How do you feel?

T A bit nervous! How did you feel when you did it?

▶ **3.44** **PART 2**

TOM How did you feel when you did it?

MARK When I asked Rachel to marry me? Um, fine, I think. You've got nothing to worry about. I'm sure it'll be ok.

T I wish I had your confidence.

M So, where are you taking her?

T I've booked a table at *Bella Vita*. It's the place where we went on our first date.

M That's a good idea.

T Do you think so? You don't think it's a bit boring?

M No, not at all.

T Hmm. I'm still worried that something will go wrong. What if she says no?

M She's definitely not going to say no. You two are perfect for each other.

T Hmm, but what if?

M All right, enough!

▶ **3.47** **PART 3**

BECKY Thank you!

TOM Thanks!

B So what are you going to get? I'm starving!

T I don't know. Maybe a pizza.

B Yeah, the pizzas do look really good.

T So, um, Becky, ever since I've known you …

B It's been a long time since we were here last.

T Yeah, we came here on our first date, didn't we?

B Really? I thought we went somewhere else. That reminds me, I need to book the restaurant for the office party. Let me just make a note of that before I forget. Were you trying to give me a ring earlier?

T A ring? What?! No!

B I've got a missed call from you on my phone.

T Oh! Oh, yeah, I just wanted to check that you knew which restaurant it was.

B Oh, OK.

T So, anyway, as I was saying, you've really changed my life.

WAITER Are you ready to order?

B Oh, we haven't even looked at the menus yet! Could you give us a couple more minutes?

W Of course.

T Becky, there's something I want to ask you.

B Oh yes, me too. Are you free this weekend? My parents are coming to stay and –

T Listen, I'm trying to ask you to marry me!

B What? Tom! Oh I had no idea. How long have you been planning this? … This ring is gorgeous. When did you buy that? Oh, I know! That's what you were doing with Rachel in the shopping centre. I was sure something was going on!

T Becky, will you marry me?

B Of course I will!

▶ **3.49**

GREG I finished training as a nurse in Auckland and I was expecting to get a job in a small hospital somewhere. But then a friend told me about *NowVolunteer* and I decided to apply. I'd always wanted to go to an African country and use my nursing skills to help people and here was a chance to do that, so I decided to take the opportunity while I could. I had to raise $500 before I went, but that was quite easy – I got two hospitals to sponsor me and then I borrowed some money from the bank.

So I went to Madagascar and joined a team of people working with a local supervisor. We set up a program where we went round villages and taught basic ways to improve hygiene and to avoid catching diseases. For example, we gave instruction about how to avoid catching malaria and distributed mosquito nets to some of the homes. I think we did some good, I hope so anyway, but I also learned a huge amount from it. I was suddenly in a completely different culture, teaching people who had such a different lifestyle from my own, so I think it made a big difference to the way I see the world. And I also made some very good friends out there, both local people and the other volunteers. We had such good times together and we've kept in touch since then.

After I came back, I got accepted straight away for a job at the university hospital, which is one of the best hospitals in Auckland. I'm sure I wouldn't have managed to do that if I hadn't worked in Madagascar and got this practical experience.

So I'd recommend *NowVolunteer* to anyone. I think their programs are great.

Phonemic Symbols

Vowel sounds

Short

/ə/	/æ/	/ʊ/	/ɒ/
teach**er**	m**a**n	p**u**t	g**o**t
/ɪ/	/i/	/e/	/ʌ/
ch**i**p	happ**y**	m**e**n	b**u**t

Long

/ɜː/	/ɑː/	/uː/	/ɔː/	/iː/
sh**ir**t	p**ar**t	wh**o**	w**a**lk	ch**ea**p

Diphthongs (two vowel sounds)

/eə/	/ɪə/	/ʊə/	/ɔɪ/	/aɪ/	/eɪ/	/əʊ/	/aʊ/
h**air**	n**ear**	t**our**	b**oy**	f**i**ne	l**a**te	wind**ow**	n**ow**

Consonants

/p/	/b/	/f/	/v/	/t/	/d/	/k/	/g/	/θ/	/ð/	/tʃ/	/dʒ/
picnic	**b**ook	**f**ace	**v**ery	**t**ime	**d**og	**c**old	**g**o	**th**ink	**the**	**ch**air	**j**ob
/s/	/z/	/ʃ/	/ʒ/	/m/	/n/	/ŋ/	/h/	/l/	/r/	/w/	/j/
sea	**z**oo	**sh**oe	televi**si**on	**m**e	**n**ow	si**ng**	**h**ot	**l**ate	**r**ed	**w**ent	**y**es

Irregular verbs

Infinitive	Past simple	Past Participle
be	was /wɒz/ / were /wɜː/	been
become	became	become
begin	began	begun
blow	blew /bluː/	blown /bləʊn/
break /breɪk/	broke /brəʊk/	broken /ˈbrəʊkən/
bring /brɪŋ/	brought /brɔːt/	brought /brɔːt/
build /bɪld/	built /bɪlt/	built /bɪlt/
buy /baɪ/	bought /bɔːt/	bought /bɔːt/
catch /kætʃ/	caught /kɔːt/	caught /kɔːt/
choose /tʃuːz/	chose /tʃəʊz/	chosen /ˈtʃəʊzən/
come	came	come
cost	cost	cost
cut	cut	cut
deal /dɪəl/	dealt /delt/	dealt /delt/
do	did	done /dʌn/
draw /drɔː/	drew /druː/	drawn /drɔːn/
drink	drank	drunk
drive /draɪv/	drove /drəʊv/	driven /ˈdrɪvən/
eat /iːt/	ate /et/	eaten /ˈiːtən/
fall	fell	fallen
feel	felt	felt
find /faɪnd/	found /faʊnd/	found /faʊnd/
fly /flaɪ/	flew /fluː/	flown /fləʊn/
forget	forgot	forgotten
get	got	got
give /gɪv/	gave /geɪv/	given /ˈgɪvən/
go	went	gone /gɒn/
grow	grew /gruː/	grown /grəʊn/
have /hæv/	had /hæd/	had /hæd/
hear /hɪə/	heard /hɜːd/	heard /hɜːd/
hit	hit	hit
hold /həʊld/	held	held
keep	kept	kept
know /nəʊ/	knew /njuː/	known /nəʊn/

Infinitive	Past simple	Past Participle
leave /liːv/	left	left
lend	lent	lent
let	let	let
lose /luːz/	lost	lost
make	made	made
meet	met	met
pay /peɪ/	paid /peɪd/	paid /peɪd/
put	put	put
read /riːd/	read /red/	read /red/
ride /raɪd/	rode /rəʊd/	ridden /ˈrɪdən/
ring	rang	rung
run	ran	run
sit	sat	sat
say /seɪ/	said /sed/	said /sed/
see	saw /sɔː/	seen
sell	sold /səʊld/	sold /səʊld/
send	sent	sent
set	set	set
sing	sang	sung
sleep	slept	slept
speak /spiːk/	spoke /spəʊk/	spoken /ˈspəʊkən/
spend	spent	spent
stand	stood /stʊd/	stood /stʊd/
steal /stiːl/	stole /stəʊl/	stolen /ˈstəʊlən/
swim /swɪm/	swam /swæm/	swum /swʌm/
take /teɪk/	took /tʊk/	taken /ˈteɪkən/
teach /tiːtʃ/	taught /tɔːt/	taught /tɔːt/
tell	told /təʊld/	told /təʊld/
think	thought /θɔːt/	thought /θɔːt/
throw /θrəʊ/	threw /θruː/	thrown /θrəʊn/
understand	understood /ʌndəˈstʊd/	understood /ʌndəˈstʊd/
wake /weɪk/	woke /wəʊk/	woken /ˈwəʊkən/
wear /weə/	wore /wɔː/	worn /wɔːn/
win	won	won
write /raɪt/	wrote /rəʊt/	written /ˈrɪtən/

Acknowledgements

The publishers would like to thank the following teachers and ELT professionals for the invaluable feedback they have provided during the development of the B1+ Student's Book:

Andre Alipio, Brazil; Peggy Altpekin, Turkey and the Gulf; Natalia Bayrak, Russia; Kate Chomacki, UK; Leonor Corradi, Argentina; Ludmila Gorodetskaya, Russia; Ludmila Kozhevnikova, Russia; Steve Laslett, UK; Rabab Marouf, Syria; Christina Maurer Smolder, Australia; Mariusz Mirecki, Poland; Catherine Morley, Spain; Antonio Mota Cosano, Spain; Julian Oakley, UK; Litany Pires Ribeiro, Brazil; Elena Pro, Spain; Wayne Rimmer, Russia; Ruth Sánchez, Spain; Hilda Zubiria, Peru.

The publishers are grateful to the following contributors:

Gareth Boden: commissioned photography
Leon Chambers: audio recordings
Hilary Luckcock: picture research
Rob Maidment and Sharp Focus Productions: video recordings, video stills
Ann Thomson: commissioned photography

The authors and publishers acknowledge the following sources of copyright material and are grateful for the permissions granted. While every effort has been made, it has not always been possible to identify the sources of all the material used, or to trace all copyright holders. If any omissions are brought to our notice, we will be happy to include the appropriate acknowledgements on reprinting.

The publisher has used its best endeavours to ensure that the URLs for external websites referred to in this book are correct and active at the time of going to press. However, the publisher has no responsibility for the websites and can make no guarantee that a site will remain live or that the content is or will remain appropriate.

The publishers are grateful to the following for permission to reproduce copyright photographs and material:
Key: L = left, C = centre, R = right, T = top, B = bottom
p7: Corbis/Andy Richter/Aurora Photos; p8(main): Alamy/OJO Images Ltd; p8(a): Alamy/ Jochen Tack; p8(b): Alamy/ipm; p8(c): Alamy/VISUM Foto GmbH; p8(d): Getty/Nicolas McComber; p11(a): Superstock/Voisin/Phanie; p11(b): CUP; p11(c): Shutterstock/AVAVA; p11(d): Alamy/Claudia Wiens; p19: Alamy/ViewPictures Ltd; p20: Alamy/Wavebreakmedia Ltd UC4; p21(a): Getty/MichaelDeleon; p21(b): Corbis/Chad Springer/Cultura; p21(c): Corbis/Sonja Pacho; p21(d): Getty/Peter Dazeley; p21(e): Corbis/ Odilon Dimier /PhotoAlto; p21(f): Thinkstock/Goodshot; p22: Getty/Mike Harrington; p23(B): Getty/Mareen Fischinger; p25: Alamy/Viktor Cap; pp28/29: Shutterstock/Lai Ching Yuen; p31: Getty/Erik Dreyer; p32: Shutterstock/Anton Gvozdikov; p33(T): Alamy/AF Archive; p33(B): Corbis/ Britta Pedersen/dpa; p35(a): Alamy/Judith Dzierzawa; p35(b): Getty/ Nancy Ney; p35(c): Corbis/68 / Larsen@Talbert/Ocean; p35(d): Masterfile; p35(e): Alamy/David Wall; p35(f): Getty/Juan Silva; p35(g): Corbis/ Paul Burns/Blend Images; p35(h): Superstock/ age fotostock; pp36/37: Superstock/ Henry Georgi/All Canada Photos; p36(T): Alamy/Janine Wiedel Photolibrary; p37(L): Alamy/MBI; p37(R): Alamy/Image Source; p40(main): Corbis/ClassicStock; p40(L): Getty/George Marks; p40(R): Topfoto/Topfoto. co.uk; p43: Getty/Ghislain & Marie David de Lossy; p44(T): The Guardian/ Graeme Robertson; p44(B): Getty/JB Lacroix; p45(TL): SA Glamour Productions/Salina Ho; p45(TR): Rex; p45(BL): Rex/Offside; p45(BR): Corbis/Andreas Lander /dpa; p46: Corbis/Kevin Dodge; p47: Random House LLC; p48(L): Alamy/Dinodia Photos; p48(R): Getty/William Philpott; p49(TL): Alamy/Mandoga Media; p49(TR): Masterfile; p49(BL): Getty / Fred Duval; p52(L): Masterfile/Robert Harding Images; p52(R): Masterfile; pp52/53: Corbis/Vstock/Tetra Images; p55: Getty/Per-Andre Hoffmann; p56(R)(forest): Whitley Fund For Nature; p56(BL): Alamy/Lou Linwei; p57(T)(logo): Whitley Fund For Nature; p57(TR): Whitley Fund For Nature; p57(T)(inset): Alamy/imageBroker; p57(CL): Whitley Fund For Nature; p57(CL)(inset): Whitley Fund For Nature; p57(BL): Alamy/F1online digitale Bildagentur GmbH; p57(BR): Whitley Fund For Nature; p57(BR)(inset): Whitley Fund For Nature; p58(T): Alamy/Kevin Schafer; p58(T)(inset): Alamy/Adrian Hepworth; p58(B): Shutterstock/Juice Team; p59(T)(a): Alamy/Stocksnapper; p59(T)(b): Getty/Anita Stizzoli; p59(1): Getty/Peter Walton Photography; p59(2): Shutterstock/v voe; p59(3): Shutterstock/zcw; p59(B)(a): Getty /AFP; p59(B)(b): Shutterstock/Sergey Skleznev; p59(B) (c): Shutterstock/violetkaipa; p60(T): Shutterstock/Svetlana Yudina; p60(B): Shutterstock/Shane Gross; p61(TL): Alamy/ Westend61GmbH; p61(TC): Alamy/Alaska Stock; p61(TR): Alamy/blickwinkel; p61(CL): Corbis/ Paul van Hoof/Buten-beeld/Minden Pictures; p61(CR): Alamy/Juniors Bildarchiv GmbH; p61(BL): Corbis/Stephen Dalton/Minden Pictures; p61(BR): Rex/Image Broker; p64(T): Alamy/World Pictures; p64(B): Rex/ Jay Town/Newspix; p65: Rex/FLPA; p67: Corbis/Hugh Sitton; pp68/69(B): Superstock/Franck Binewald/Imagebroker.net; p69(L)(firefighters): PA/

Eraldo Peres/AP; p69(L)(jeep): Alamy/patrick nairne; p69(L)(hospital): Rex/Sipa Press; p69(TR): BBC Photo Sales; p70: Alamy/imageBroker; p71(a): Alamy/Julie Woodhouse; p71(b): Alamy/Martin Turzak; p71(c): Alamy/Food and Drink Photos; p71(d): Alamy/amana images inc.; p71(e): Shutterstock/Sean Wandzilak; p71(B): Alamy/Robert Harding Picture Library Ltd; p72(TL): Shutterstock/racorn; p72(TR): Alamy/MBI; p72(B): Alamy/JLImages; p73(L): Corbis/Inspirestock; p73(C): Alamy/ Simon Reddy; p73(R): Alamy/ Bon Appetit; p76(1): Shutterstock/Radu Bercan; p76(2): Alamy/Robert Harding Picture Library Ltd; p76(3): Shutterstock/ jan kranendonk; p77: Shutterstock/posztos; p79: Corbis/Michael Freeman; p80(a): Shutterstock/Natali Glado; p80(b): Superstock/View Pictures Ltd; p80(c): Alamy/Peter Donaldson; p80(d): Alamy/ CulturalEyes-N; p81(T): Shutterstock/Breadmaker; p81(BL): Alamy/Greg Balfour Evans; p81(BR): Superstock/View Pictures Ltd; p82(L): Alamy/les polders; p82(a): Alamy/ Jon Arnold Images Ltd; p82(b): Alamy/Images&Stories; p82(c): Alamy/ David J. Green; p82(d): Alamy/Adam Burton; p82(e): Alamy/Clive Sawyer; p82(f): Alamy/Doug Houghton; p83(T): Getty/Folio Images; p83(B): Alamy/ David Lyon; pp84/85: Corbis/Atlantide Phototravel; p85(Pablo): Masterfile; p85(Jen): Masterfile/Beth Dixson; p85(Kira): Masterfile; p88(TR): Shutterstock/Richard Goldberg; p88(CR): Alamy/North Wind Picture Archives; p88(main): Science Photo Library/National Reconnaissance Office; p89: Shutterstock/Richard Cavalleri; p91: Real Madrid via Getty Images; p93(T): Corbis/Gary Hershorn/Reuters; p93(B): Science Photo Library/Ria Novosti; p94: Getty/Nicolas McComber; p95(TR): Shutterstock/ Goodluz; p95(CL): Corbis/Rick Friedman; p95(BL): Masterfile/Al Accardo; p100(a): Shutterstock/pio3; p100(b): Rex/Isopix; p100(c): Getty/Daniel Reiter/Stock4B; p103: Corbis/Lucas Jackson/Reuters; p104(TR): Rex/ Moviestore; p104(CL): Rex/Moviestore; p104(CC): Rex/c.W. Disney/ Everett; p104(CR): Kobal/Lucasfilm/20th Century Fox; p104(BL): Ronald Grant Archive/New Line Cinema/Wingnut Films/Lord Dritte Productions Deutschland Filmproduktion GmbH/Saul Zaentz Co.; p105(TR): Rex/ Courtesy Everett Collection; p105(CL): Capital Pictures/NFS; p105(CR): Alamy/AF Archive; p105(BL): Capital Pictures/NFS; p105(BR): Photofest/ Walt Disney Studios; p106: Corbis/enewsimage.com/Splash News; p107(L) (1): Alamy/Rob Ball; p107(L)(2): Alamy/Juice Images; p107(L)(3): Alamy/ Ted Foxx; p107(R)(a): Shutterstock/ Igor Bulgarin; p107(R)(b): Lebrecht Music & Arts/Leemage; p107(R)(c): Alamy/Jose Elias/StockPhotosArt – Events; p108/109: Splash UK; p108(L): Rex/Gonzales Photo/Christian Hjorth/PYMCA; p109: Getty Images Entertainment; p112(T): Alamy/John Warburton-Lee Photography; p112(B): Alamy/Juice Images; p113(L): Alamy/Geraint Lewis; p113(C): Shutterstock/ Martin Lehmann; p113(TR): Rex/ Benjamin Lozovsky/BFAnyc.com; p113(BR): Lebrecht Music & Arts/ Chris Christodoulou; p115: Corbis/Andrew Fox; p116(TL): Getty Images Sport; p116(BL): Alamy/Zuma Press Inc.; p116(BR): Getty/Shannon Stent; p117(T): Shutterstock/Richard Whitcombe; p117(B): Corbis/ Remko de Waal/epa; p118(CL): Alamy/Mikhail Kondrashov "fotomik"; p118(BL): Alamy/imageBroker; p118(BR): Rex/Terry Harris; p119(a)(T): Shutterstock/Monkey Business Images; p119(b)(C): Shutterstock/Jacek Fulawka; p119(c)(L): Alamy/Robert Stainforth; p119(c)(R): Alamy/PYMCA; p119(c)(B): Shutterstock/Brian Eichhorn; p119(background): Shutterstock/ Songquan Deng; p120(TR): Shutterstock/Monkey Business Images; p120(BR): Shutterstock/ Image Point Fr; p124(T): Masterfile; p124(B): Masterfile/R. Ian Lloyd; p125(T): Corbis/Oliver Rossi; p125(B): Alamy/ Yvette Cardozo; p130: Kobal/RKO; p154(T): Shutterstock/Pu Su Lan; p154(C): Alamy/Global Warming Images; p154(B): Alamy/Tips Images/Tips Italia Srl a socio unico; p155(R)(1): Shutterstock/ alslutsky; p155(R)(2): Getty/ Visuals Unlimited. Inc; p155(R)(3): Alamy/Images&Stories; p155(R) (4): Rex/Image Broker; p155(R)(5): Masterfile/Minden Pictures; p155(R) (6): Shutterstock/Cathy Keifer; p160(1): Kobal/ Paramount Pictures; p160(2): Corbis/Radius Images; p160(3): Rex/Ken McKay; p160(4): Kobal/New Line Productions/Michael Ginsberg; p160(5): Disney-ABC via Getty Images; p160(6): Kobal/Universal; p160(7): Ronald Grant Archive/ Walt Disney Pictures/Pixar Animation Studios; p160(8): Rex/ITV; p160(9): Kobal/Dream Works Animation; p160(10): Rex/FremantleMedia Ltd; p160(11): Ronald Grant Archive/Ariescope Pictures; p160(12): Kobal/ Samson Films/Summit Entertainment.

Commissioned photography by Gareth Boden: pp10(T,B), 16(all), 28, 95(BR), 119(a)(C), p119 (b)(T,B) and 120(L).

We are grateful to Barratt Developments plc and Neide's Deli Cafe for their help with the commissioned photography.

Front cover photograph by Alamy/imageBROKER.

The publishers would like to thank the following illustrators: Beatrice Bencivenni, Mark Bird, Mark Duffin, Jo Goodberry, Mark (KJA Artists), Jerome Mireault, Gavin Reece, Gregory Roberts, Sean (KJA Artists), David Semple, Sean Sims, Marie-Eve-Tremblay.

Corpus Development of this publication has made use of the Cambridge English Corpus (CEC). The CEC is a computer database of contemporary spoken and written English, which currently stands at over one billion words. It includes British English, American English and other varieties of English. It also includes the Cambridge Learner Corpus, developed in collaboration with the University of Cambridge ESOL Examinations. Cambridge University Press has built up the CEC to provide evidence about language use that helps to produce better language teaching materials.

English Profile This product is informed by the English Vocabulary Profile, built as part of English Profile, a collaborative programme designed to enhance the learning, teaching and assessment of English worldwide. Its main funding partners are Cambridge University Press and Cambridge ESOL and its aim is to create a 'profile' for English linked to the Common European Framework of Reference for Languages (CEFR). English Profile outcomes, such as the English Vocabulary Profile, will provide detailed information about the language that learners can be expected to demonstrate at each CEFR level, offering a clear benchmark for learners' proficiency. For more information, please visit www.englishprofile.org

CALD The Cambridge Advanced Learner's Dictionary is the world's most widely used dictionary for learners of English. Including all the words and phrases that learners are likely to come across, it also has easy-to-understand definitions and example sentences to show how the word is used in context. The Cambridge Advanced Learner's Dictionary is available online at dictionary.cambridge.org. © Cambridge University Press, Third Edition, 2008 reproduced with permission.